BE BEAUTIFUL • BE INTELLIGENT • BE HEALTHY • BE IMMORTAL

BE SUPERIOR

EXTREMIS 3.0

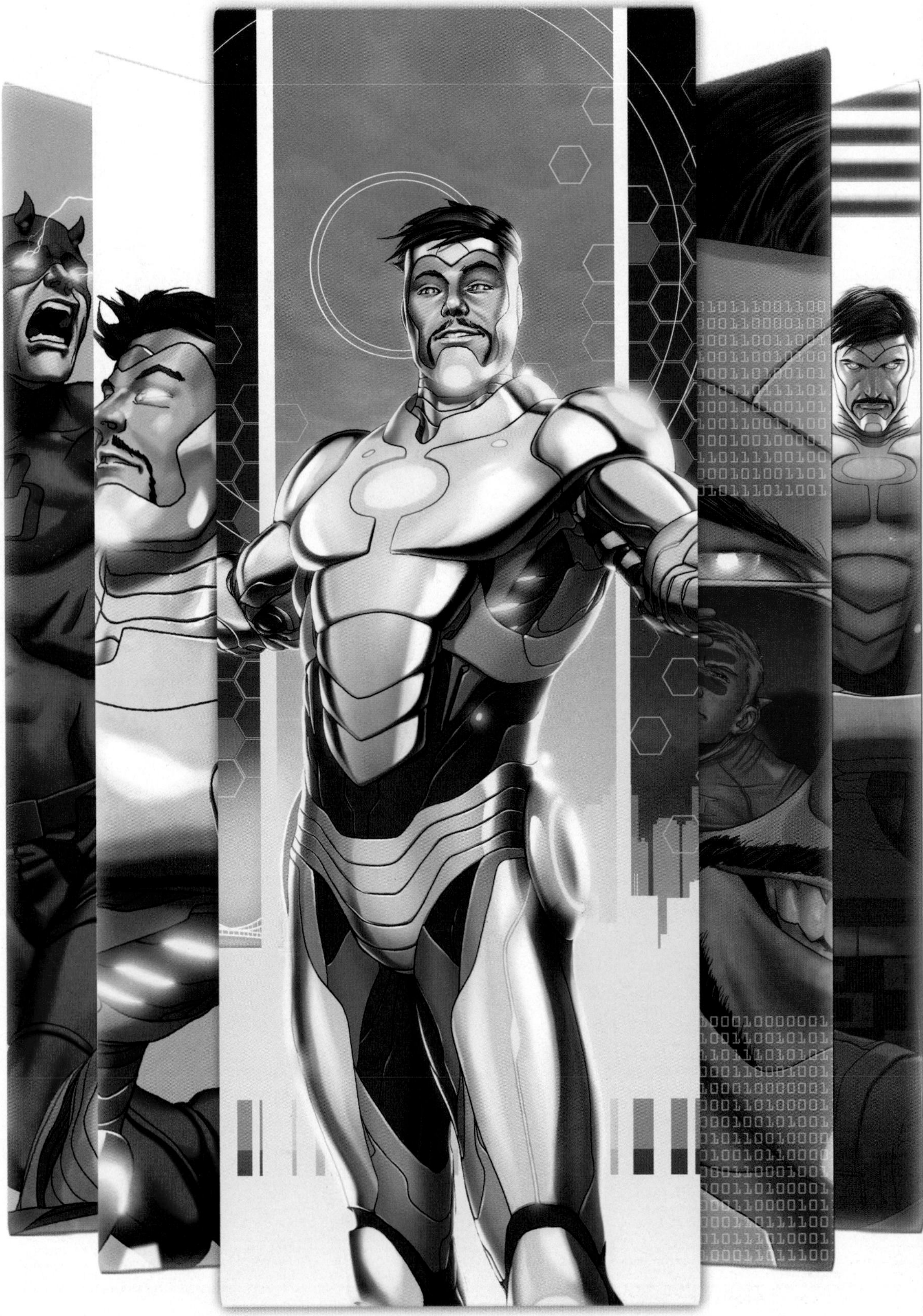

SUPERIOR IRON MAN

INFAMOUS

Writer Tom Taylor   *Withdrawn*

ISSUES #1-3
Artist Yildiray Çinar
Ink Assists Ruy Jose & Juan Vlasco

ISSUE #4
Penciler Yildiray Çinar
Inkers Cory Hamscher (pp. 1-15)
& Tom Palmer (pp. 16-20)

ISSUE #5
Artist Laura Braga

Colorist Guru-eFX
Letterer VC's Clayton Cowles
Cover Art Mike Choi
Assistant Editor Jon Moisan
Editor Mark Paniccia

Iron Man created by Stan Lee, Don Heck, Larry Lieber & Jack Kirby

Collection Editor Jennifer Grünwald   **Assistant Editor** Sarah Brunstad
Associate Managing Editor Alex Starbuck   **Editor, Special Projects** Mark D. Beazley
Senior Editor, Special Projects Jeff Youngquist   **SVP Print, Sales & Marketing** David Gabriel

Editor in Chief Axel Alonso   **Chief Creative Officer** Joe Quesada
Publisher Dan Buckley   **Executive Producer** Alan Fine

SUPERIOR IRON MAN VOL. 1: INFAMOUS. Contains material originally published in magazine form as SUPERIOR IRON MAN #1-5. First printing 2015. ISBN# 978-0-7851-9249-7. Published by MARVEL WORLDWIDE, INC., a subsidiary of MARVEL ENTERTAINMENT, LLC. OFFICE OF PUBLICATION: 135 West 50th Street, New York, NY 10020. Copyright © 2015 MARVEL No similarity between any of the names, characters, persons, and/or institutions in this magazine with those of any living or dead person or institution is intended, and any such similarity which may exist is purely coincidental. **Printed in the U.S.A.** ALAN FINE, President, Marvel Entertainment; DAN BUCKLEY, President, TV, Publishing and Brand Management; JOE QUESADA, Chief Creative Officer; TOM BREVOORT, SVP of Publishing; DAVID BOGART, SVP of Operations & Procurement, Publishing; C.B. CEBULSKI, VP of International Development & Brand Management; DAVID GABRIEL, SVP Print, Sales & Marketing; JIM O'KEEFE, VP of Operations & Logistics; DAN CARR, Executive Director of Publishing Technology; SUSAN CRESPI, Editorial Operations Manager; ALEX MORALES, Publishing Operations Manager; STAN LEE, Chairman Emeritus. For information regarding advertising in Marvel Comics or on Marvel.com, please contact Jonathan Rheingold, VP of Custom Solutions & Ad Sales, at jrheingold@marvel.com. For Marvel subscription inquiries, please call 800-217-9158. **Manufactured between 11/6/2015 and 12/14/2015 by R.R. DONNELLEY, INC., SALEM, VA, USA.**

10 9 8 7 6 5 4 3 2 1

Tony Stark is a technological visionary...a famous, wealthy and unparalleled inventor. With the world's most advanced and powerful suit of armor, Stark has valiantly protected the innocent as an invincible bright knight known as IRON MAN.

But when his mind was altered, a more selfish and devious personality surfaced. Can Tony Stark still be a hero when he thinks he's superior?

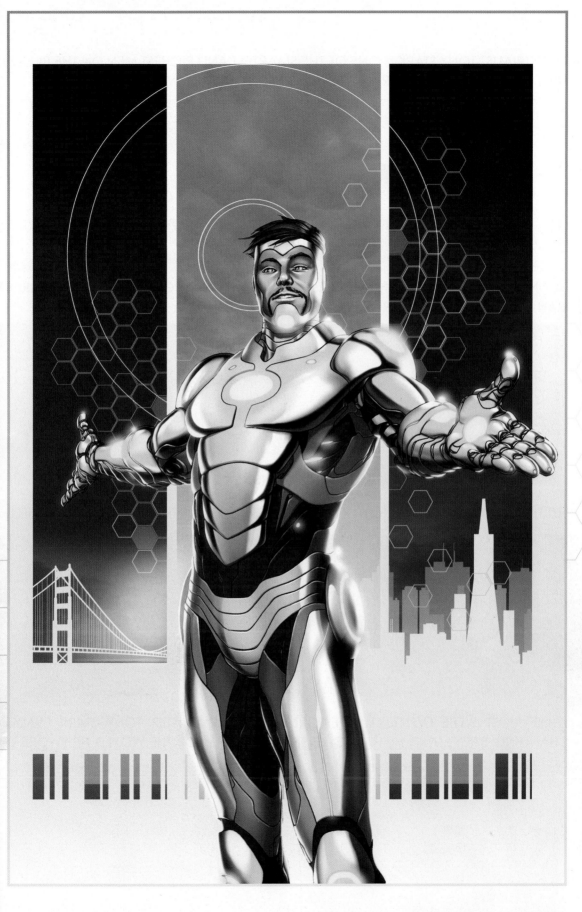

1: NIGHTMARE SCENARIO

WHAT HAS GONE BEFORE...

INDUSTRIALIST TONY STARK IS ONE OF THE SMARTEST AND RICHEST MEN ON THE PLANET. WITH HIS HIGH-TECH ARMOR HE PROTECTS EARTH AS THE INVINCIBLE IRON MAN.

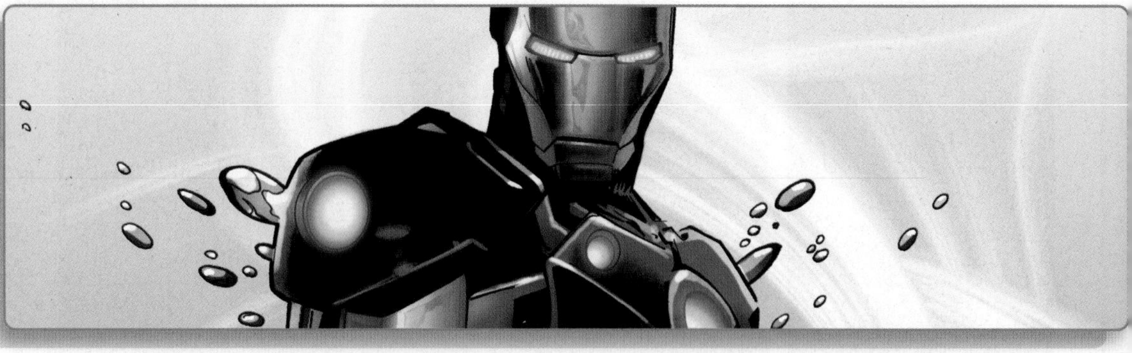

DURING A WORLD-THREATENING BATTLE WITH A PSYCHIC-POWERED RED SKULL, IRON MAN AND AN ARMY OF HEROES DEFEATED THE VILLAIN...

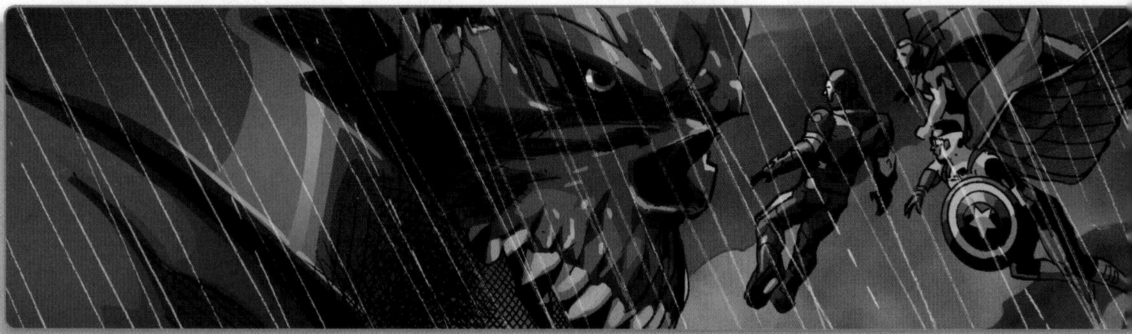

BUT THE PSYCHIC FALLOUT CHANGED THE PERSONALITIES OF THOSE ON THE BATTLEFIELD.

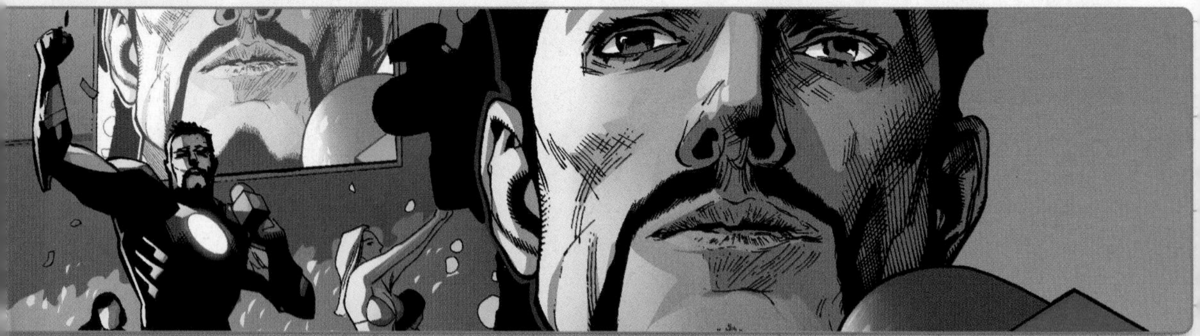

WHILE MOST WERE EVENTUALLY RESTORED, A MORE SINISTER TONY STARK EVADED CHANGING BACK...AND HE HAS SOME SPECIAL PLANS FOR THE WORLD HE SWORE TO PROTECT.

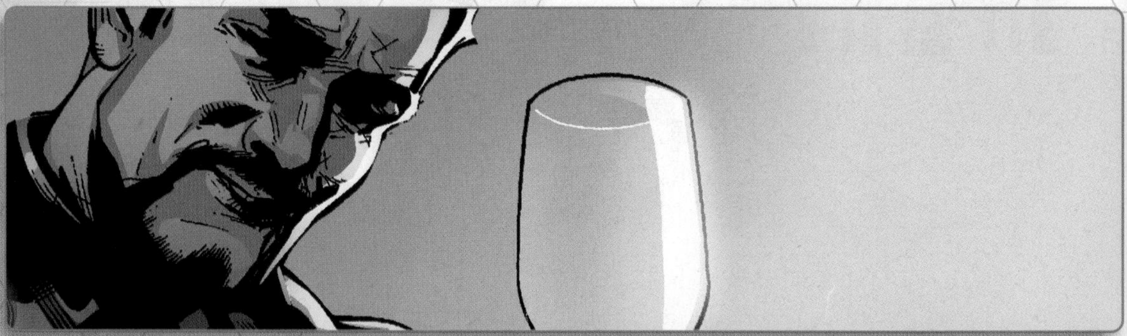

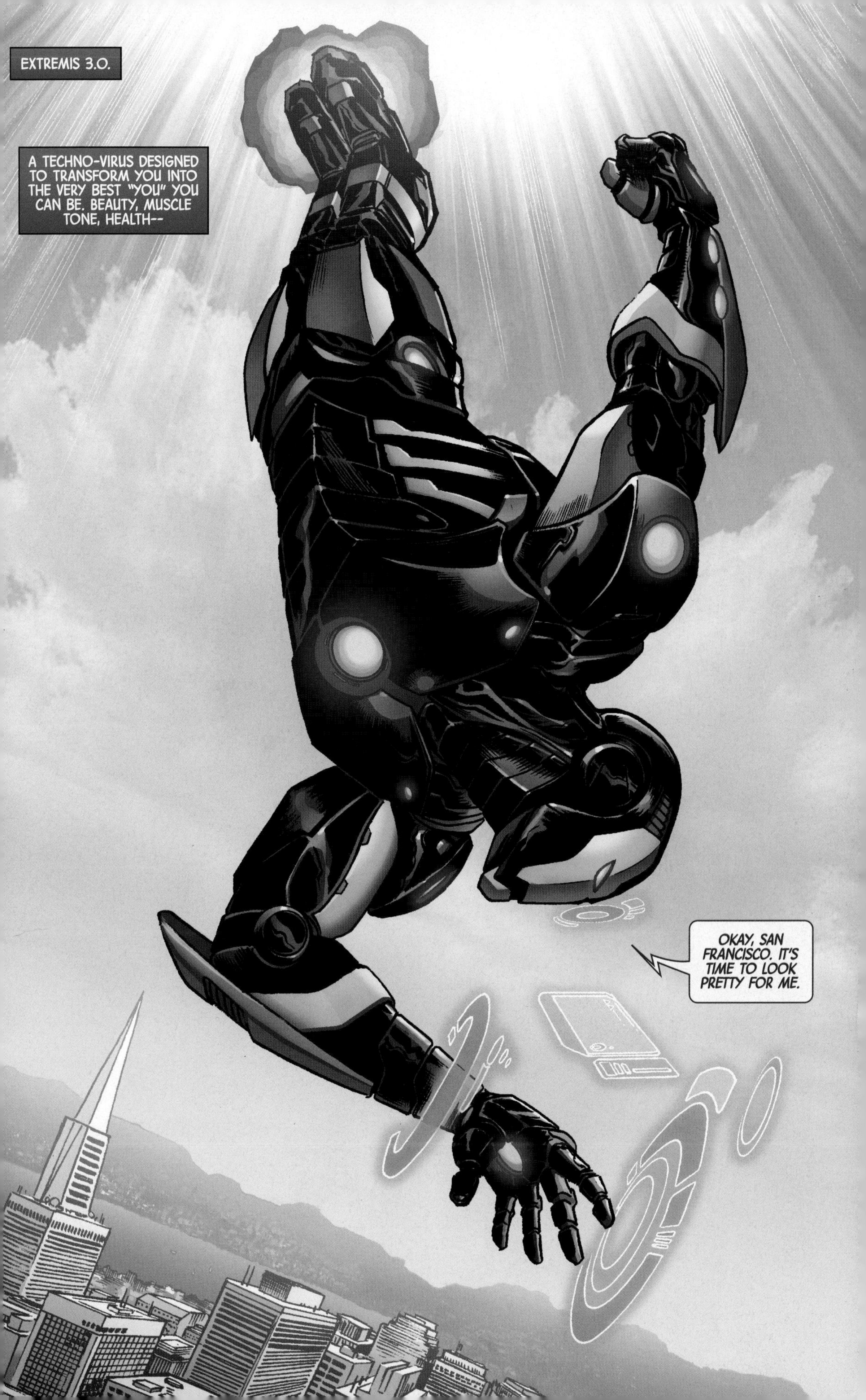
EXTREMIS 3.O.
A TECHNO-VIRUS DESIGNED TO TRANSFORM YOU INTO THE VERY BEST "YOU" YOU CAN BE. BEAUTY, MUSCLE TONE, HEALTH--
OKAY, SAN FRANCISCO. IT'S TIME TO LOOK PRETTY FOR ME.

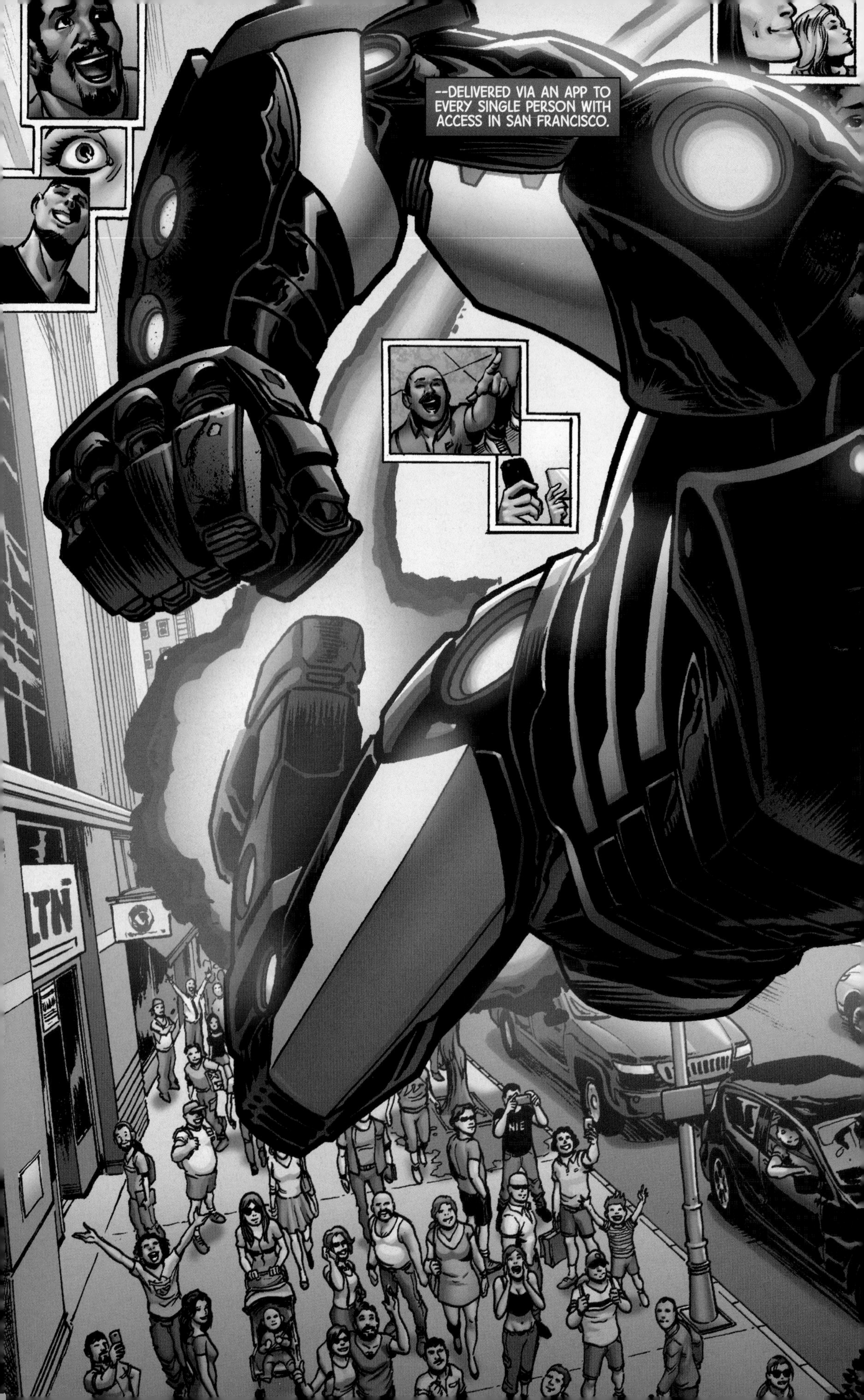
--DELIVERED VIA AN APP TO EVERY SINGLE PERSON WITH ACCESS IN SAN FRANCISCO.
LTN
NIE

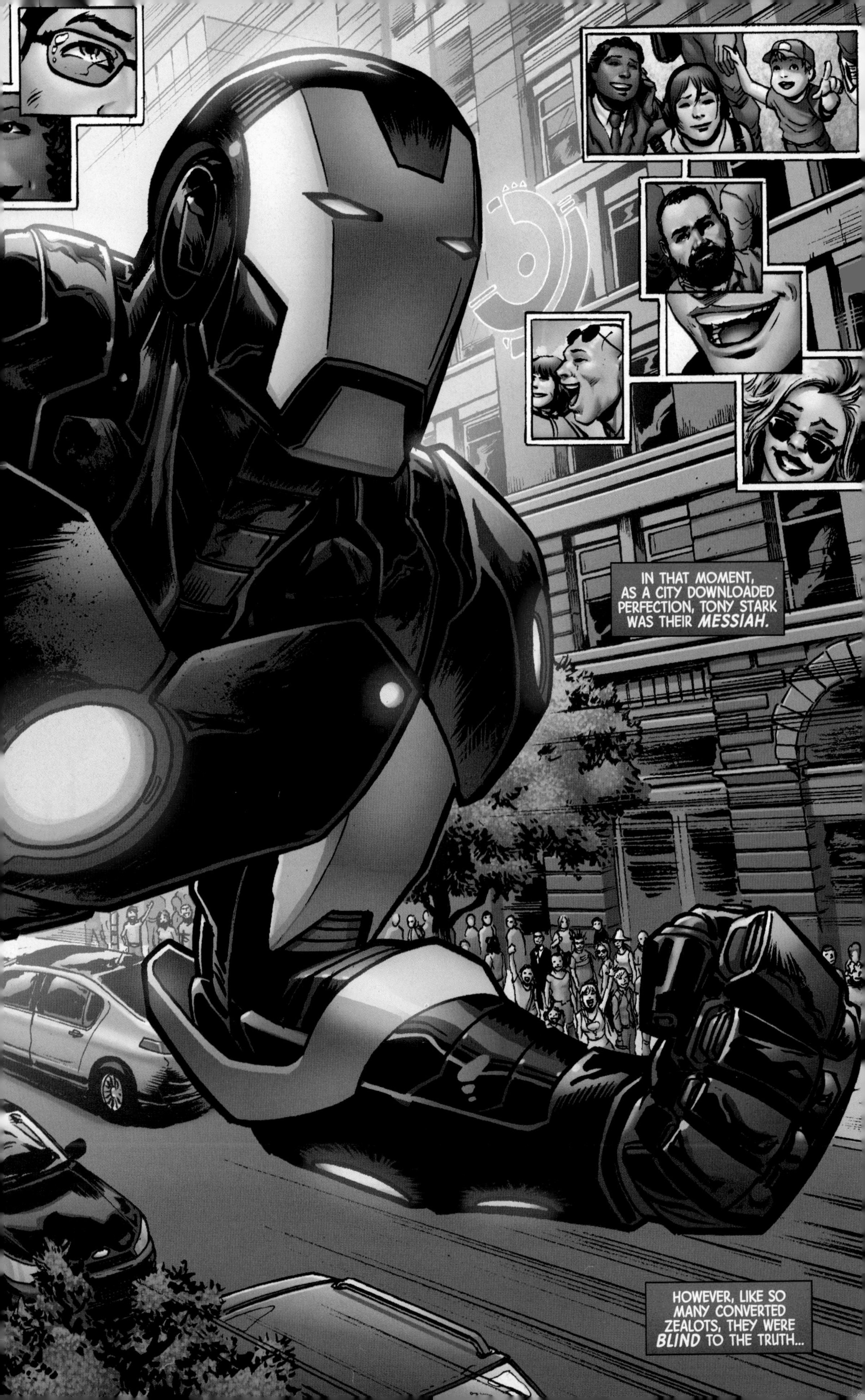
IN THAT MOMENT, AS A CITY DOWNLOADED PERFECTION, TONY STARK WAS THEIR *MESSIAH.*
HOWEVER, LIKE SO MANY CONVERTED ZEALOTS, THEY WERE *BLIND* TO THE TRUTH...

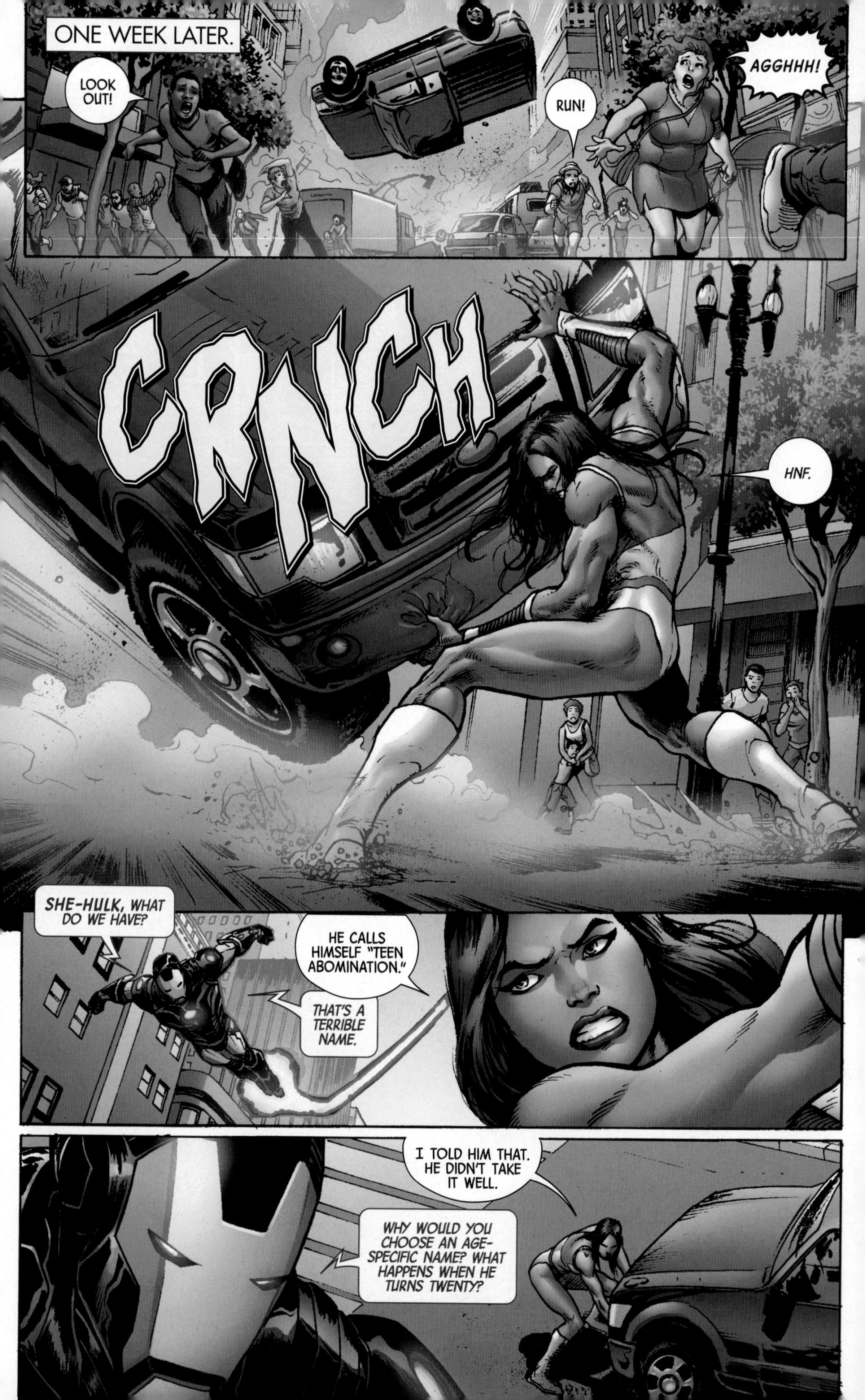
ONE WEEK LATER.
LOOK OUT!
RUN!
AGGHHH!
CRNCH
HNF.
SHE-HULK, WHAT DO WE HAVE?
HE CALLS HIMSELF "TEEN ABOMINATION."
THAT'S A TERRIBLE NAME.
I TOLD HIM THAT. HE DIDN'T TAKE IT WELL.
WHY WOULD YOU CHOOSE AN AGE-SPECIFIC NAME? WHAT HAPPENS WHEN HE TURNS TWENTY?

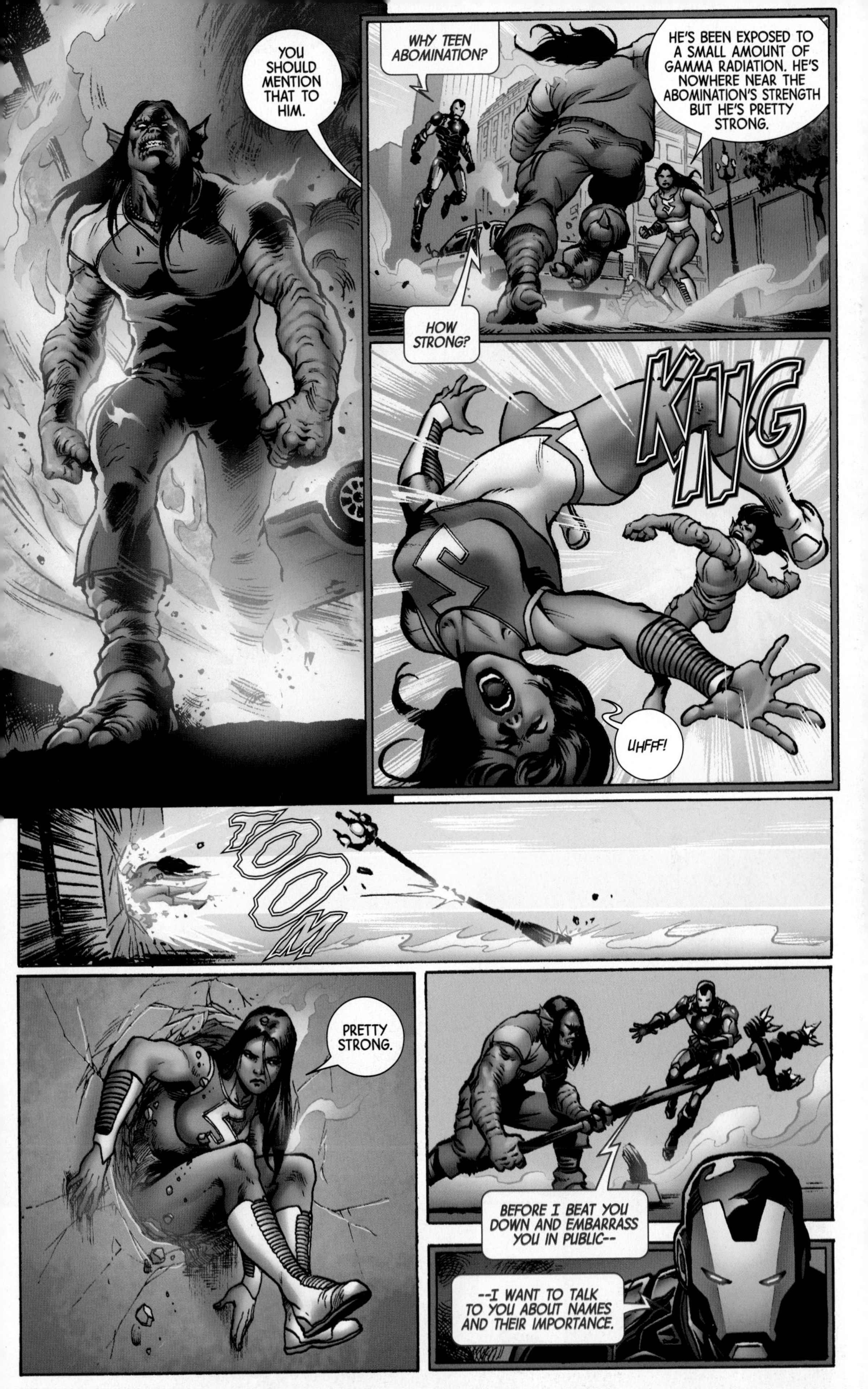
YOU SHOULD MENTION THAT TO HIM.
WHY TEEN ABOMINATION?
HE'S BEEN EXPOSED TO A SMALL AMOUNT OF GAMMA RADIATION. HE'S NOWHERE NEAR THE ABOMINATION'S STRENGTH BUT HE'S PRETTY STRONG.
HOW STRONG?
KNNG
UHFFF!
TOOOM
PRETTY STRONG.
BEFORE I BEAT YOU DOWN AND EMBARRASS YOU IN PUBLIC--
--I WANT TO TALK TO YOU ABOUT NAMES AND THEIR IMPORTANCE.

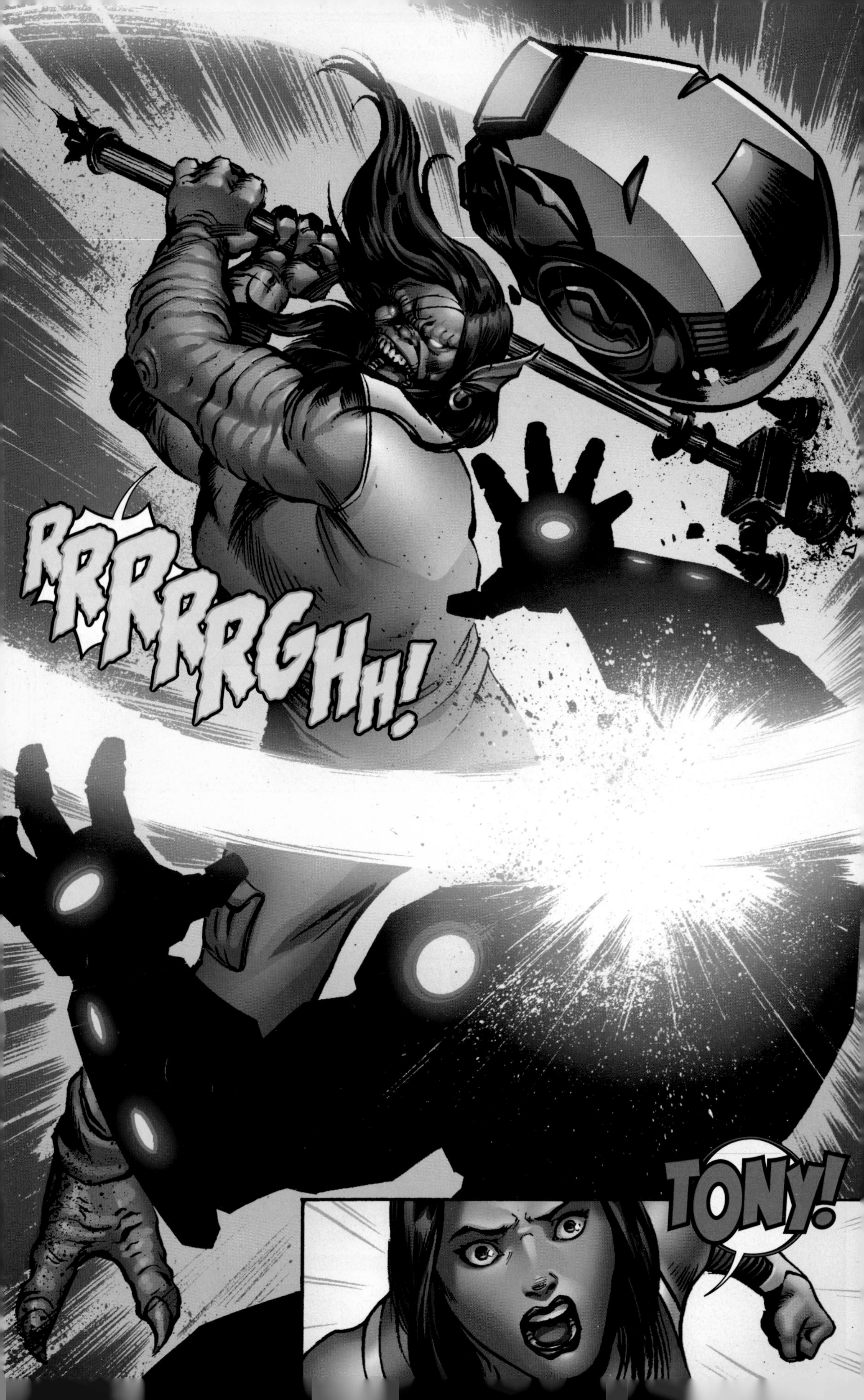
RRRRRGHH!
TONY!

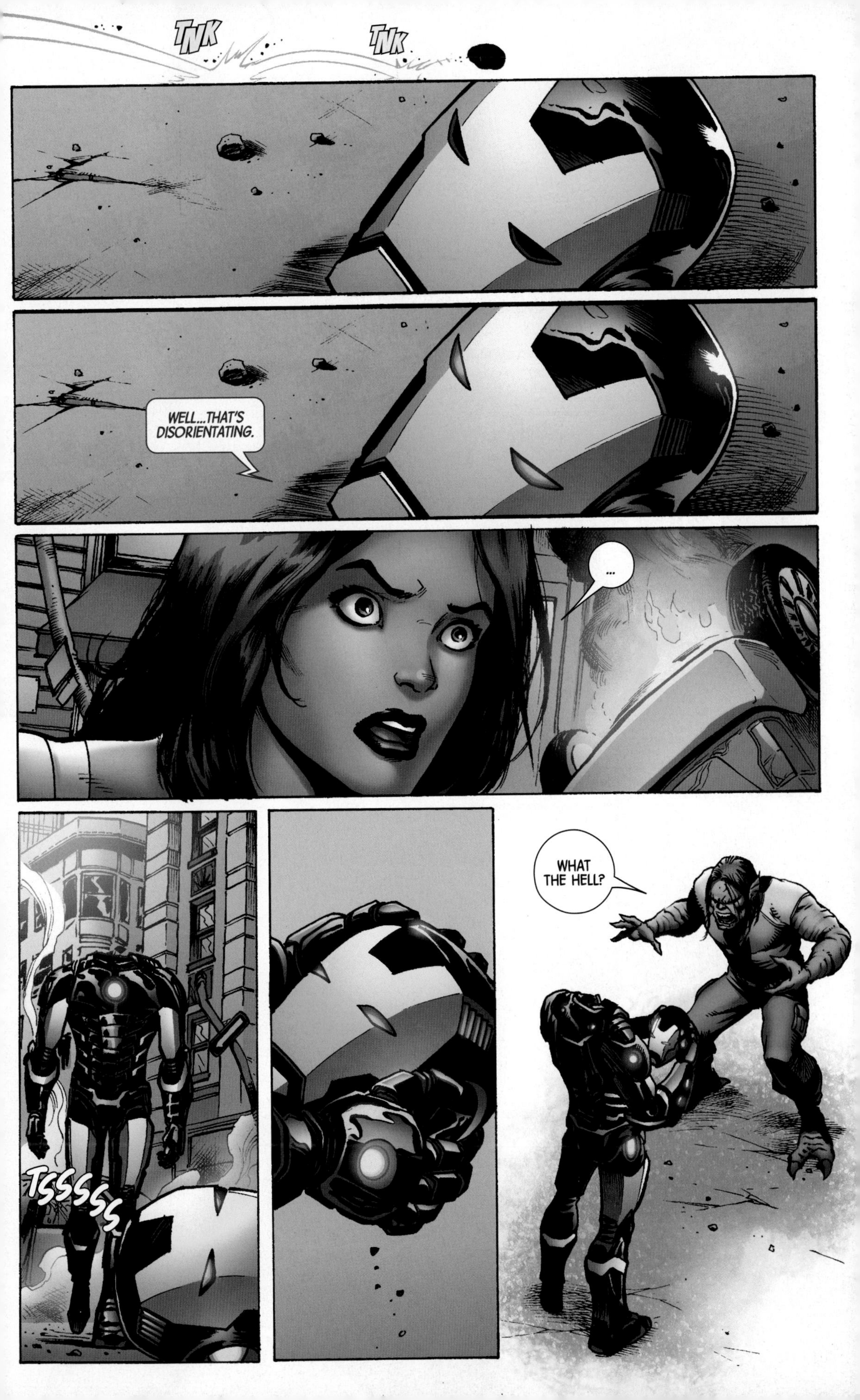
TNK
TNK
WELL...THAT'S DISORIENTATING.
...
TSSSSS
WHAT THE HELL?

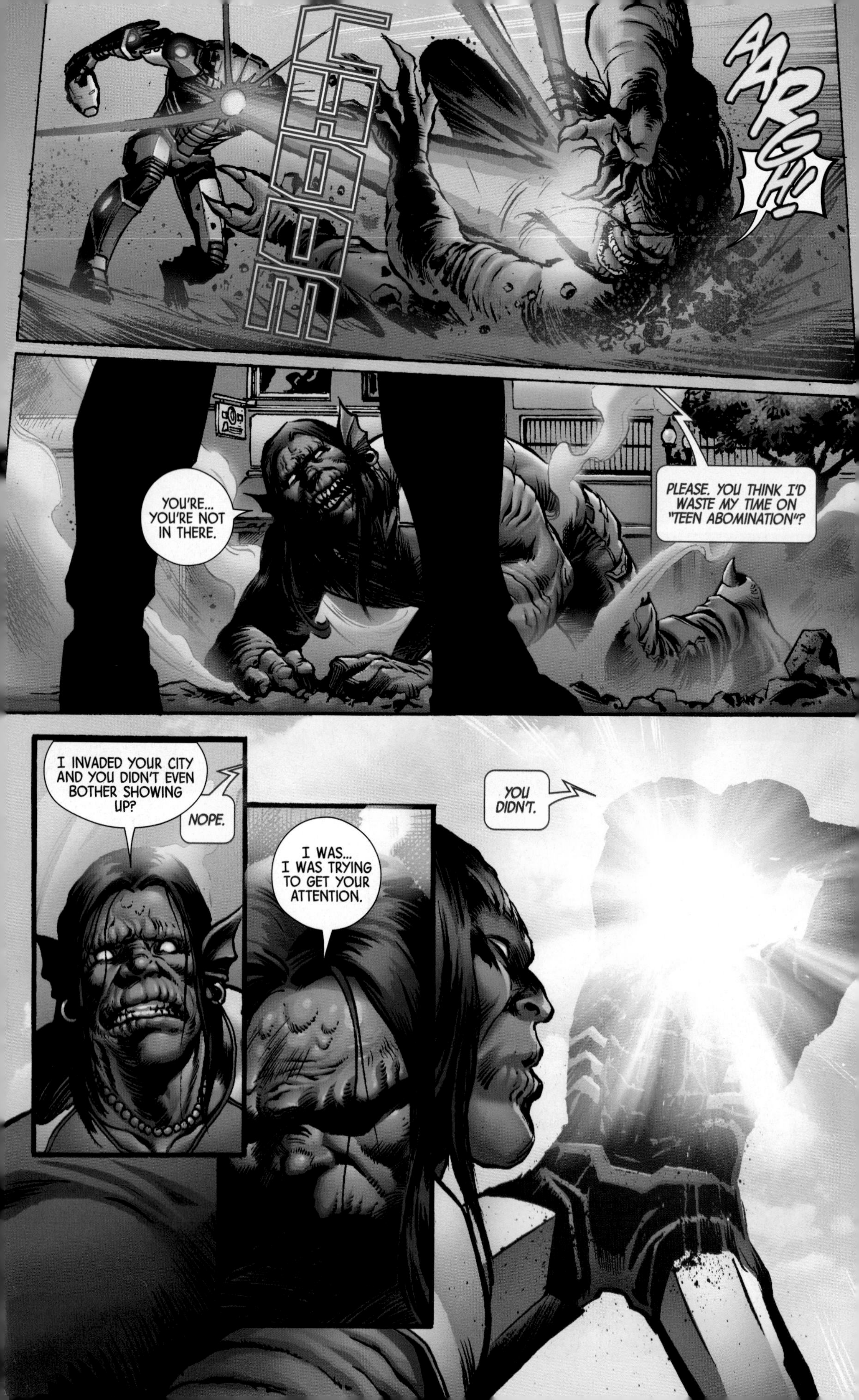
AARGH!
YOU'RE... YOU'RE NOT IN THERE.
PLEASE. YOU THINK I'D WASTE MY TIME ON "TEEN ABOMINATION"?
I INVADED YOUR CITY AND YOU DIDN'T EVEN BOTHER SHOWING UP?
NOPE.
I WAS... I WAS TRYING TO GET YOUR ATTENTION.
YOU DIDN'T.

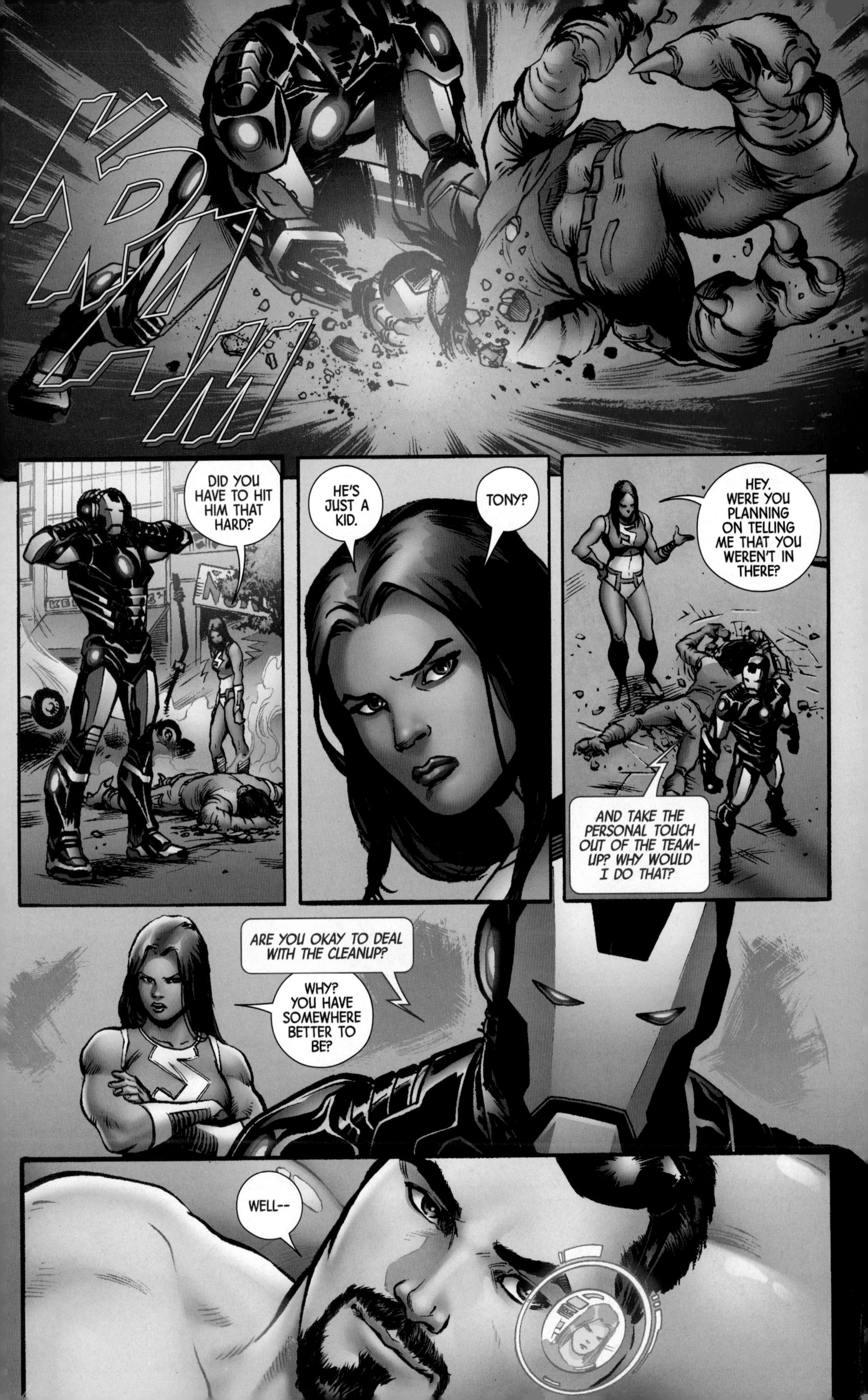

KRAKAM
DID YOU HAVE TO HIT HIM THAT HARD?
HE'S JUST A KID.
TONY?
HEY. WERE YOU PLANNING ON TELLING ME THAT YOU WEREN'T IN THERE?
AND TAKE THE PERSONAL TOUCH OUT OF THE TEAM-UP? WHY WOULD I DO THAT?
ARE YOU OKAY TO DEAL WITH THE CLEANUP?
WHY? YOU HAVE SOMEWHERE BETTER TO BE?
WELL--

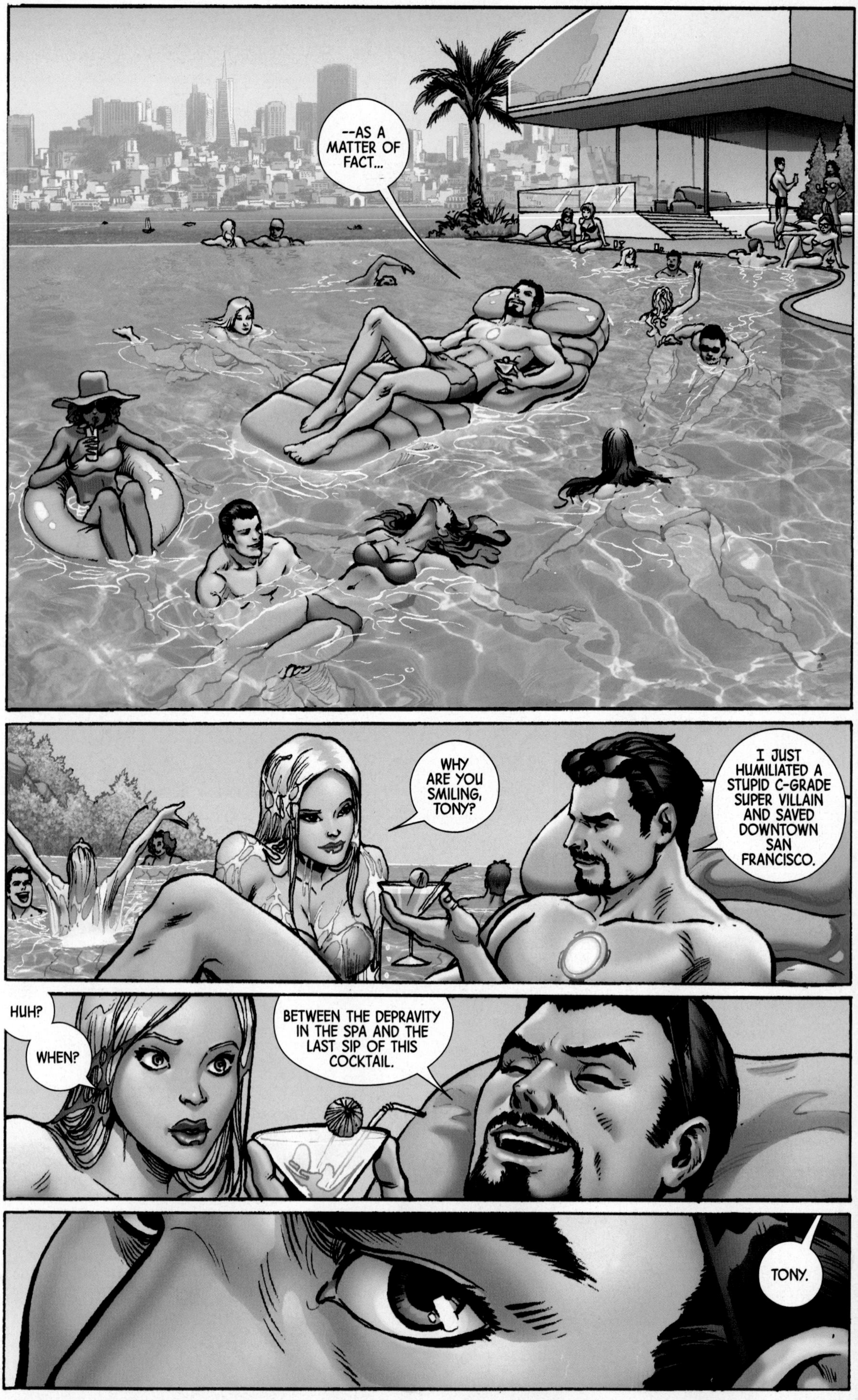
--AS A MATTER OF FACT...
WHY ARE YOU SMILING, TONY?
I JUST HUMILIATED A STUPID C-GRADE SUPER VILLAIN AND SAVED DOWNTOWN SAN FRANCISCO.
HUH?
WHEN?
BETWEEN THE DEPRAVITY IN THE SPA AND THE LAST SIP OF THIS COCKTAIL.
TONY.

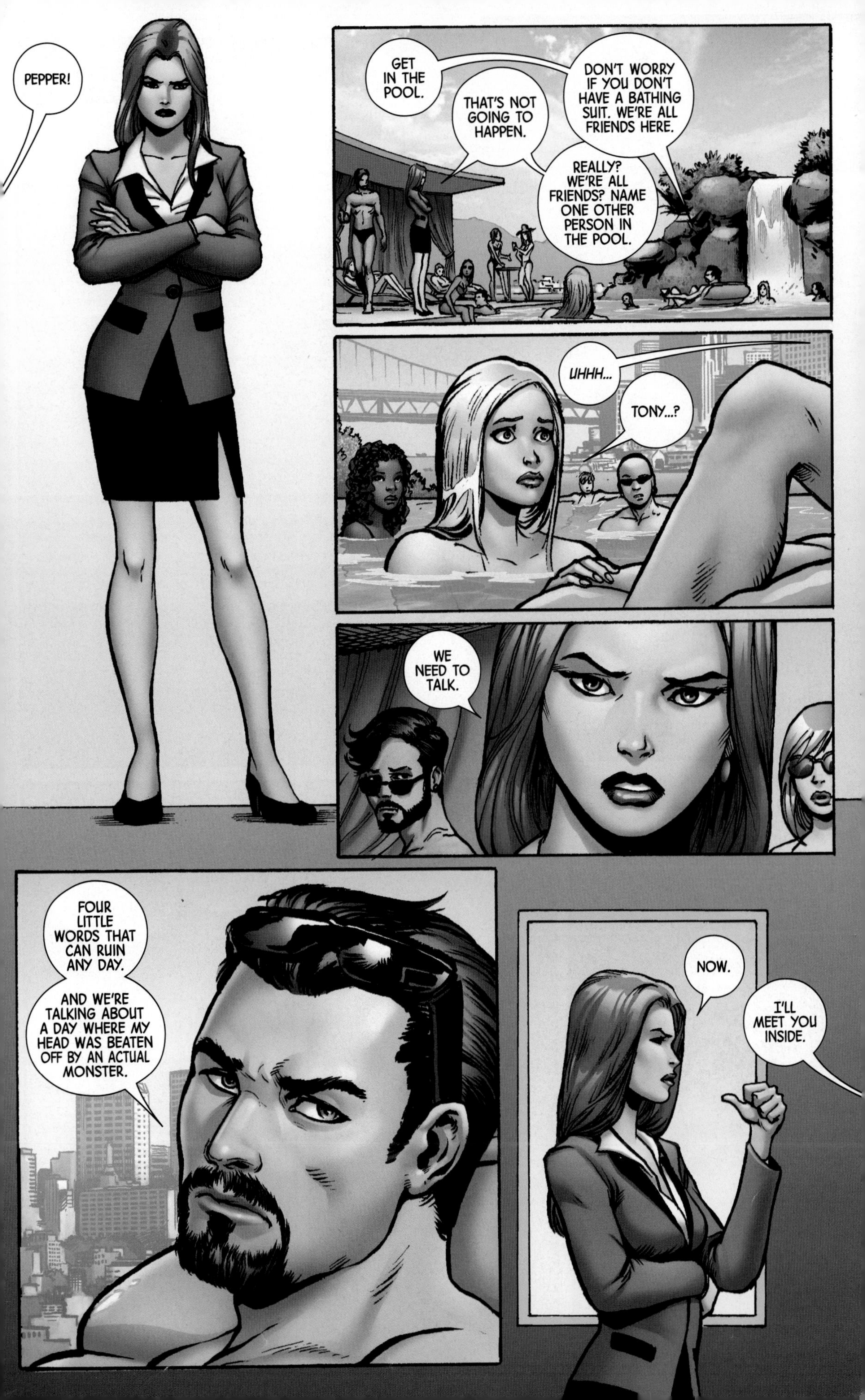
PEPPER!
GET IN THE POOL.
DON'T WORRY IF YOU DON'T HAVE A BATHING SUIT. WE'RE ALL FRIENDS HERE.
THAT'S NOT GOING TO HAPPEN.
REALLY? WE'RE ALL FRIENDS? NAME ONE OTHER PERSON IN THE POOL.
UHHH...
TONY...?
WE NEED TO TALK.
FOUR LITTLE WORDS THAT CAN RUIN ANY DAY.
AND WE'RE TALKING ABOUT A DAY WHERE MY HEAD WAS BEATEN OFF BY AN ACTUAL MONSTER.
NOW.
I'LL MEET YOU INSIDE.

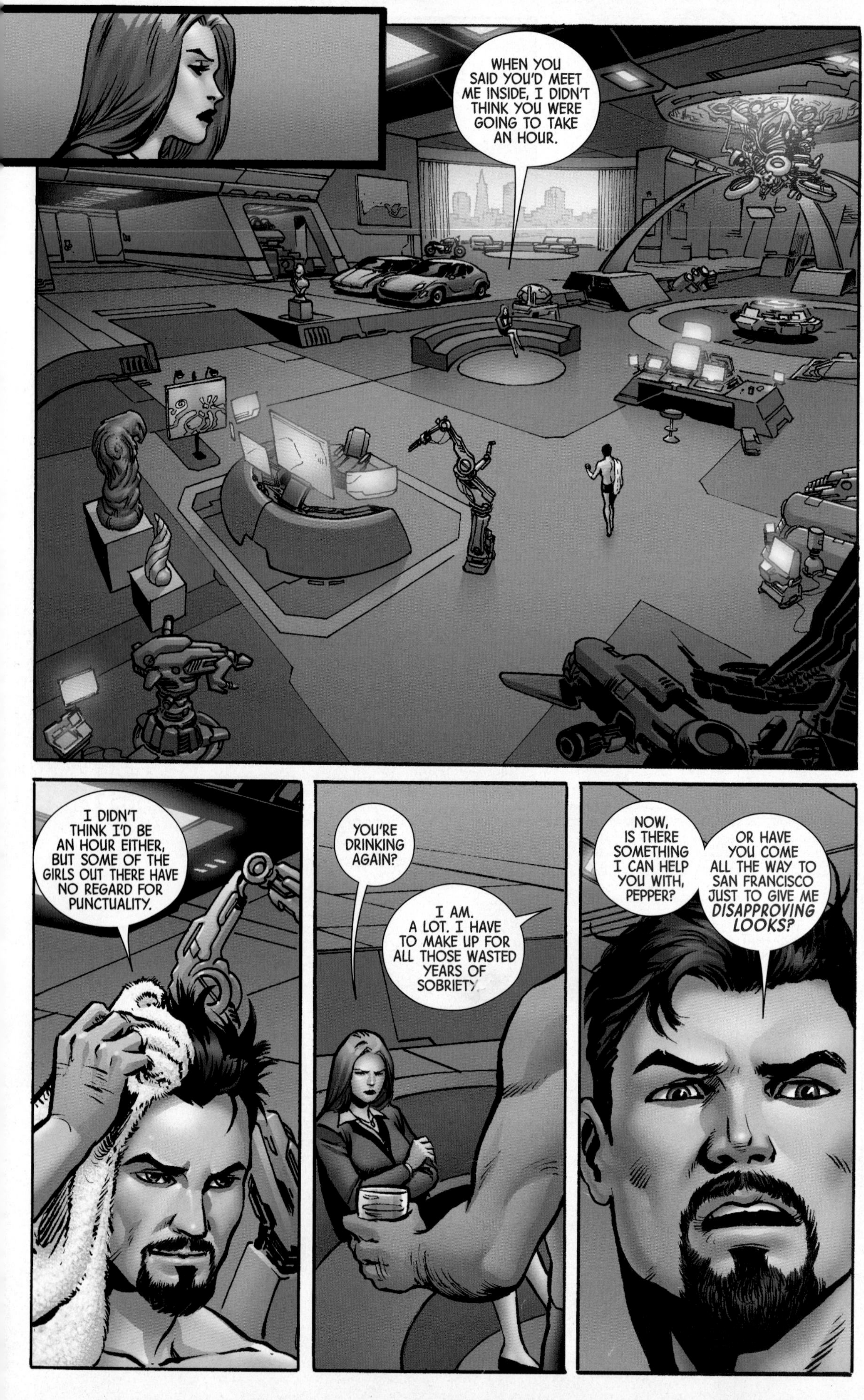
WHEN YOU SAID YOU'D MEET ME INSIDE, I DIDN'T THINK YOU WERE GOING TO TAKE AN HOUR.
I DIDN'T THINK I'D BE AN HOUR EITHER, BUT SOME OF THE GIRLS OUT THERE HAVE NO REGARD FOR PUNCTUALITY.
YOU'RE DRINKING AGAIN?
I AM. A LOT. I HAVE TO MAKE UP FOR ALL THOSE WASTED YEARS OF SOBRIETY.
NOW, IS THERE SOMETHING I CAN HELP YOU WITH, PEPPER?
OR HAVE YOU COME ALL THE WAY TO SAN FRANCISCO JUST TO GIVE ME *DISAPPROVING LOOKS?*

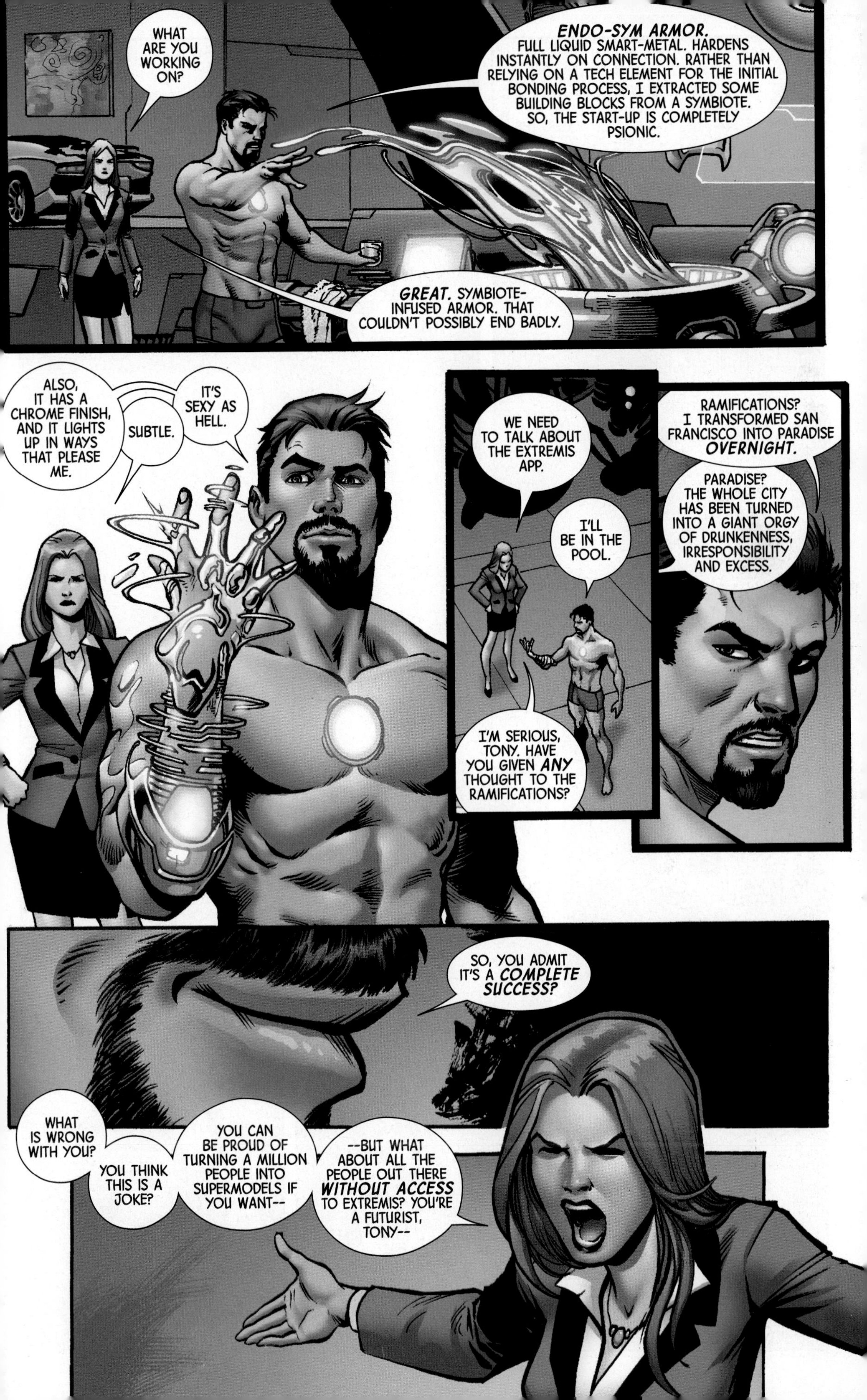
WHAT ARE YOU WORKING ON?
ENDO-SYM ARMOR. FULL LIQUID SMART-METAL. HARDENS INSTANTLY ON CONNECTION. RATHER THAN RELYING ON A TECH ELEMENT FOR THE INITIAL BONDING PROCESS, I EXTRACTED SOME BUILDING BLOCKS FROM A SYMBIOTE. SO, THE START-UP IS COMPLETELY PSIONIC.
GREAT. SYMBIOTE-INFUSED ARMOR. THAT COULDN'T POSSIBLY END BADLY.
ALSO, IT HAS A CHROME FINISH, AND IT LIGHTS UP IN WAYS THAT PLEASE ME.
SUBTLE.
IT'S SEXY AS HELL.
WE NEED TO TALK ABOUT THE EXTREMIS APP.
I'LL BE IN THE POOL.
I'M SERIOUS, TONY. HAVE YOU GIVEN ANY THOUGHT TO THE RAMIFICATIONS?
RAMIFICATIONS? I TRANSFORMED SAN FRANCISCO INTO PARADISE OVERNIGHT.
PARADISE? THE WHOLE CITY HAS BEEN TURNED INTO A GIANT ORGY OF DRUNKENNESS, IRRESPONSIBILITY AND EXCESS.
SO, YOU ADMIT IT'S A COMPLETE SUCCESS?
WHAT IS WRONG WITH YOU?
YOU THINK THIS IS A JOKE?
YOU CAN BE PROUD OF TURNING A MILLION PEOPLE INTO SUPERMODELS IF YOU WANT--
--BUT WHAT ABOUT ALL THE PEOPLE OUT THERE WITHOUT ACCESS TO EXTREMIS? YOU'RE A FUTURIST, TONY--

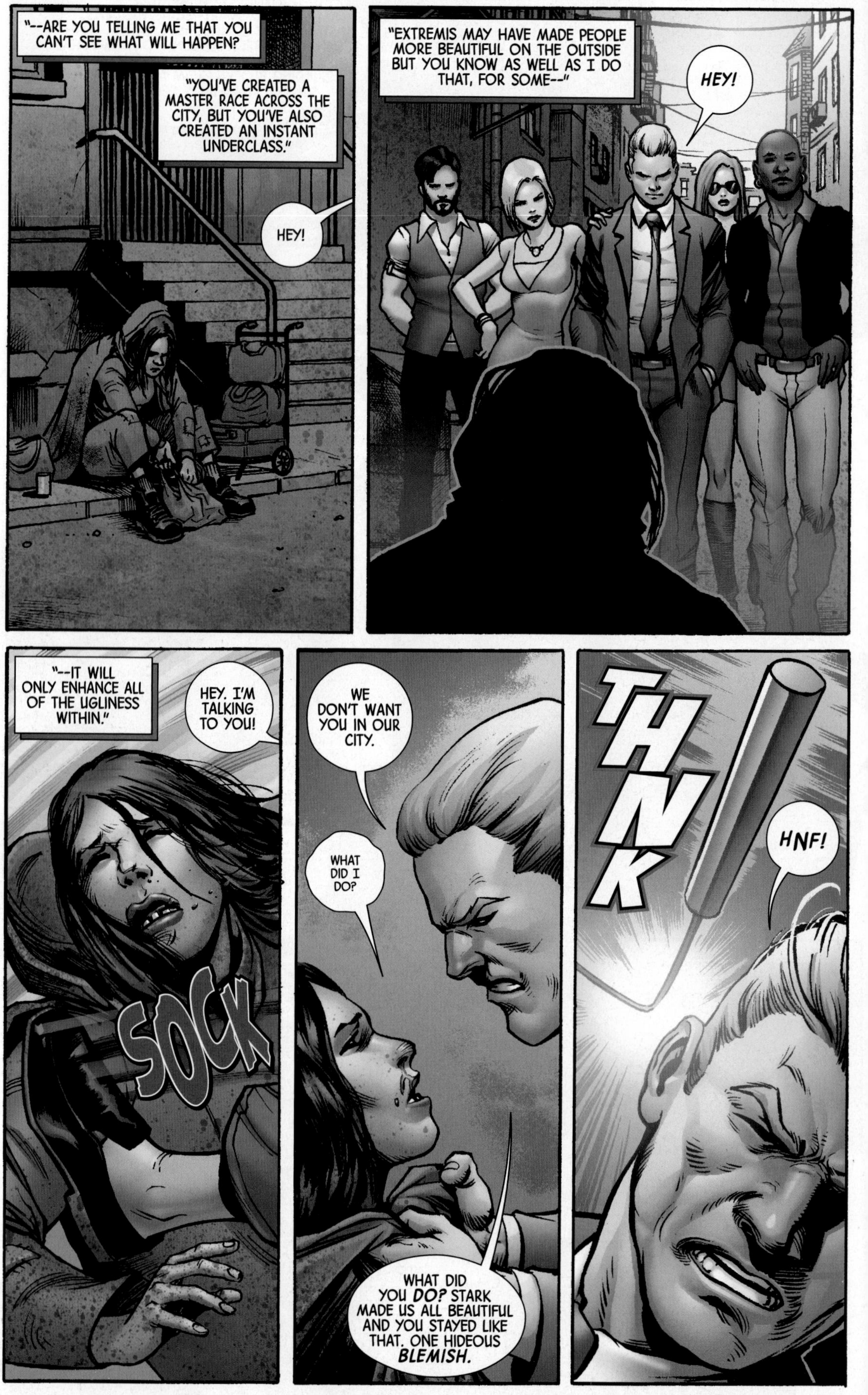
"--ARE YOU TELLING ME THAT YOU CAN'T SEE WHAT WILL HAPPEN?
"YOU'VE CREATED A MASTER RACE ACROSS THE CITY, BUT YOU'VE ALSO CREATED AN INSTANT UNDERCLASS."
HEY!
"EXTREMIS MAY HAVE MADE PEOPLE MORE BEAUTIFUL ON THE OUTSIDE BUT YOU KNOW AS WELL AS I DO THAT, FOR SOME--"
HEY!
"--IT WILL ONLY ENHANCE ALL OF THE UGLINESS WITHIN."
HEY. I'M TALKING TO YOU!
SOCK
WE DON'T WANT YOU IN OUR CITY.
WHAT DID I DO?
WHAT DID YOU DO? STARK MADE US ALL BEAUTIFUL AND YOU STAYED LIKE THAT. ONE HIDEOUS BLEMISH.
THNK
HNF!

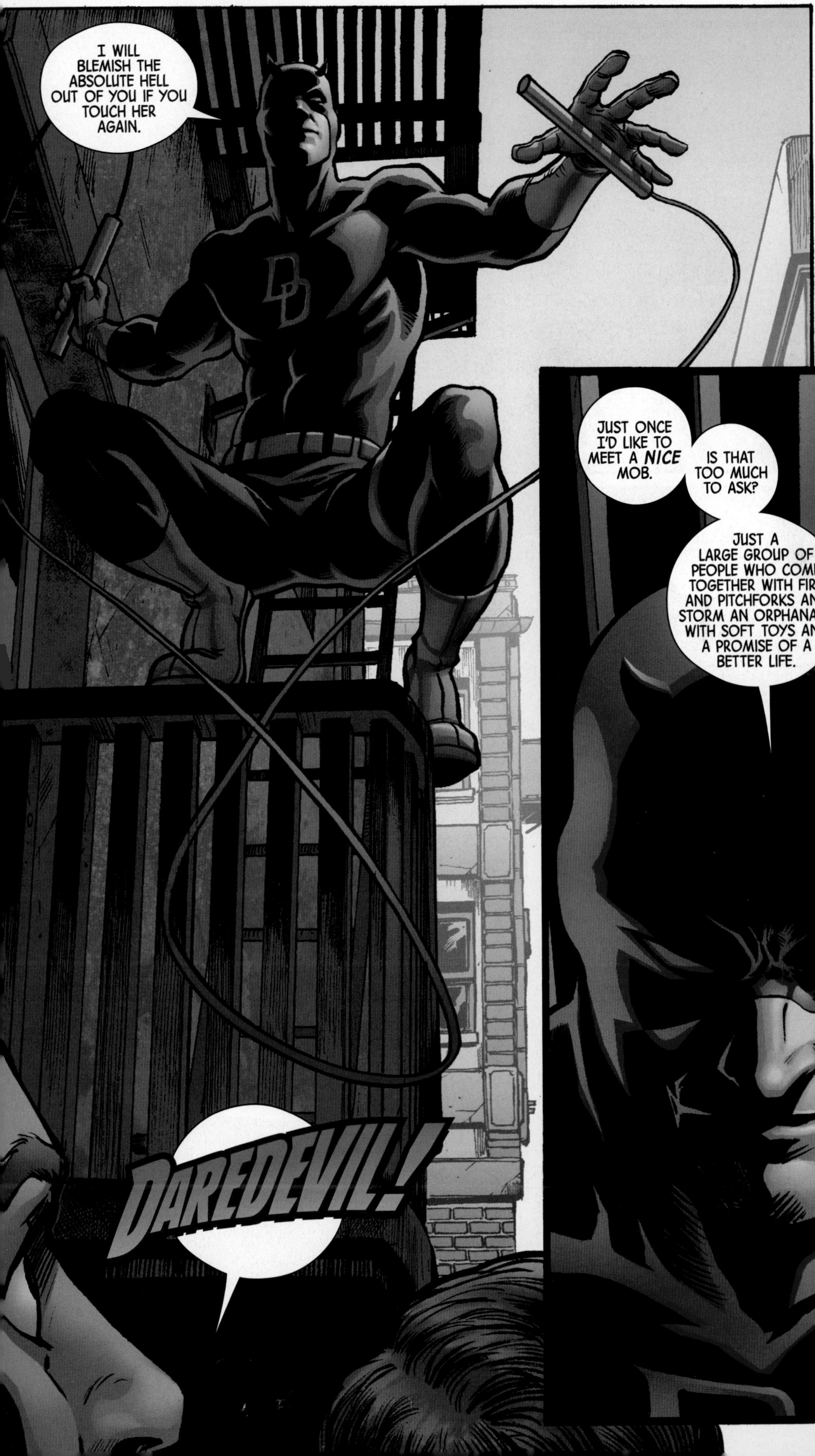
I WILL BLEMISH THE ABSOLUTE HELL OUT OF YOU IF YOU TOUCH HER AGAIN.
DAREDEVIL!
JUST ONCE I'D LIKE TO MEET A NICE MOB.
IS THAT TOO MUCH TO ASK?
JUST A LARGE GROUP OF PEOPLE WHO COME TOGETHER WITH FIRE AND PITCHFORKS AND STORM AN ORPHANAGE WITH SOFT TOYS AND A PROMISE OF A BETTER LIFE.

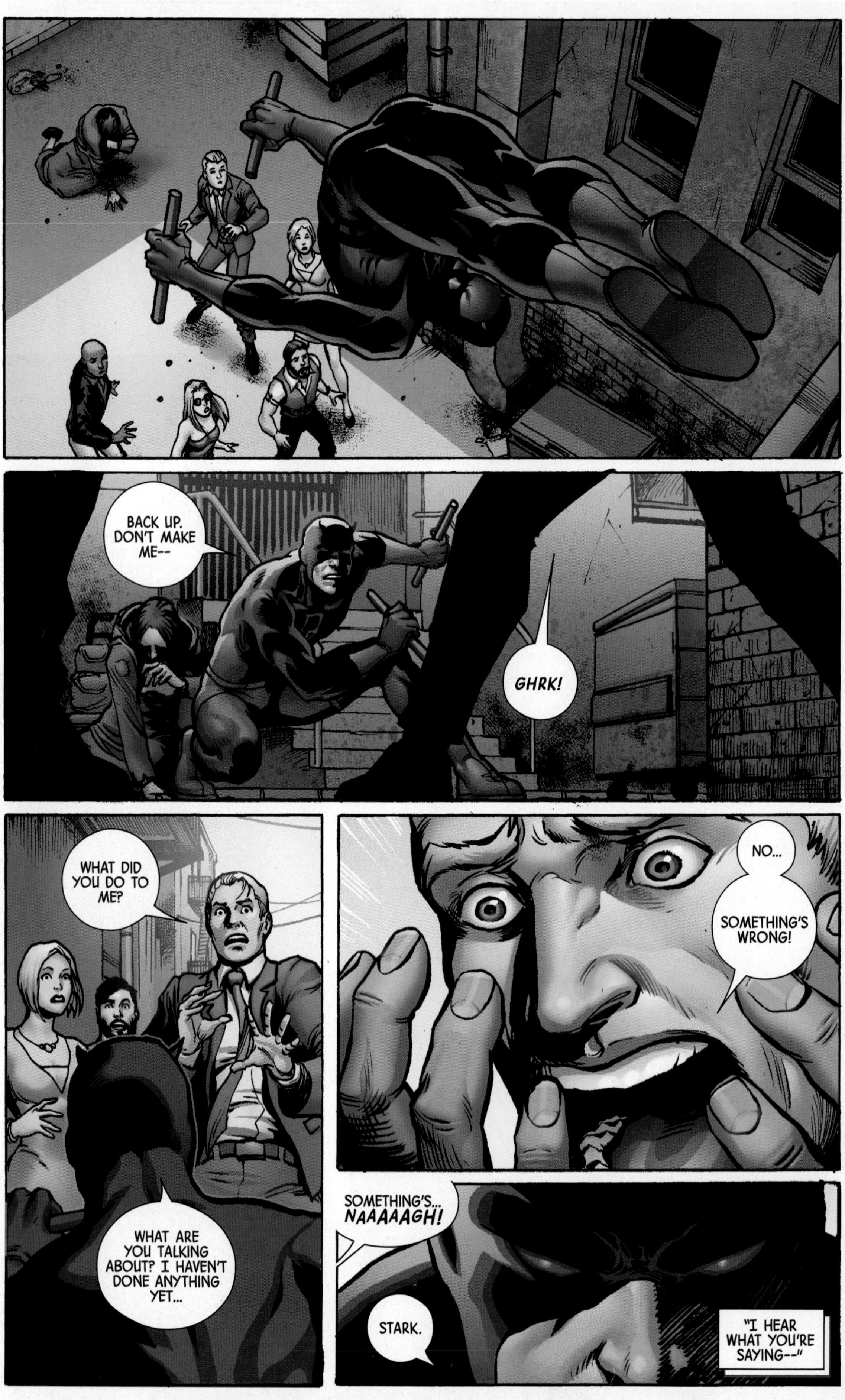

BACK UP. DON'T MAKE ME--
GHRK!
WHAT DID YOU DO TO ME?
WHAT ARE YOU TALKING ABOUT? I HAVEN'T DONE ANYTHING YET...
NO...
SOMETHING'S WRONG!
SOMETHING'S... NAAAAAGH!
STARK.
"I HEAR WHAT YOU'RE SAYING--"

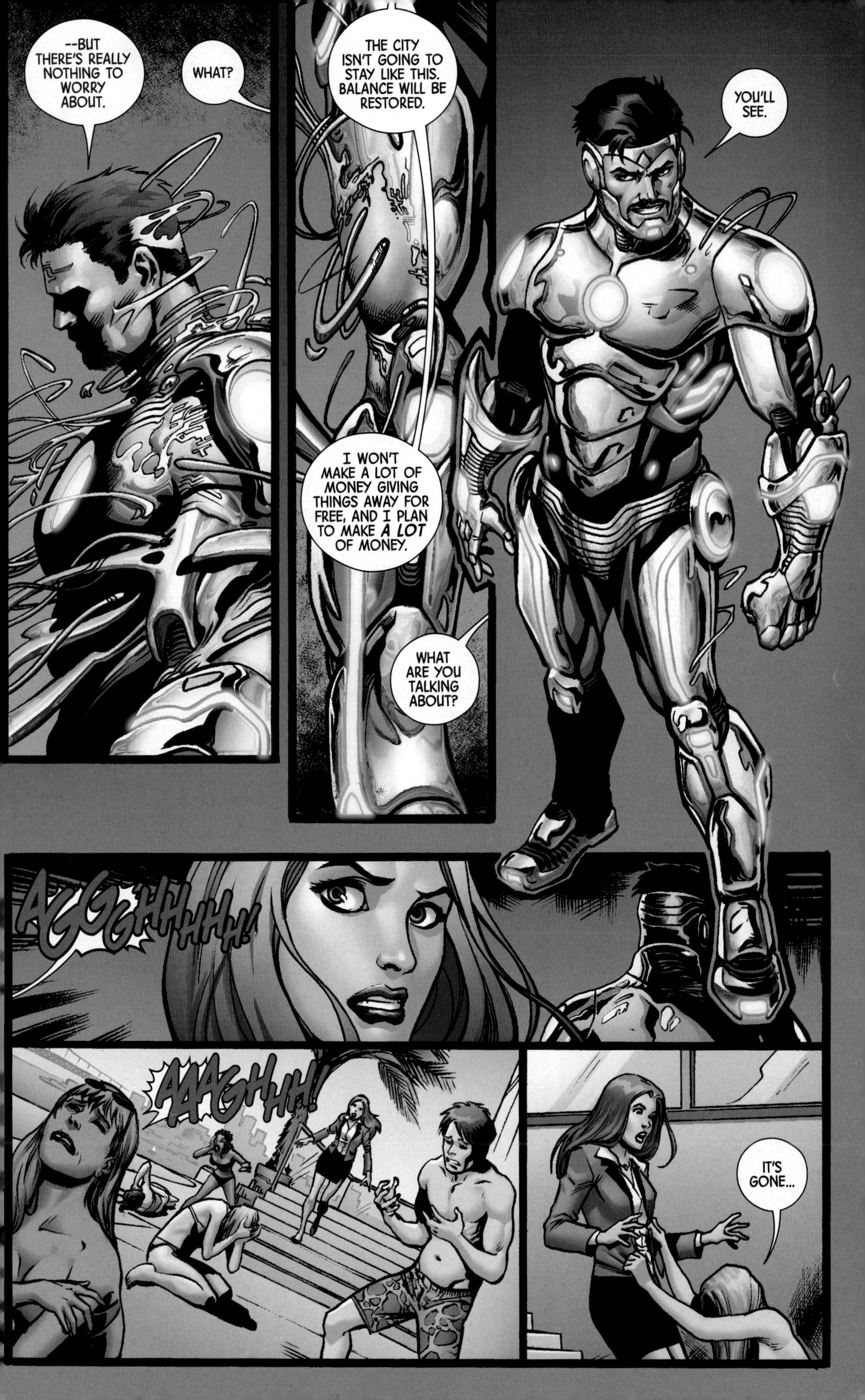
--BUT THERE'S REALLY NOTHING TO WORRY ABOUT.
WHAT?
THE CITY ISN'T GOING TO STAY LIKE THIS. BALANCE WILL BE RESTORED.
YOU'LL SEE.
I WON'T MAKE A LOT OF MONEY GIVING THINGS AWAY FOR FREE, AND I PLAN TO MAKE *A LOT* OF MONEY.
WHAT ARE YOU TALKING ABOUT?
AGGGHHHHHH!
AAAGHHH!
IT'S GONE...

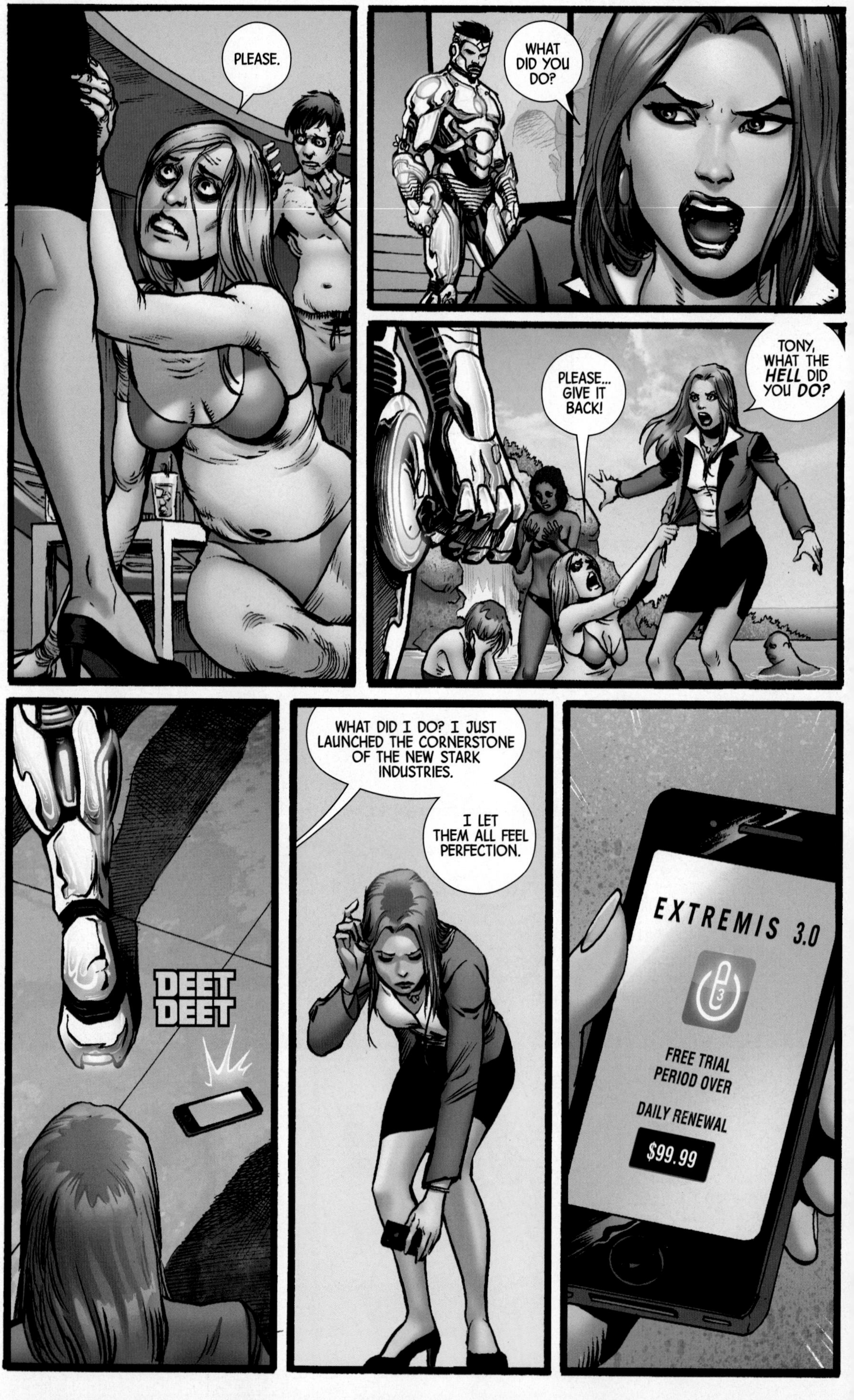
PLEASE.
WHAT DID YOU DO?
PLEASE... GIVE IT BACK!
TONY, WHAT THE HELL DID YOU DO?
DEET DEET
WHAT DID I DO? I JUST LAUNCHED THE CORNERSTONE OF THE NEW STARK INDUSTRIES.
I LET THEM ALL FEEL PERFECTION.
EXTREMIS 3.0
FREE TRIAL PERIOD OVER
DAILY RENEWAL
$99.99

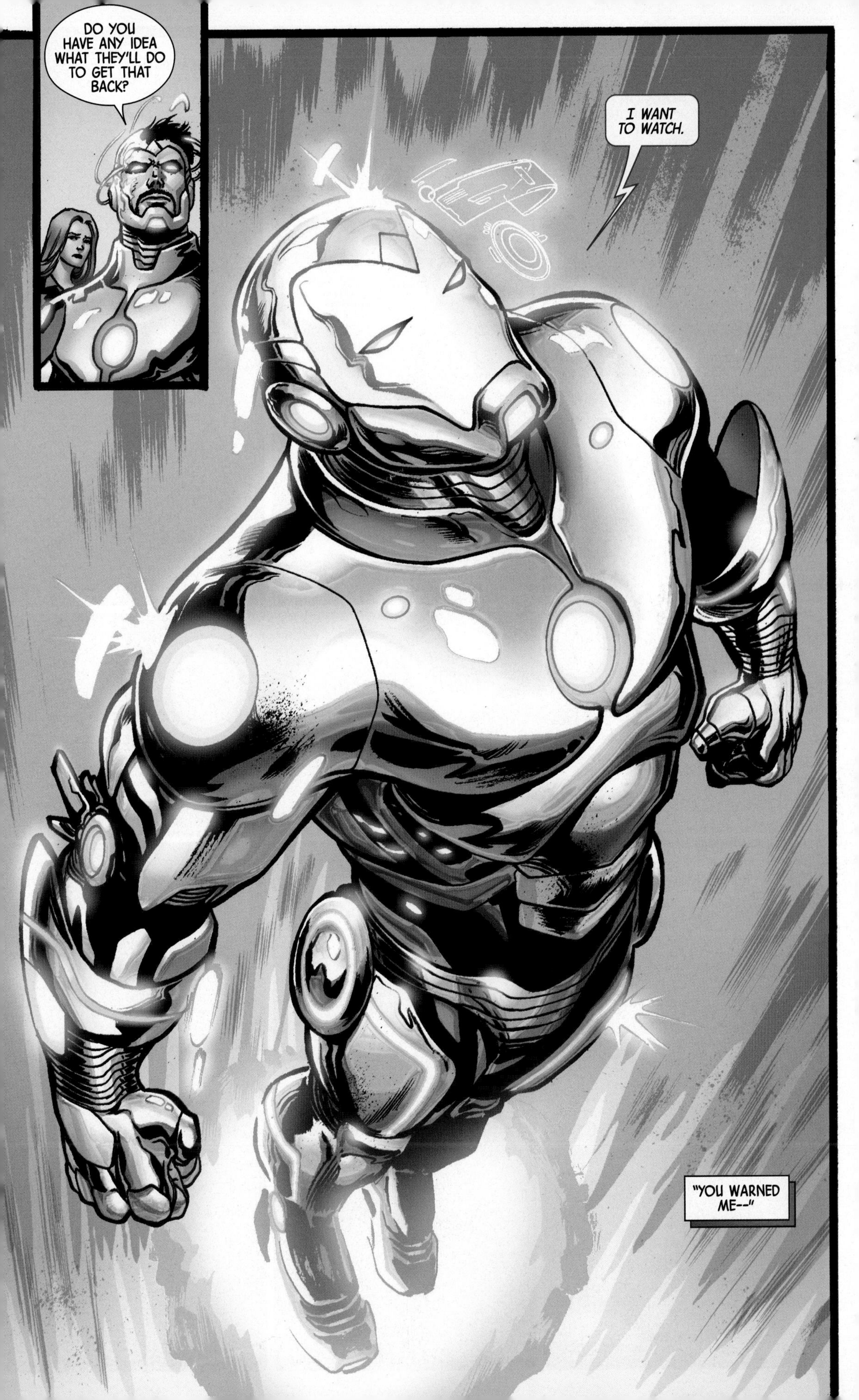
DO YOU HAVE ANY IDEA WHAT THEY'LL DO TO GET THAT BACK?
I WANT TO WATCH.
"YOU WARNED ME--"

--TONY ALWAYS SAID HIS BIGGEST FEAR WASN'T THE WRONG PEOPLE GETTING THEIR HANDS ON HIS TECHNOLOGY, HIS WEAPONS, HIS FRIENDS OR EVEN HIS LOVERS.

WHEN HE TOLD ME WHAT IT WAS, I THOUGHT IT WAS EGO. BUT I UNDERSTAND NOW.

BECAUSE THE NIGHTMARE SCENARIO HAS HAPPENED.

HIS *MIND* HAS BEEN *TAKEN.*

WE NEED TO ACTIVATE THE CONTINGENCY.

UNDERSTOOD.

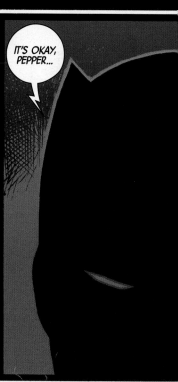

IT'S OKAY, PEPPER...

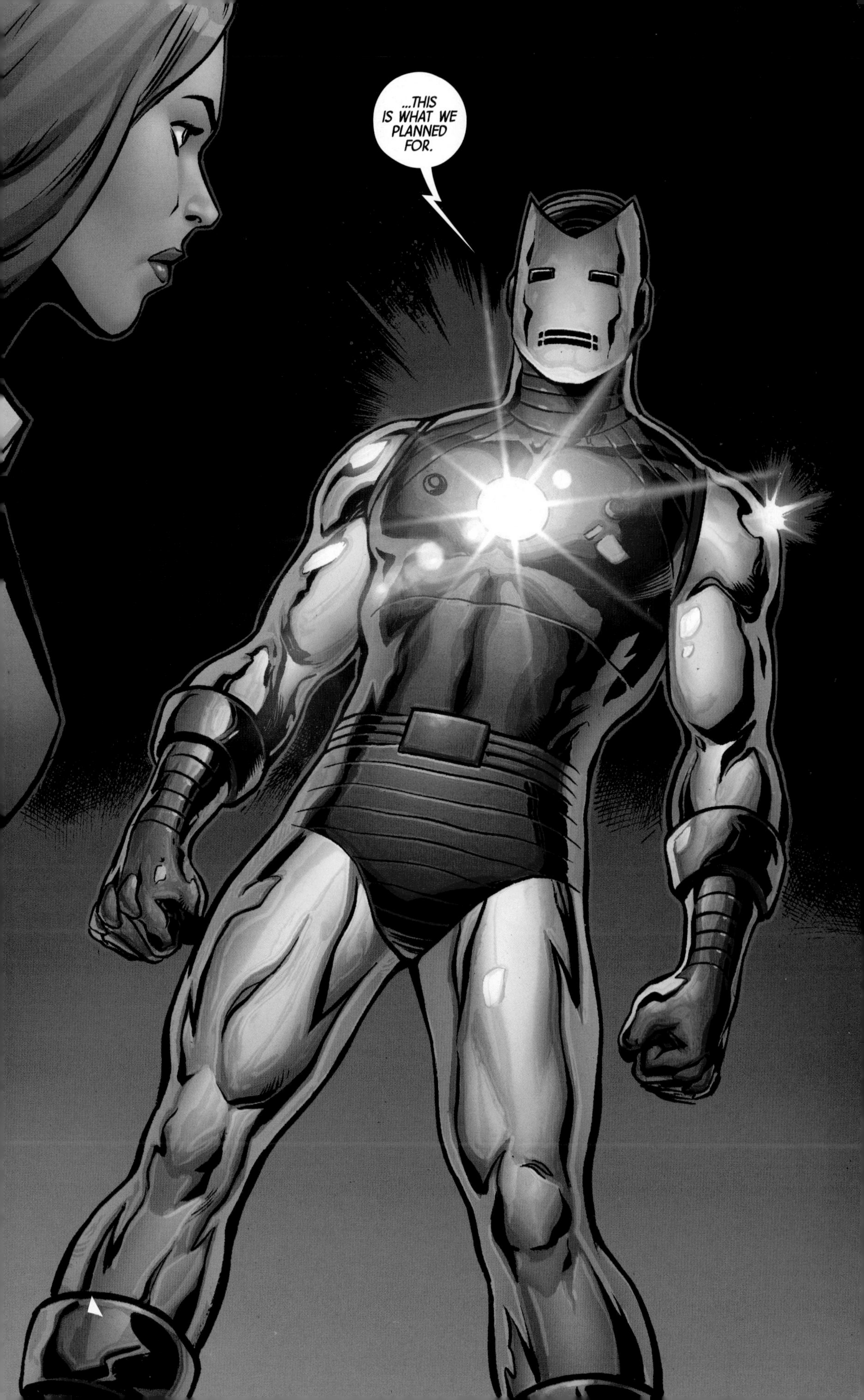
...THIS IS WHAT WE PLANNED FOR.

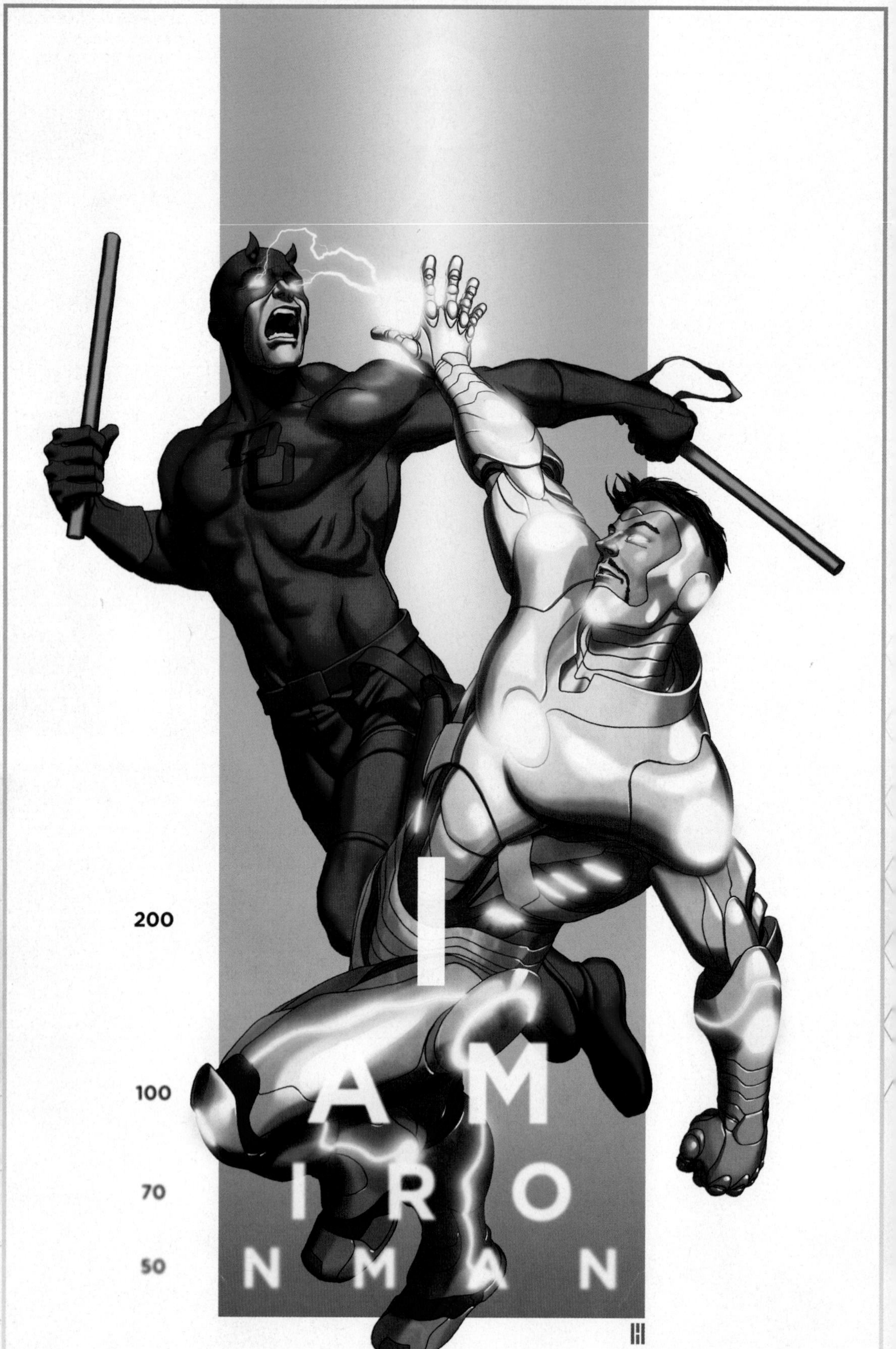
200
I
100
A M
70
I R O
50
N M A N

2: DAREDEVIL VS. IRON MAN

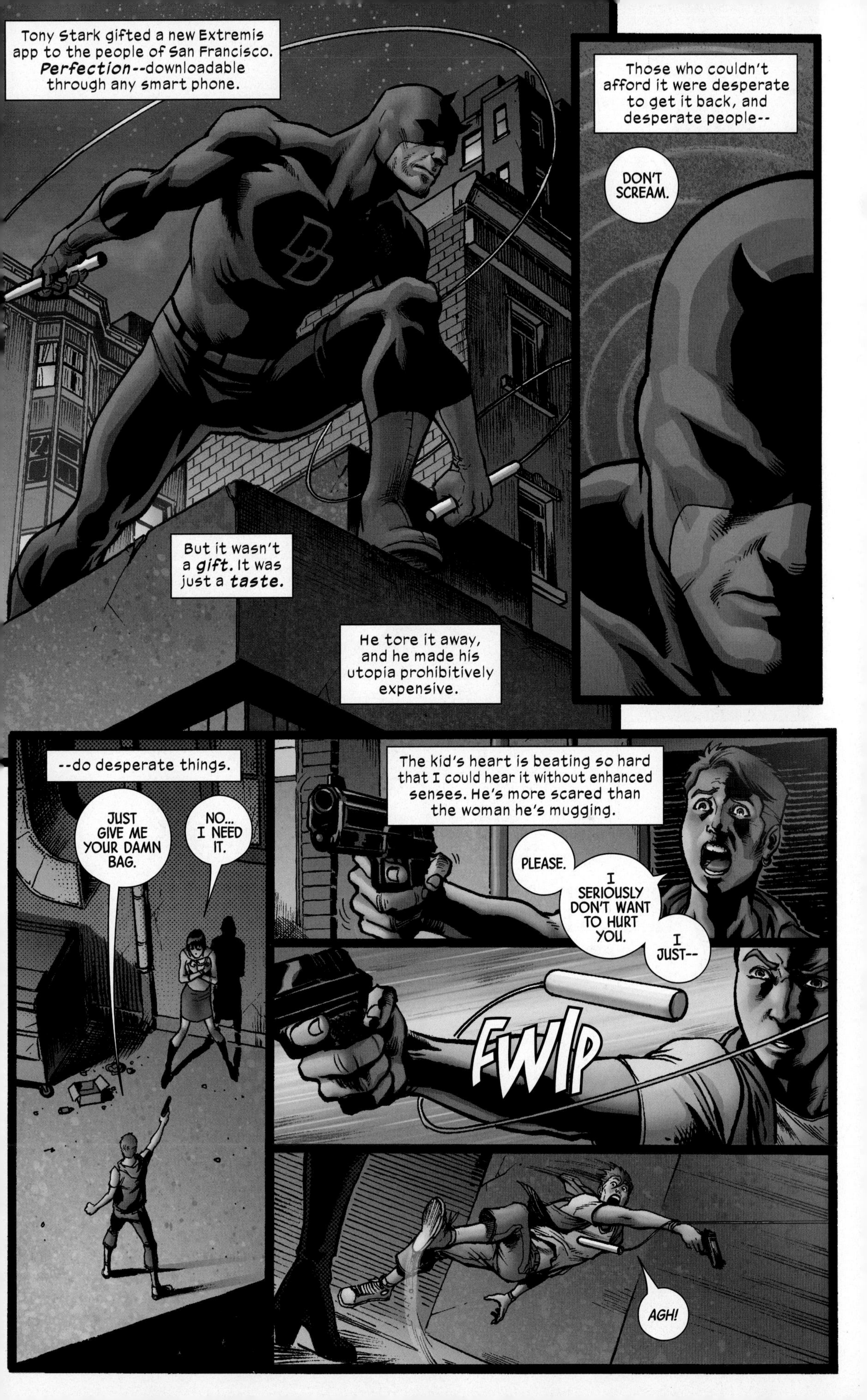
Tony Stark gifted a new Extremis app to the people of San Francisco. *Perfection*--downloadable through any smart phone.
But it wasn't a *gift*. It was just a *taste*.
He tore it away, and he made his utopia prohibitively expensive.
Those who couldn't afford it were desperate to get it back, and desperate people--
DON'T SCREAM.
--do desperate things.
JUST GIVE ME YOUR DAMN BAG.
NO... I NEED IT.
The kid's heart is beating so hard that I could hear it without enhanced senses. He's more scared than the woman he's mugging.
PLEASE.
I SERIOUSLY DON'T WANT TO HURT YOU.
I JUST--
FWIP
AGH!

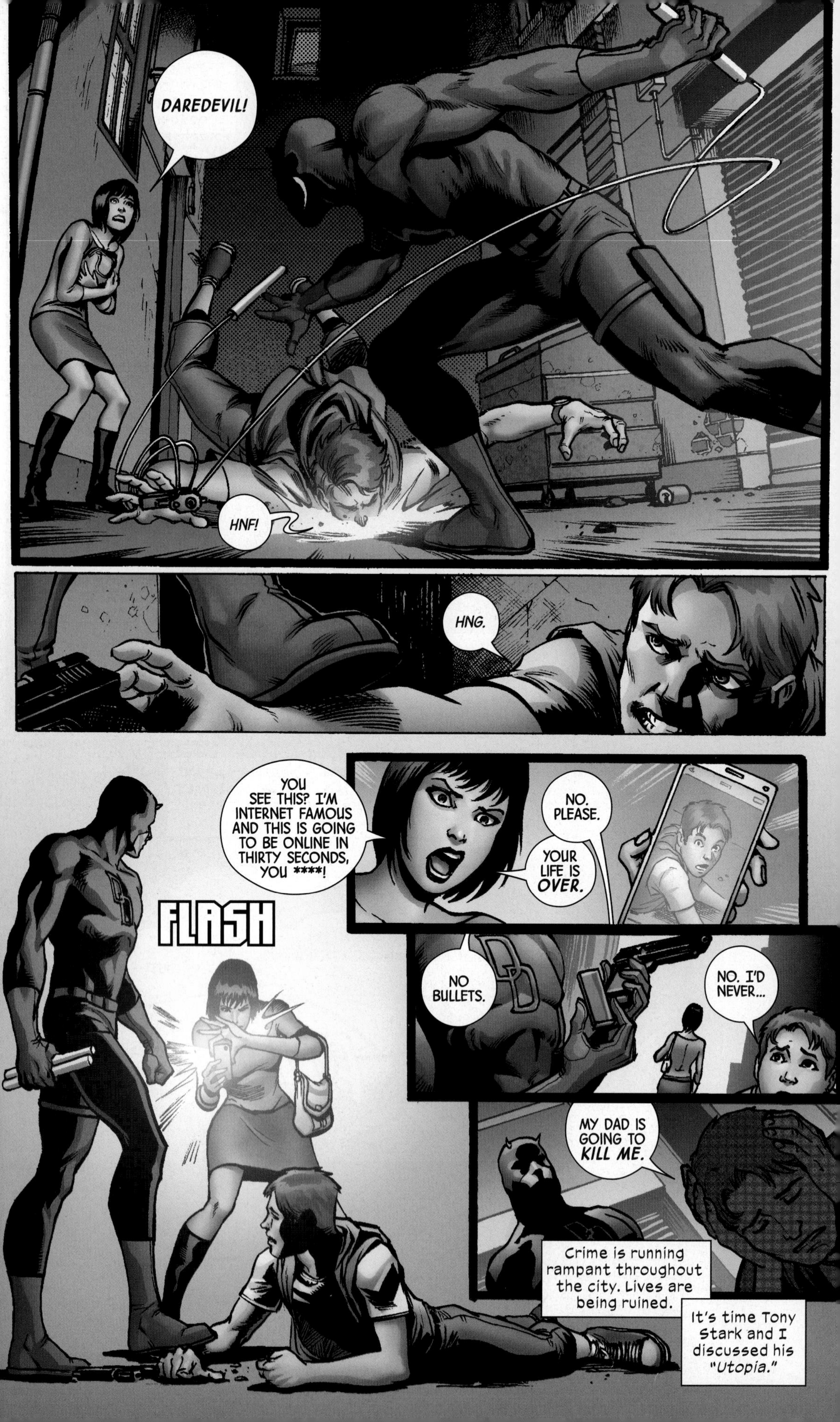
DAREDEVIL!
HNF!
HNG.
YOU SEE THIS? I'M INTERNET FAMOUS AND THIS IS GOING TO BE ONLINE IN THIRTY SECONDS, YOU ****!
FLASH
NO. PLEASE.
YOUR LIFE IS OVER.
NO BULLETS.
NO. I'D NEVER...
MY DAD IS GOING TO KILL ME.
Crime is running rampant throughout the city. Lives are being ruined.
It's time Tony Stark and I discussed his "Utopia."

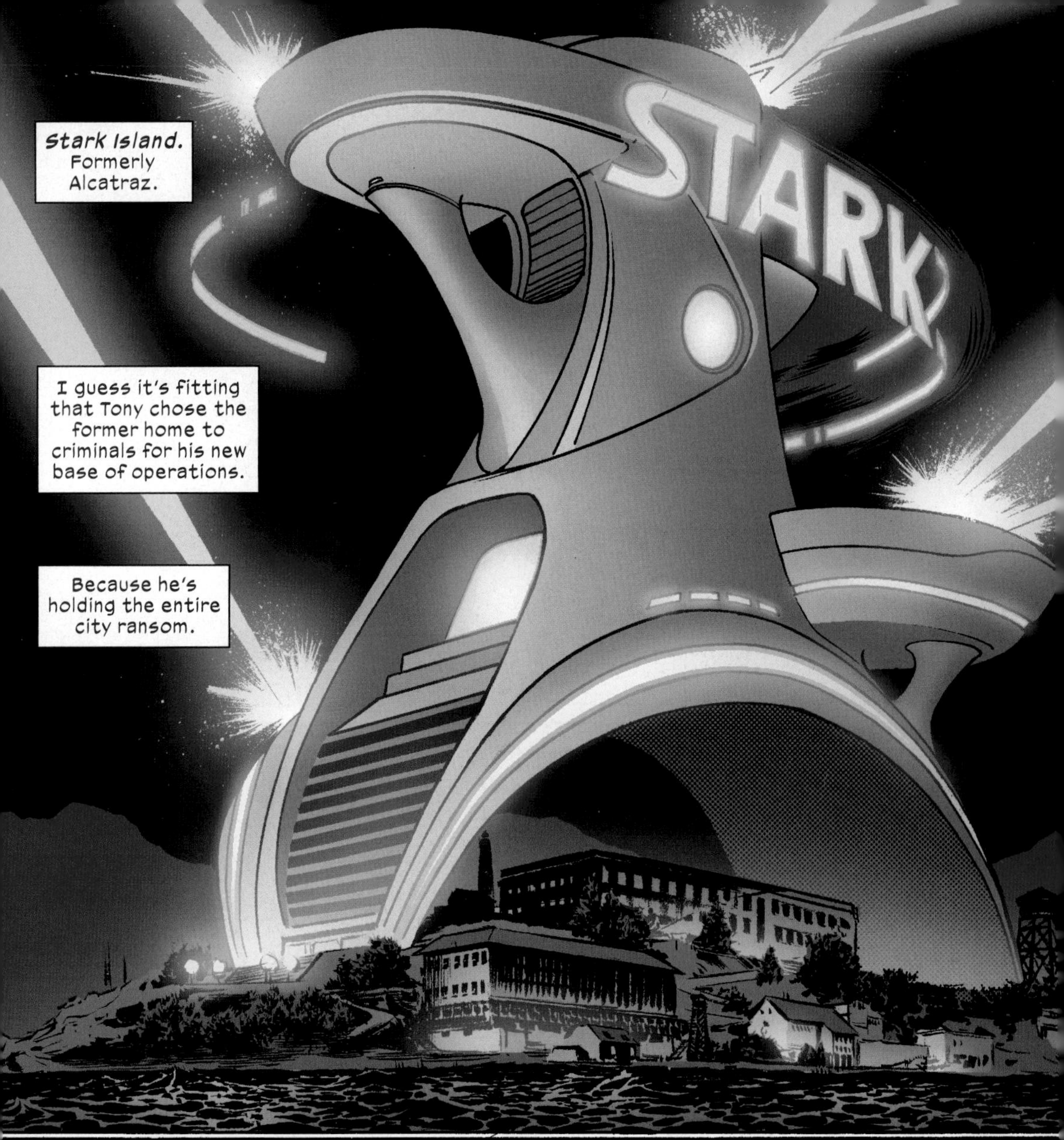
Stark Island. Formerly Alcatraz.
STARK
I guess it's fitting that Tony chose the former home to criminals for his new base of operations.
Because he's holding the entire city ransom.

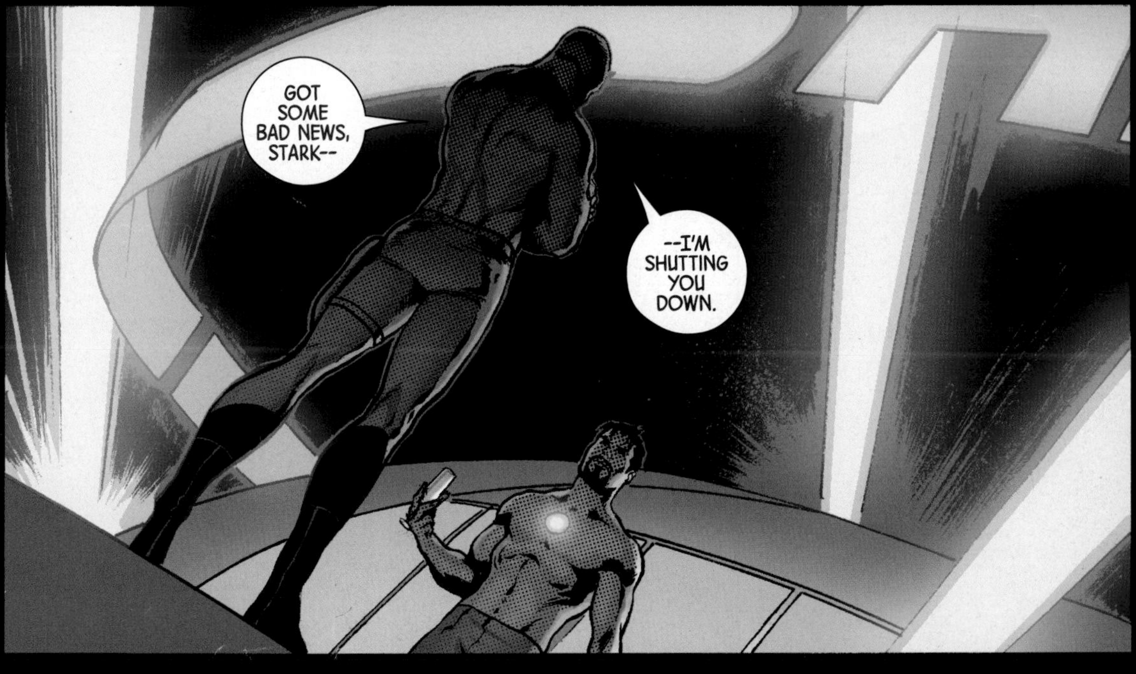
GOT SOME BAD NEWS, STARK--
--I'M SHUTTING YOU DOWN.

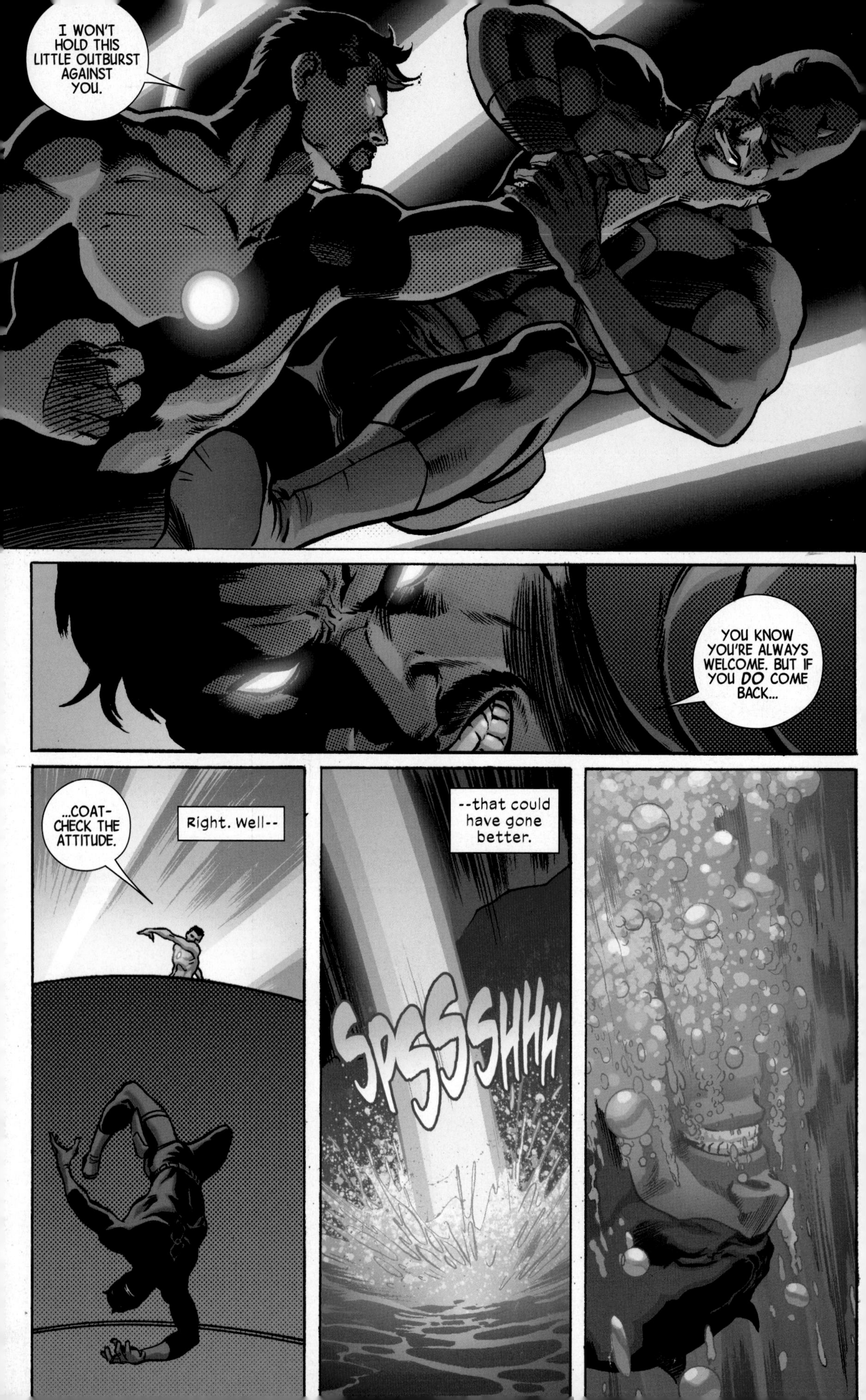

I WON'T HOLD THIS LITTLE OUTBURST AGAINST YOU.
YOU KNOW YOU'RE ALWAYS WELCOME. BUT IF YOU *DO* COME BACK...
...COAT-CHECK THE ATTITUDE.
Right. Well--
--that could have gone better.
SPSSSHHH

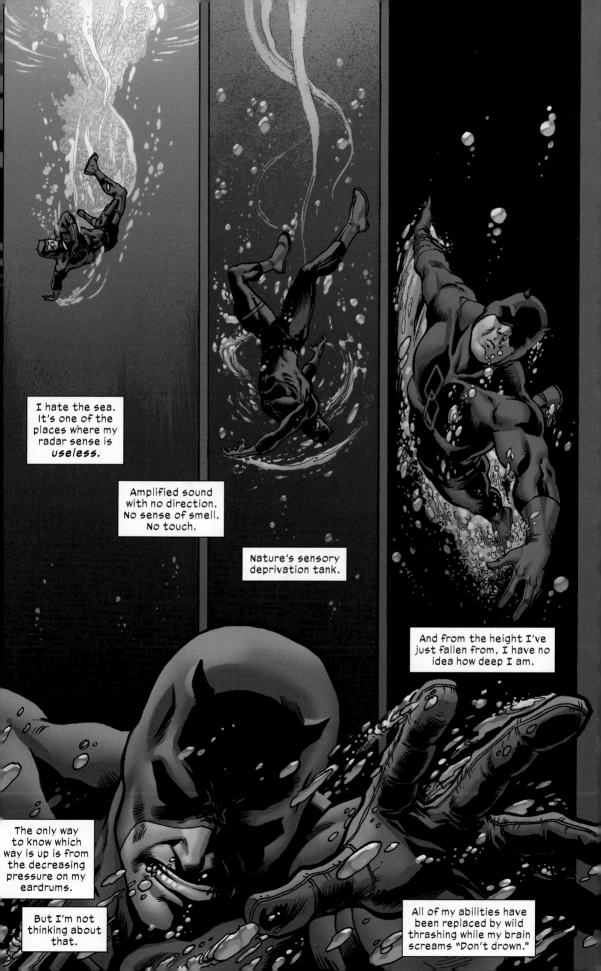

I hate the sea. It's one of the places where my radar sense is *useless*.

Amplified sound with no direction. No sense of smell. No touch.

Nature's sensory deprivation tank.

And from the height I've just fallen from, I have no idea how deep I am.

The only way to know which way is up is from the decreasing pressure on my eardrums.

But I'm not thinking about that.

All of my abilities have been replaced by wild thrashing while my brain screams "Don't drown."

HUUURGH!

I can hear the party. I can hear the excitement. The adrenaline. Everything has increased. Tony's guests have been fueled by him throwing me out of there.

Confronting him at home was stupid. Way too public. I just gave him a chance to *show off.*

And Tony Stark has always loved an audience.

LADIES AND GENTLEMEN. THAT WAS OUR ENTERTAINMENT FOR THE EVENING, DAREDEVIL, THE MAN WITHOUT FEAR!

THOUGH I HAVE TO SAY, FOR A *"MAN WITHOUT FEAR,"* AS HE WAS FALLING THROUGH THE AIR, HE LOOKED JUST A TEENSY-BIT WORRIED.

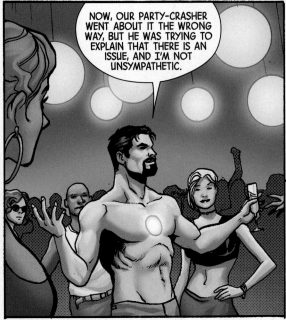

NOW, OUR PARTY-CRASHER WENT ABOUT IT THE WRONG WAY, BUT HE WAS TRYING TO EXPLAIN THAT THERE IS AN ISSUE, AND I'M NOT UNSYMPATHETIC.

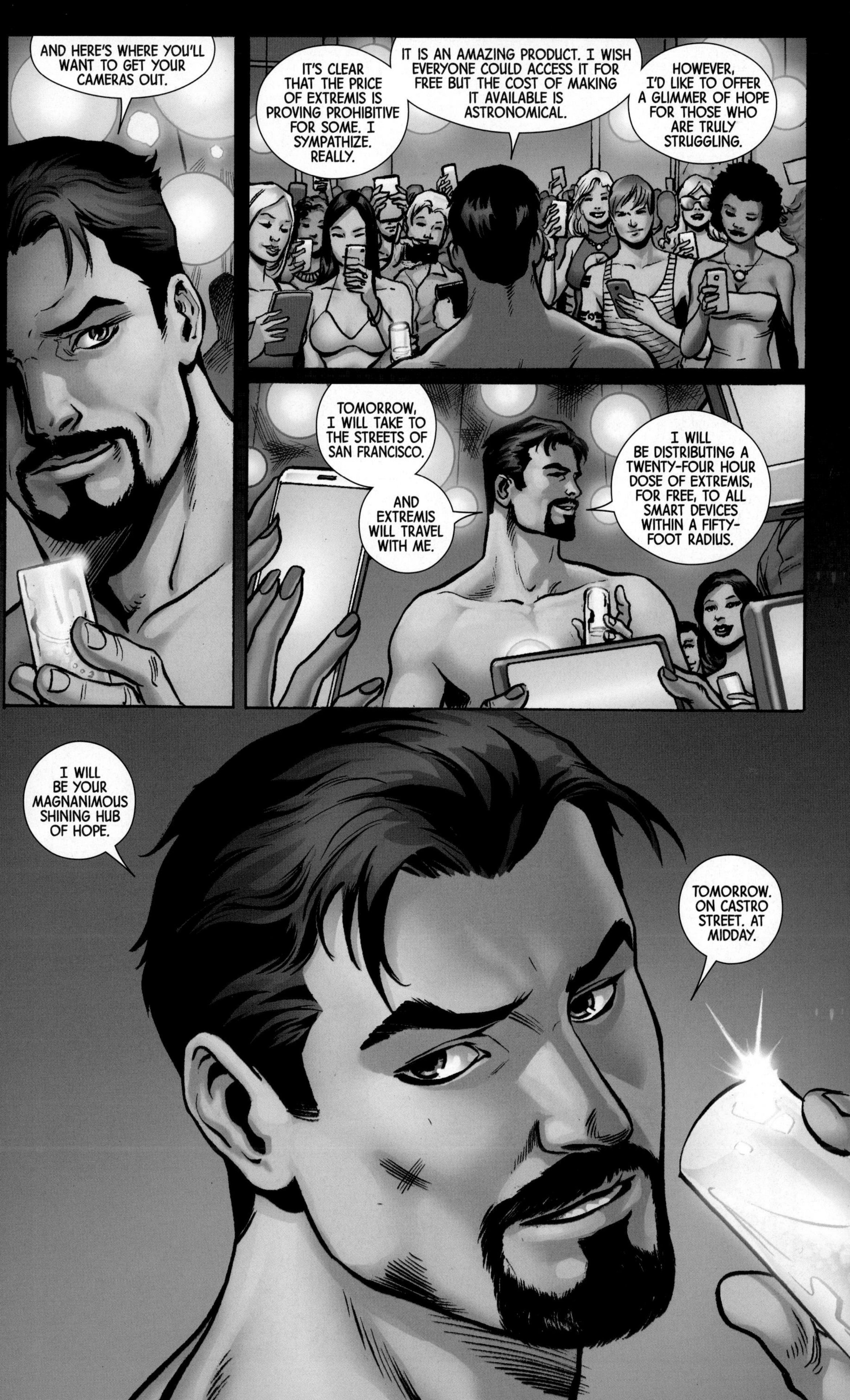
AND HERE'S WHERE YOU'LL WANT TO GET YOUR CAMERAS OUT.
IT'S CLEAR THAT THE PRICE OF EXTREMIS IS PROVING PROHIBITIVE FOR SOME. I SYMPATHIZE. REALLY.
IT IS AN AMAZING PRODUCT. I WISH EVERYONE COULD ACCESS IT FOR FREE BUT THE COST OF MAKING IT AVAILABLE IS ASTRONOMICAL.
HOWEVER, I'D LIKE TO OFFER A GLIMMER OF HOPE FOR THOSE WHO ARE TRULY STRUGGLING.
TOMORROW, I WILL TAKE TO THE STREETS OF SAN FRANCISCO.
AND EXTREMIS WILL TRAVEL WITH ME.
I WILL BE DISTRIBUTING A TWENTY-FOUR HOUR DOSE OF EXTREMIS, FOR FREE, TO ALL SMART DEVICES WITHIN A FIFTY-FOOT RADIUS.
I WILL BE YOUR MAGNANIMOUS SHINING HUB OF HOPE.
TOMORROW. ON CASTRO STREET. AT MIDDAY.

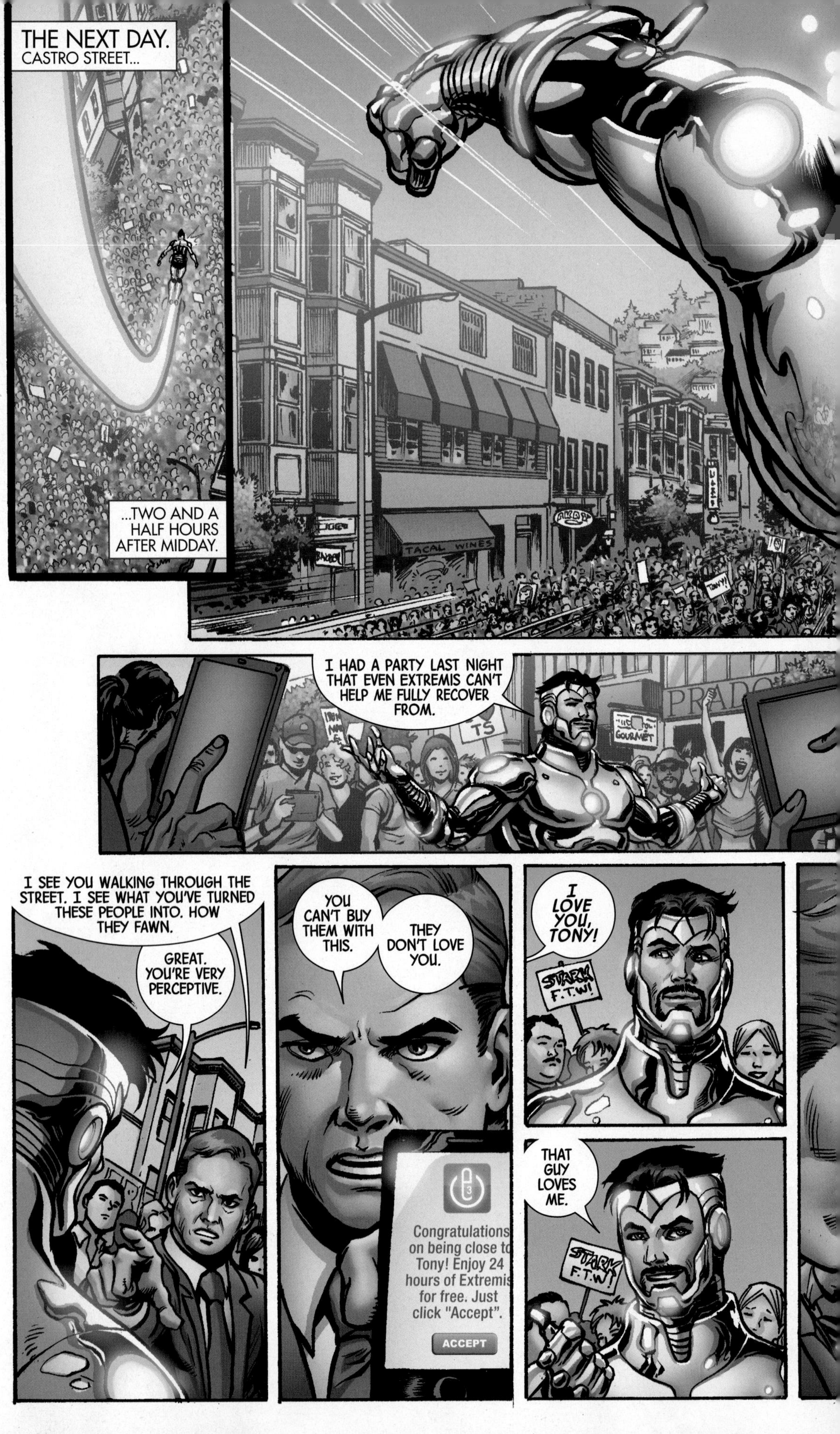
THE NEXT DAY. CASTRO STREET...
...TWO AND A HALF HOURS AFTER MIDDAY.
TACAL WINES
TONY!
I HAD A PARTY LAST NIGHT THAT EVEN EXTREMIS CAN'T HELP ME FULLY RECOVER FROM.
TS
GOURMET
PRADO
I SEE YOU WALKING THROUGH THE STREET. I SEE WHAT YOU'VE TURNED THESE PEOPLE INTO. HOW THEY FAWN.
GREAT. YOU'RE VERY PERCEPTIVE.
YOU CAN'T BUY THEM WITH THIS.
THEY DON'T LOVE YOU.
Congratulations on being close to Tony! Enjoy 24 hours of Extremis for free. Just click "Accept".
ACCEPT
I LOVE YOU, TONY!
STARK F.T.W!
THAT GUY LOVES ME.
STARK F.T.W!

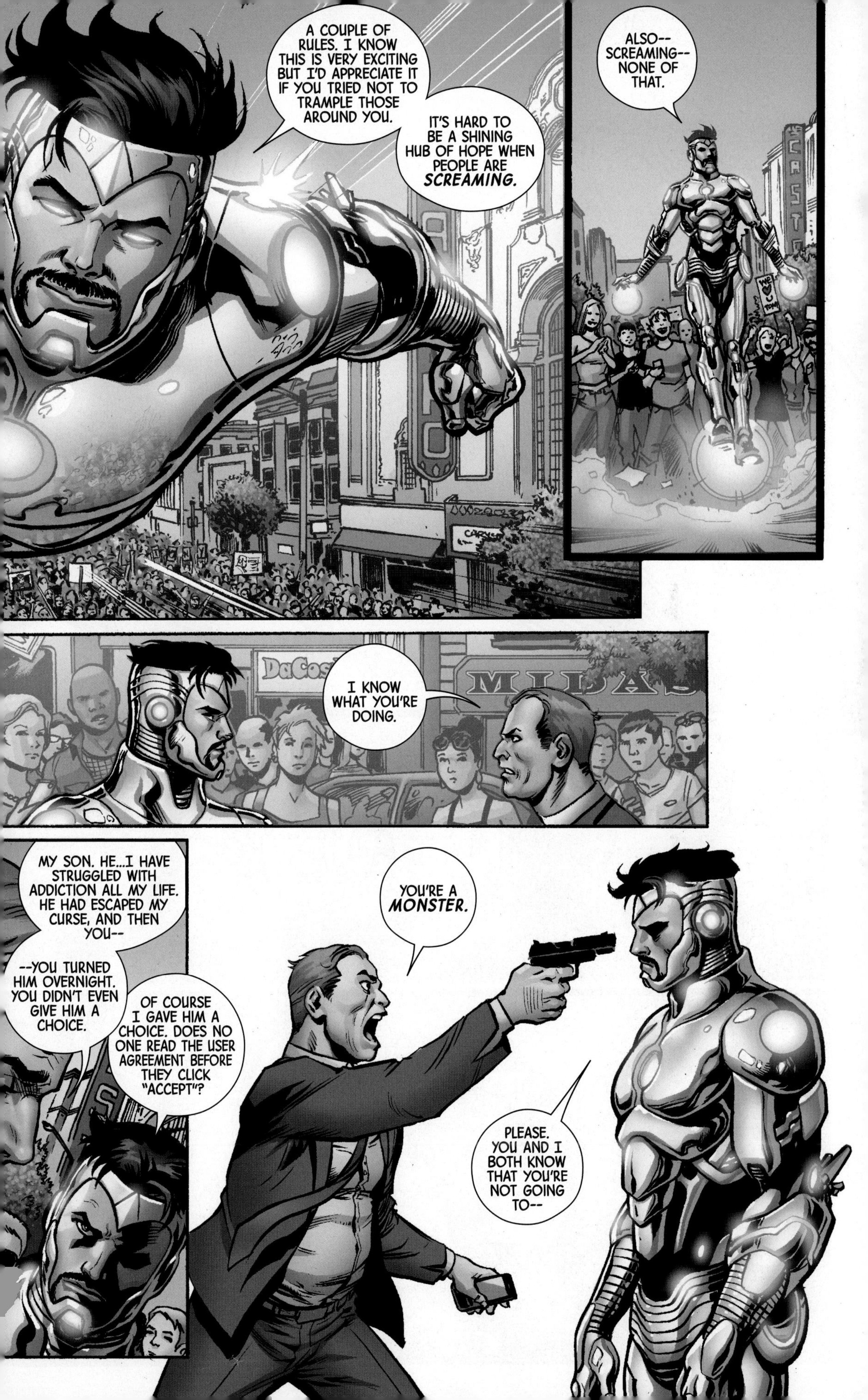
A COUPLE OF RULES. I KNOW THIS IS VERY EXCITING BUT I'D APPRECIATE IT IF YOU TRIED NOT TO TRAMPLE THOSE AROUND YOU.
IT'S HARD TO BE A SHINING HUB OF HOPE WHEN PEOPLE ARE *SCREAMING.*
ALSO-- SCREAMING-- NONE OF THAT.
I KNOW WHAT YOU'RE DOING.
MY SON. HE...I HAVE STRUGGLED WITH ADDICTION ALL MY LIFE. HE HAD ESCAPED MY CURSE, AND THEN YOU--
--YOU TURNED HIM OVERNIGHT. YOU DIDN'T EVEN GIVE HIM A CHOICE.
OF COURSE I GAVE HIM A CHOICE. DOES NO ONE READ THE USER AGREEMENT BEFORE THEY CLICK "ACCEPT"?
YOU'RE A *MONSTER.*
PLEASE. YOU AND I BOTH KNOW THAT YOU'RE NOT GOING TO--

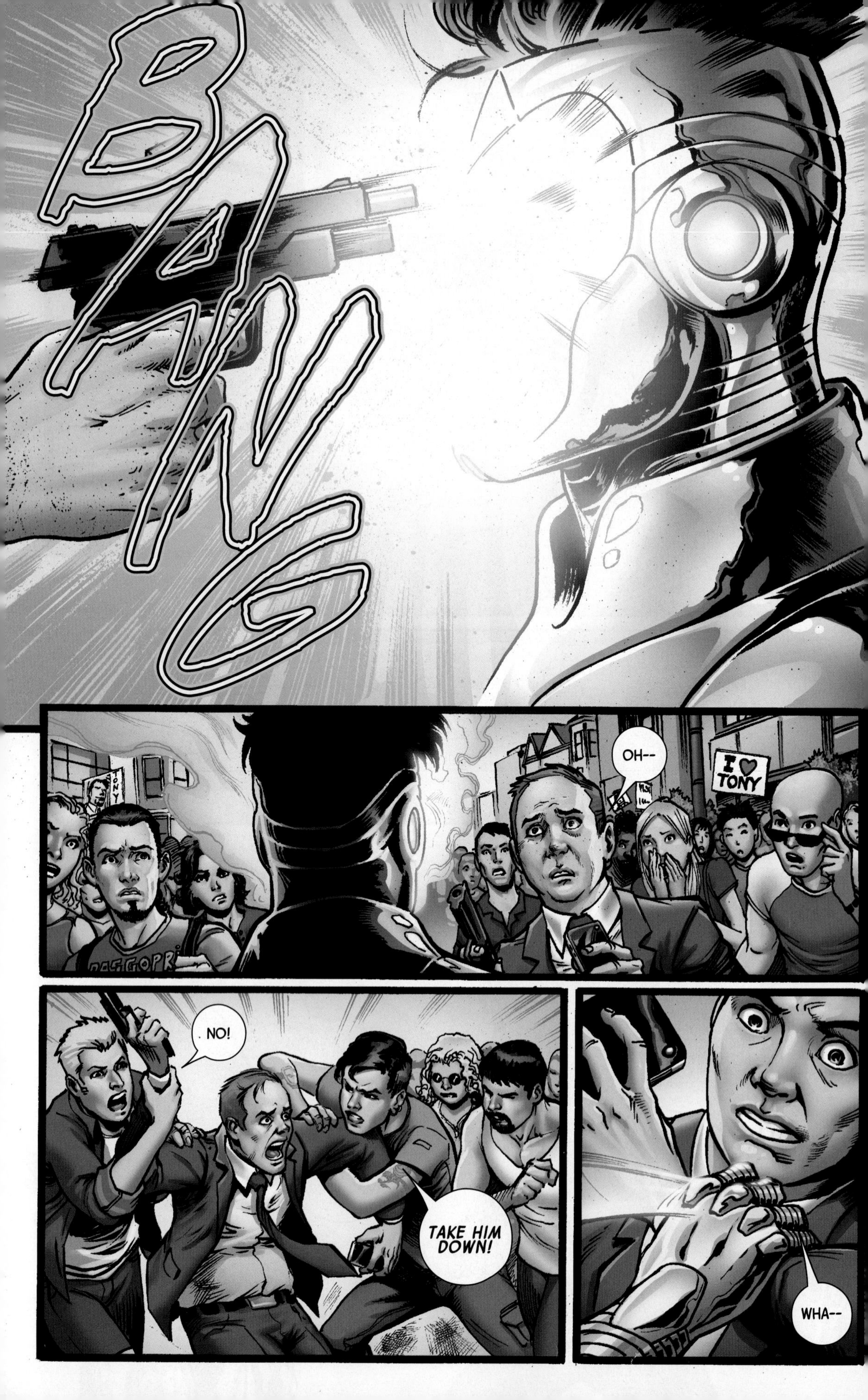
BANG
OH--
I ♥ TONY
NO!
TAKE HIM DOWN!
WHA--

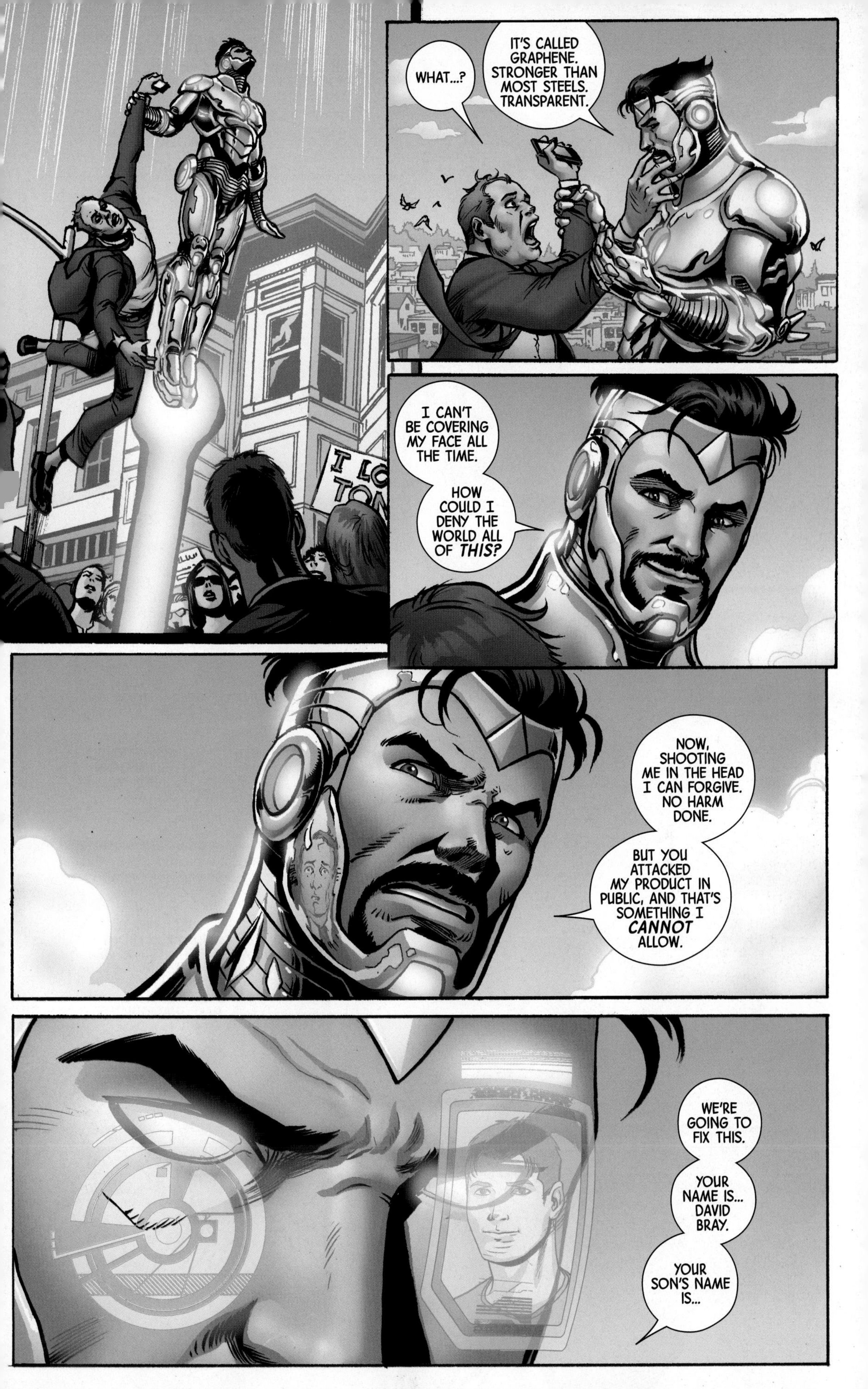

WHAT...?
IT'S CALLED GRAPHENE. STRONGER THAN MOST STEELS. TRANSPARENT.
I LO
TON
I CAN'T BE COVERING MY FACE ALL THE TIME.
HOW COULD I DENY THE WORLD ALL OF *THIS?*
NOW, SHOOTING ME IN THE HEAD I CAN FORGIVE. NO HARM DONE.
BUT YOU ATTACKED MY PRODUCT IN PUBLIC, AND THAT'S SOMETHING I ***CANNOT*** ALLOW.
WE'RE GOING TO FIX THIS.
YOUR NAME IS... DAVID BRAY.
YOUR SON'S NAME IS...

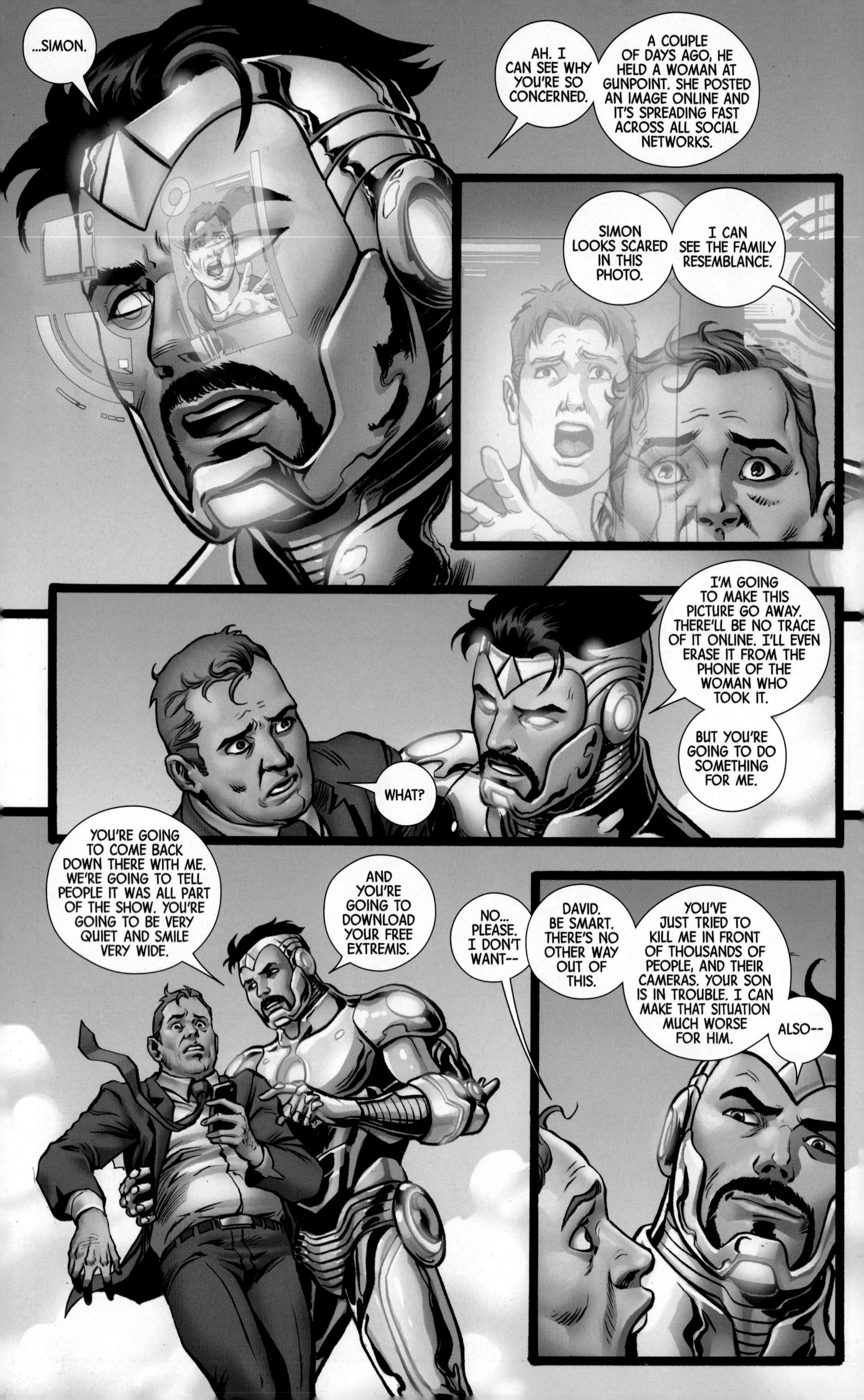
...SIMON.
AH. I CAN SEE WHY YOU'RE SO CONCERNED.
A COUPLE OF DAYS AGO, HE HELD A WOMAN AT GUNPOINT. SHE POSTED AN IMAGE ONLINE AND IT'S SPREADING FAST ACROSS ALL SOCIAL NETWORKS.
SIMON LOOKS SCARED IN THIS PHOTO.
I CAN SEE THE FAMILY RESEMBLANCE.
I'M GOING TO MAKE THIS PICTURE GO AWAY. THERE'LL BE NO TRACE OF IT ONLINE. I'LL EVEN ERASE IT FROM THE PHONE OF THE WOMAN WHO TOOK IT.
BUT YOU'RE GOING TO DO SOMETHING FOR ME.
WHAT?
YOU'RE GOING TO COME BACK DOWN THERE WITH ME. WE'RE GOING TO TELL PEOPLE IT WAS ALL PART OF THE SHOW. YOU'RE GOING TO BE VERY QUIET AND SMILE VERY WIDE.
AND YOU'RE GOING TO DOWNLOAD YOUR FREE EXTREMIS.
NO... PLEASE. I DON'T WANT--
DAVID. BE SMART. THERE'S NO OTHER WAY OUT OF THIS.
YOU'VE JUST TRIED TO KILL ME IN FRONT OF THOUSANDS OF PEOPLE, AND THEIR CAMERAS. YOUR SON IS IN TROUBLE. I CAN MAKE THAT SITUATION MUCH WORSE FOR HIM.
ALSO--

--IT'S A *VERY* LONG WAY DOWN.

YOU BASTARD.

Congratulations on being close to Tony! Enjoy 24 hours of f---mis DEET for f---click "accept".

THERE. WAS THAT SO HARD?

HOW DO YOU FEEL?

INCREDIBLE.

DAMN STRAIGHT.

NOW SMILE.

No one else heard their conversation.

But I heard every word--

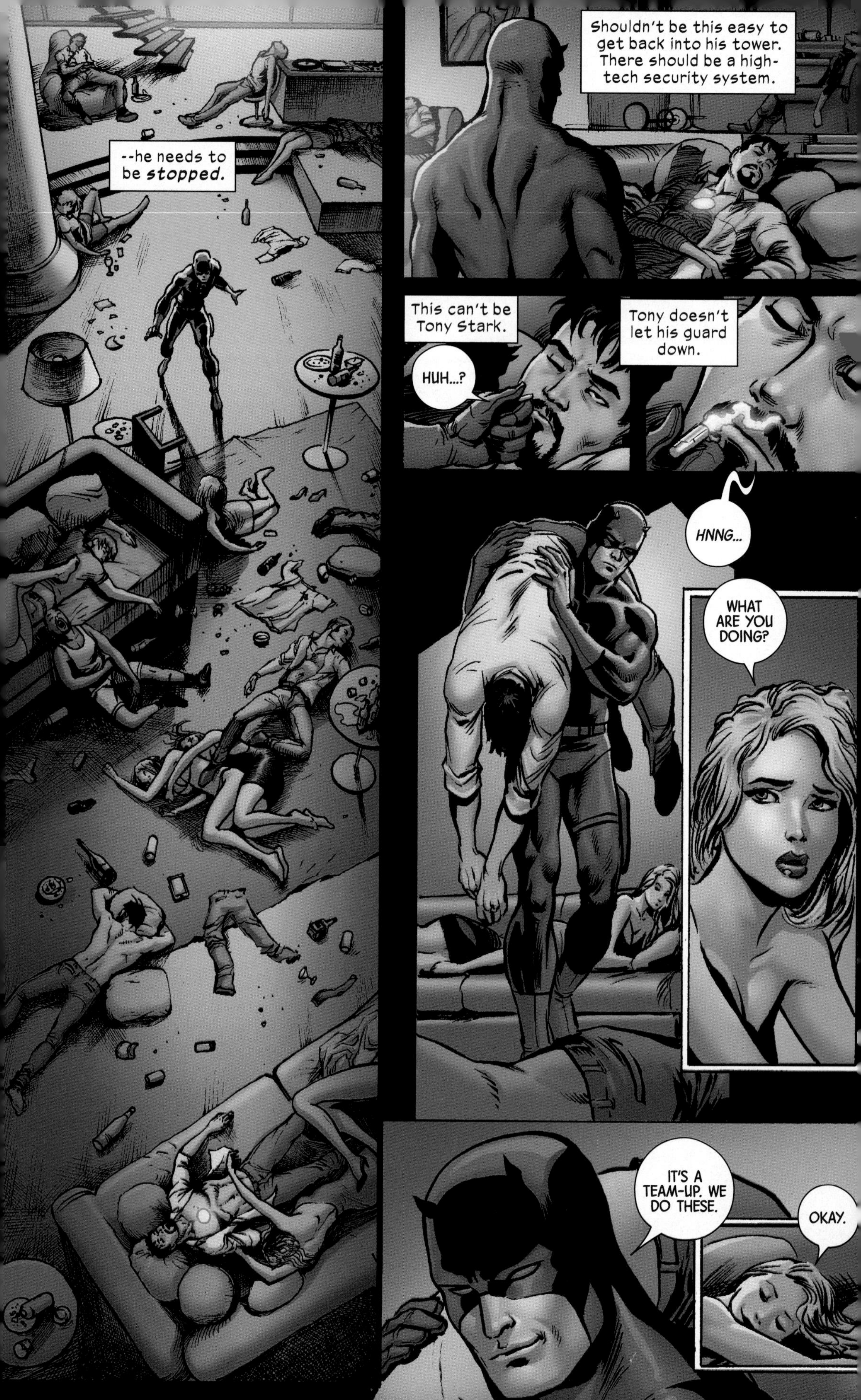
--he needs to be *stopped.*
Shouldn't be this easy to get back into his tower. There should be a high-tech security system.
This can't be Tony Stark.
HUH...?
Tony doesn't let his guard down.
HNNG...
WHAT ARE YOU DOING?
IT'S A TEAM-UP. WE DO THESE.
OKAY.

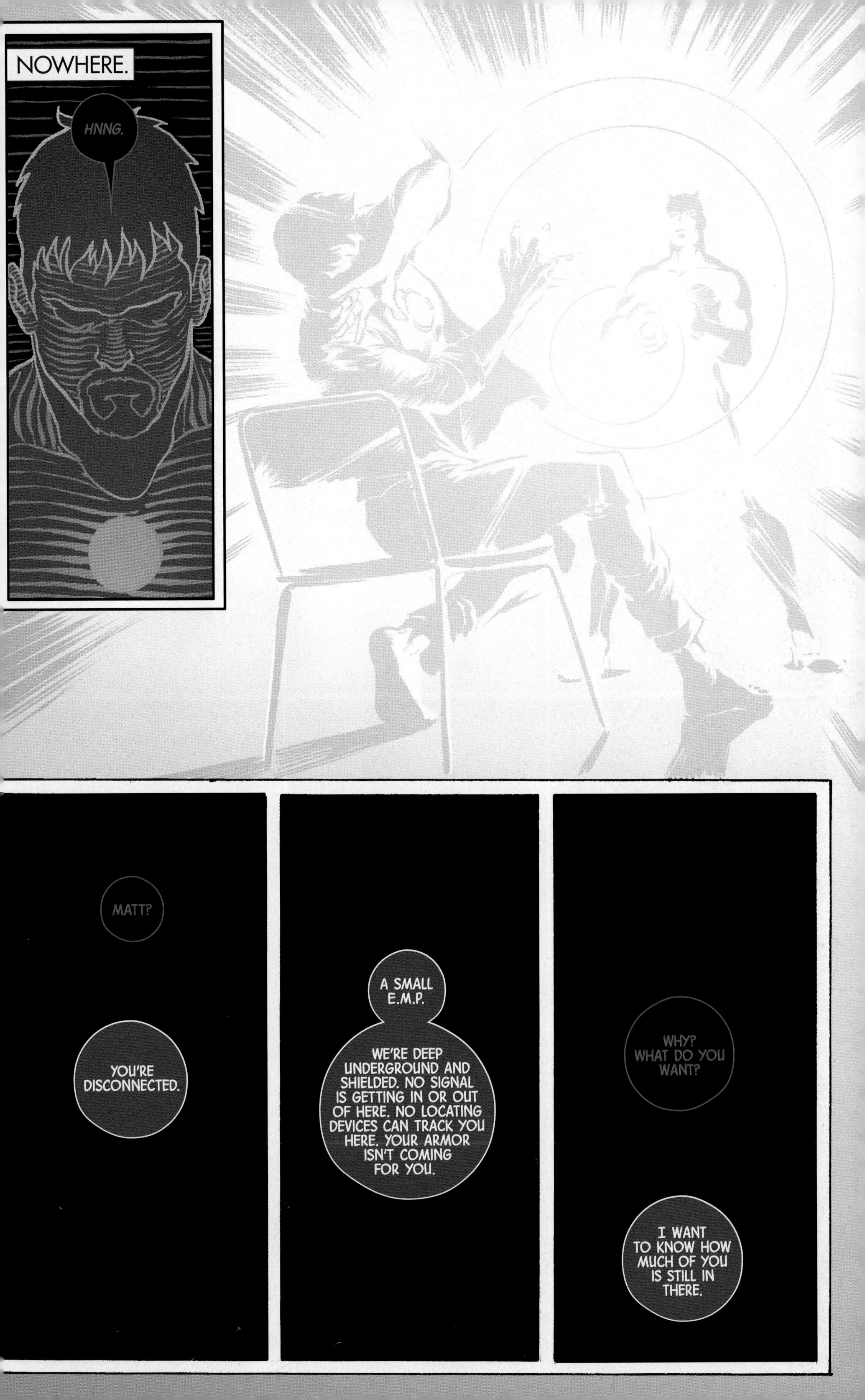
NOWHERE.
HNNG.
MATT?
YOU'RE DISCONNECTED.
A SMALL E.M.P.
WE'RE DEEP UNDERGROUND AND SHIELDED. NO SIGNAL IS GETTING IN OR OUT OF HERE. NO LOCATING DEVICES CAN TRACK YOU HERE. YOUR ARMOR ISN'T COMING FOR YOU.
WHY? WHAT DO YOU WANT?
I WANT TO KNOW HOW MUCH OF YOU IS STILL IN THERE.

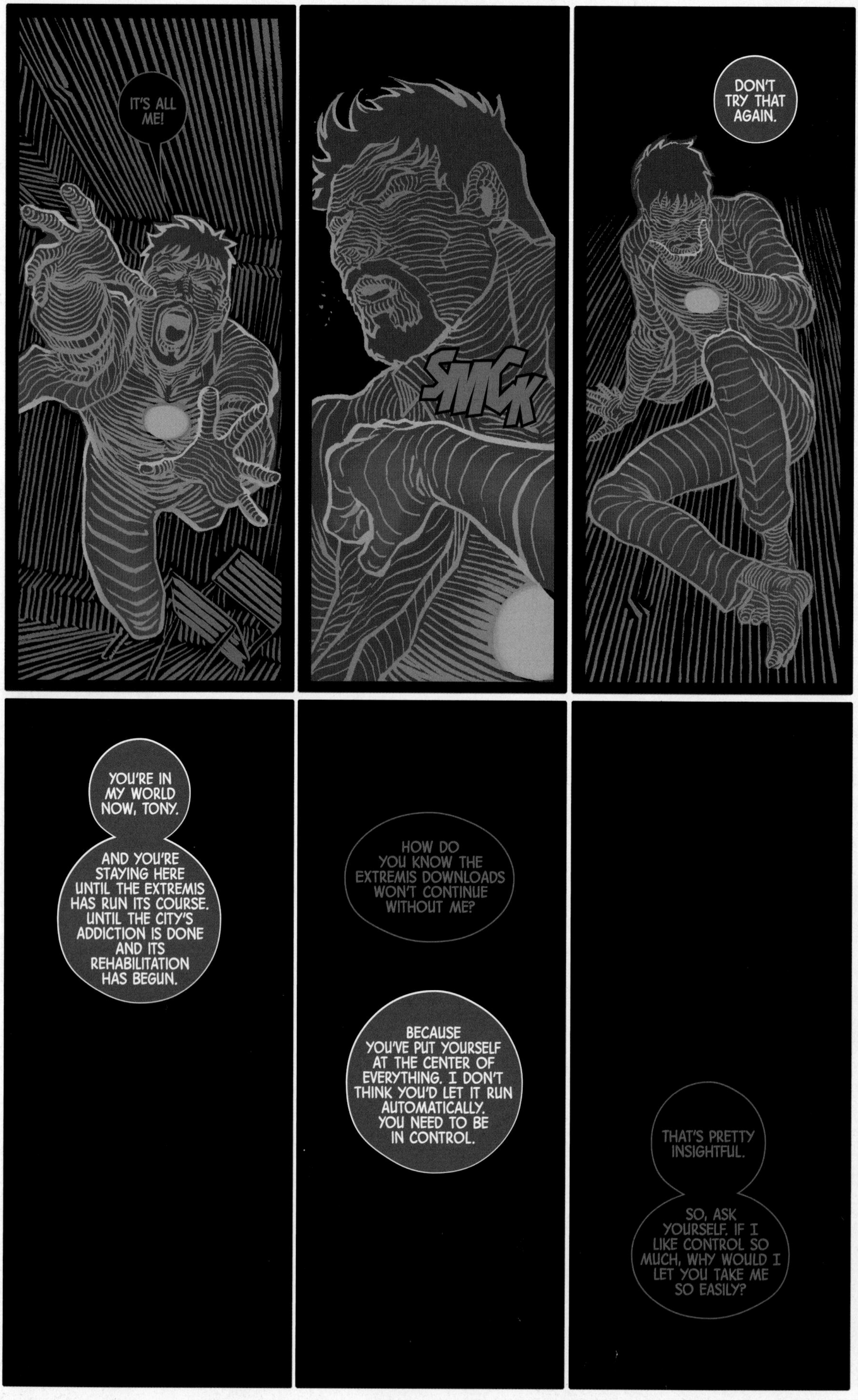

IT'S ALL ME!

SMICK

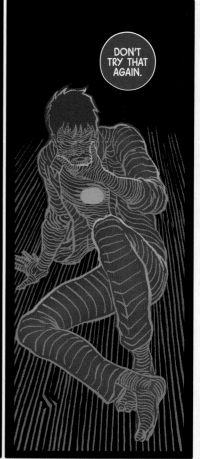

DON'T TRY THAT AGAIN.

YOU'RE IN MY WORLD NOW, TONY.

AND YOU'RE STAYING HERE UNTIL THE EXTREMIS HAS RUN ITS COURSE. UNTIL THE CITY'S ADDICTION IS DONE AND ITS REHABILITATION HAS BEGUN.

HOW DO YOU KNOW THE EXTREMIS DOWNLOADS WON'T CONTINUE WITHOUT ME?

BECAUSE YOU'VE PUT YOURSELF AT THE CENTER OF EVERYTHING. I DON'T THINK YOU'D LET IT RUN AUTOMATICALLY. YOU NEED TO BE IN CONTROL.

THAT'S PRETTY INSIGHTFUL.

SO, ASK YOURSELF. IF I LIKE CONTROL SO MUCH, WHY WOULD I LET YOU TAKE ME SO EASILY?

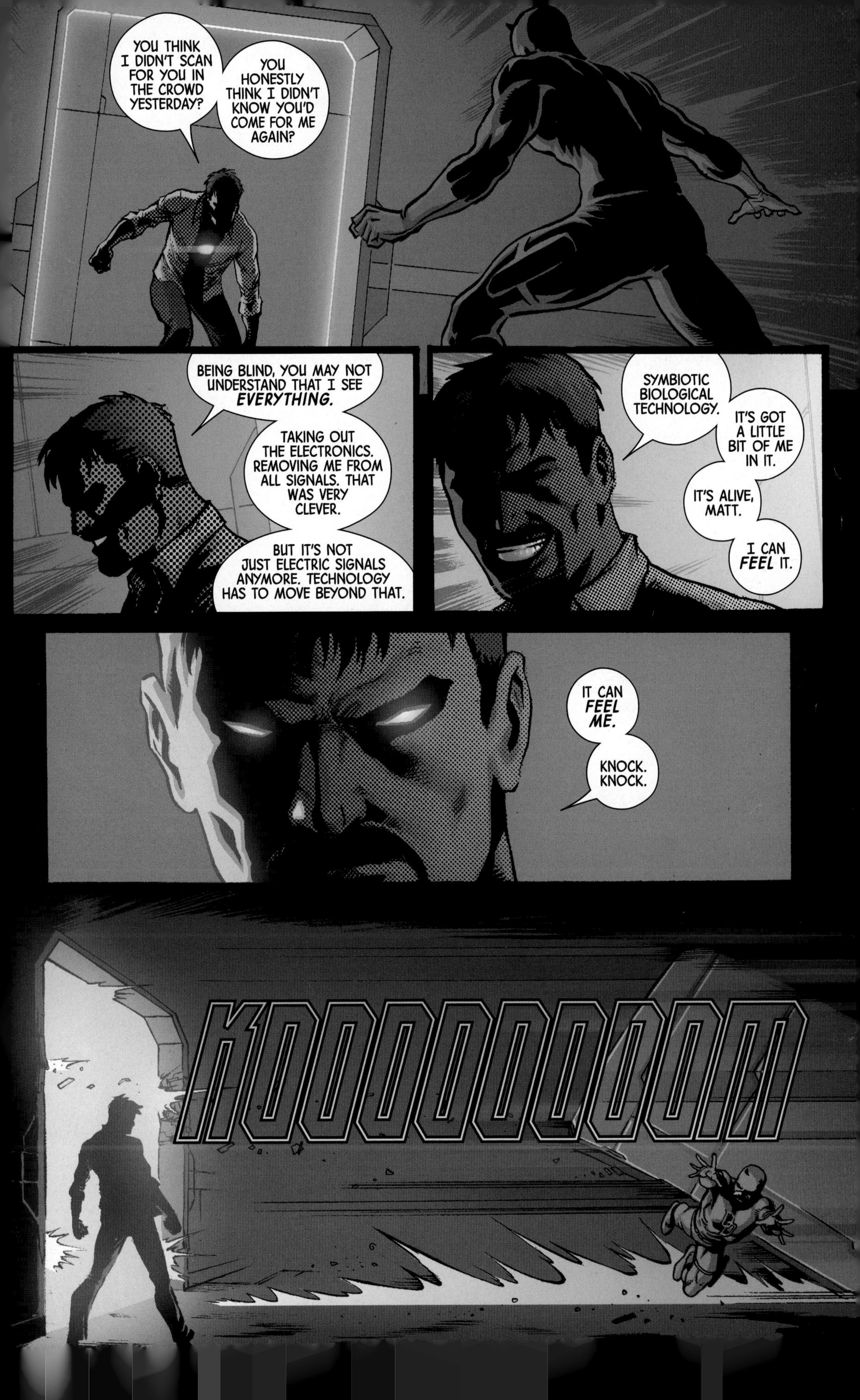
YOU THINK I DIDN'T SCAN FOR YOU IN THE CROWD YESTERDAY?
YOU HONESTLY THINK I DIDN'T KNOW YOU'D COME FOR ME AGAIN?
BEING BLIND, YOU MAY NOT UNDERSTAND THAT I SEE *EVERYTHING.*
TAKING OUT THE ELECTRONICS. REMOVING ME FROM ALL SIGNALS. THAT WAS VERY CLEVER.
BUT IT'S NOT JUST ELECTRIC SIGNALS ANYMORE. TECHNOLOGY HAS TO MOVE BEYOND THAT.
SYMBIOTIC BIOLOGICAL TECHNOLOGY.
IT'S GOT A LITTLE BIT OF ME IN IT.
IT'S ALIVE, MATT.
I CAN *FEEL* IT.
IT CAN *FEEL ME.*
KNOCK. KNOCK.
KOOOOOOOOOM

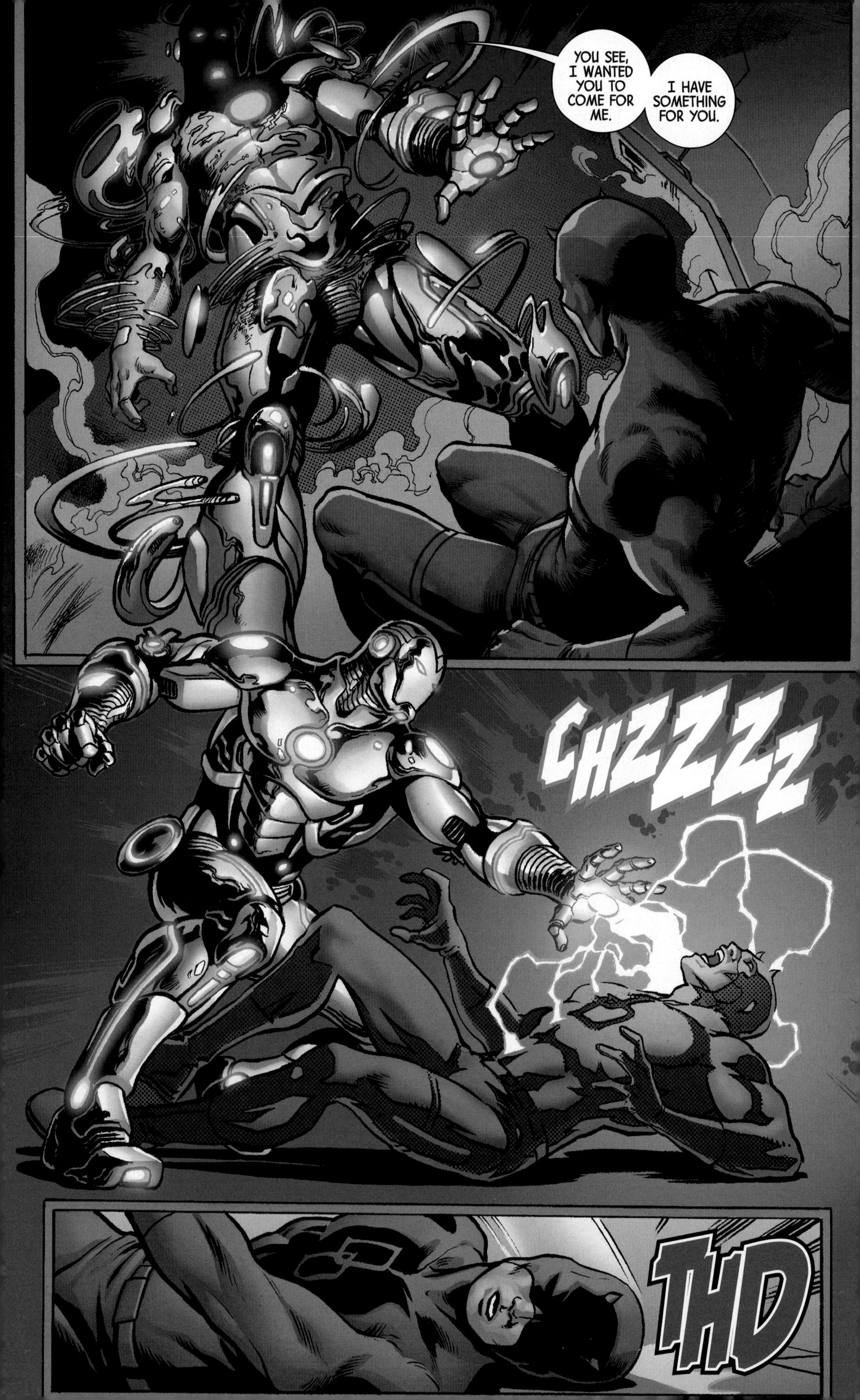
YOU SEE, I WANTED YOU TO COME FOR ME.
I HAVE SOMETHING FOR YOU.
CHZZZZ
THD

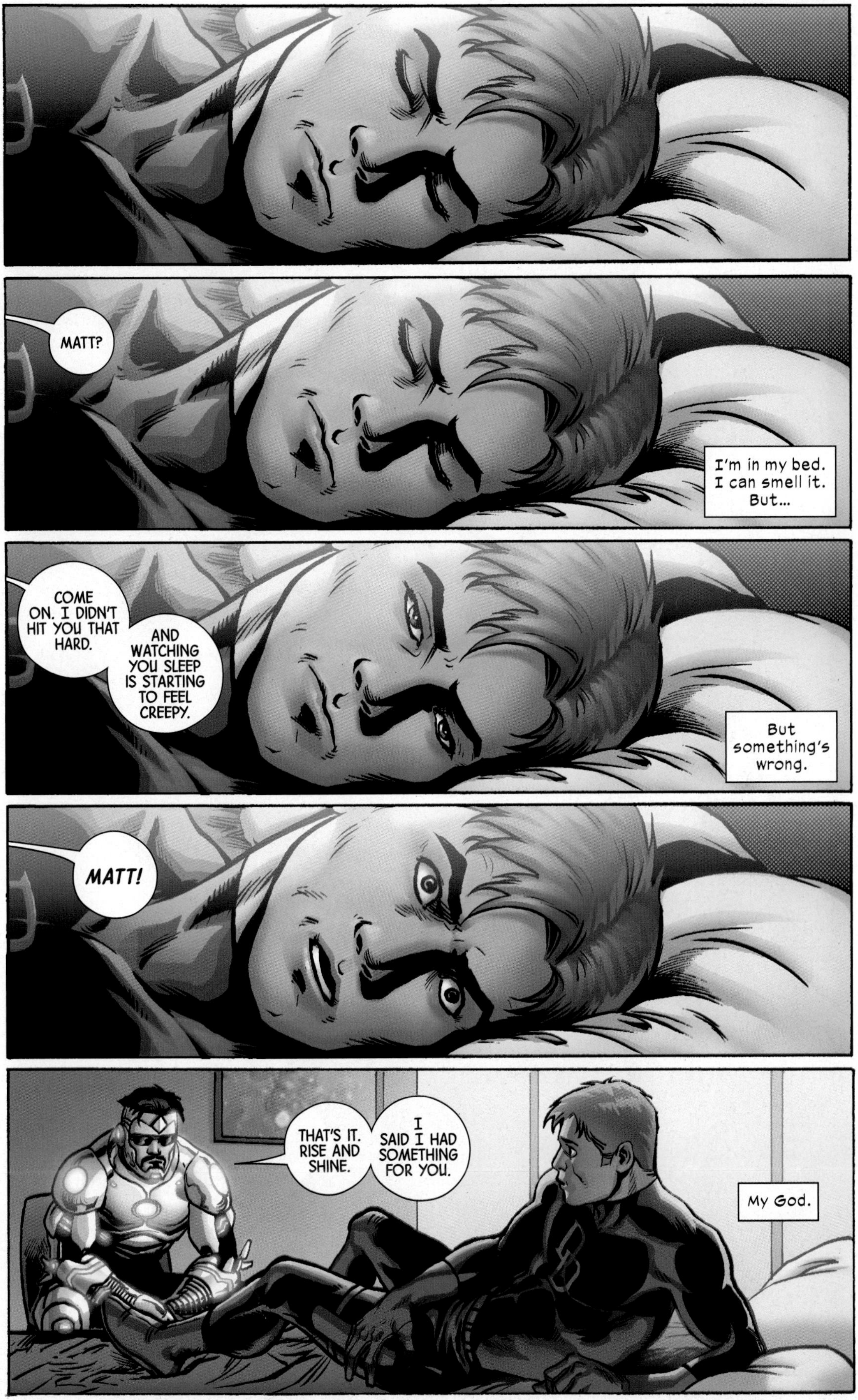
MATT?
I'm in my bed. I can smell it. But...
COME ON. I DIDN'T HIT YOU THAT HARD.
AND WATCHING YOU SLEEP IS STARTING TO FEEL CREEPY.
But something's wrong.
MATT!
THAT'S IT. RISE AND SHINE.
I SAID I HAD SOMETHING FOR YOU.
My God.

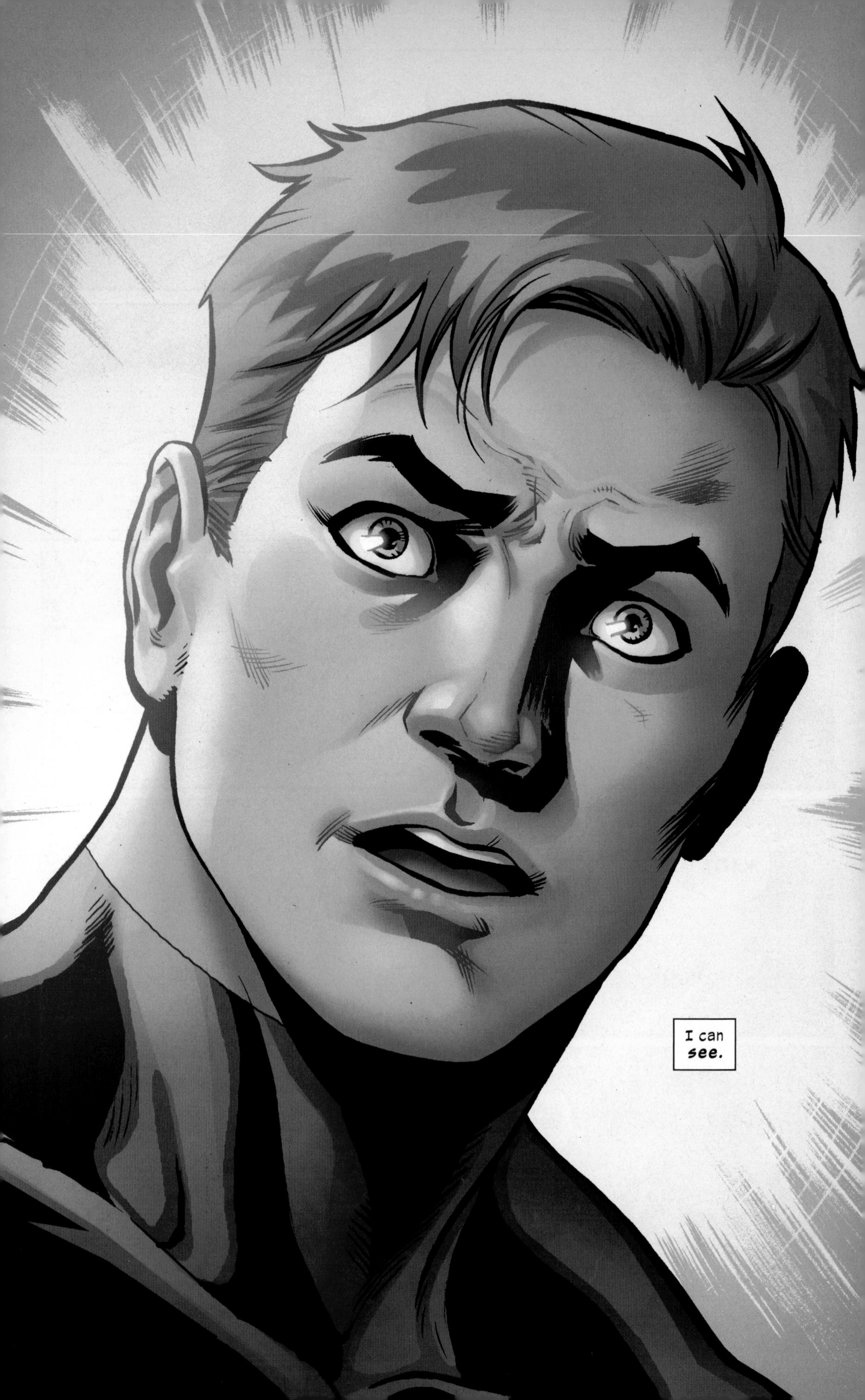
I can see.

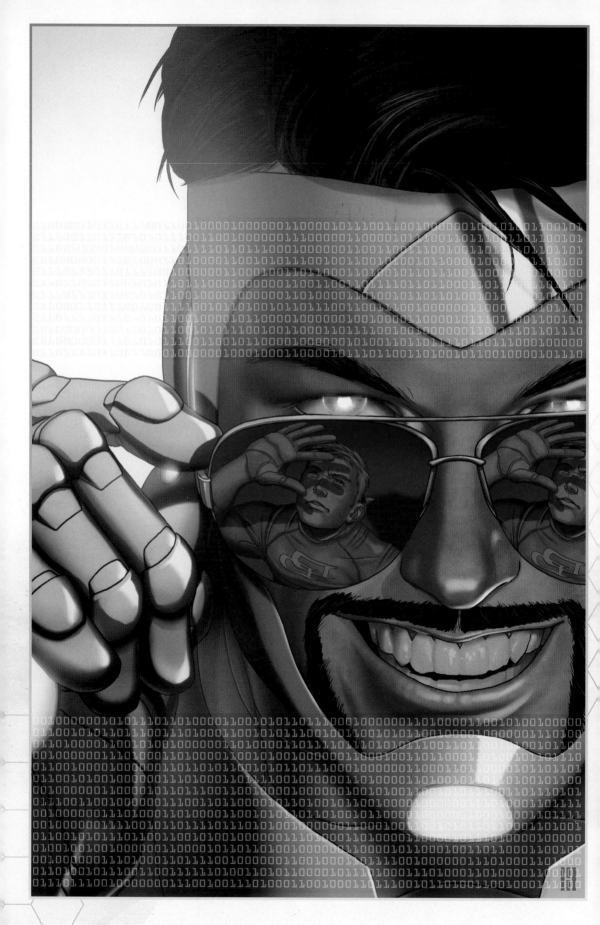

3: MAN OF VISION

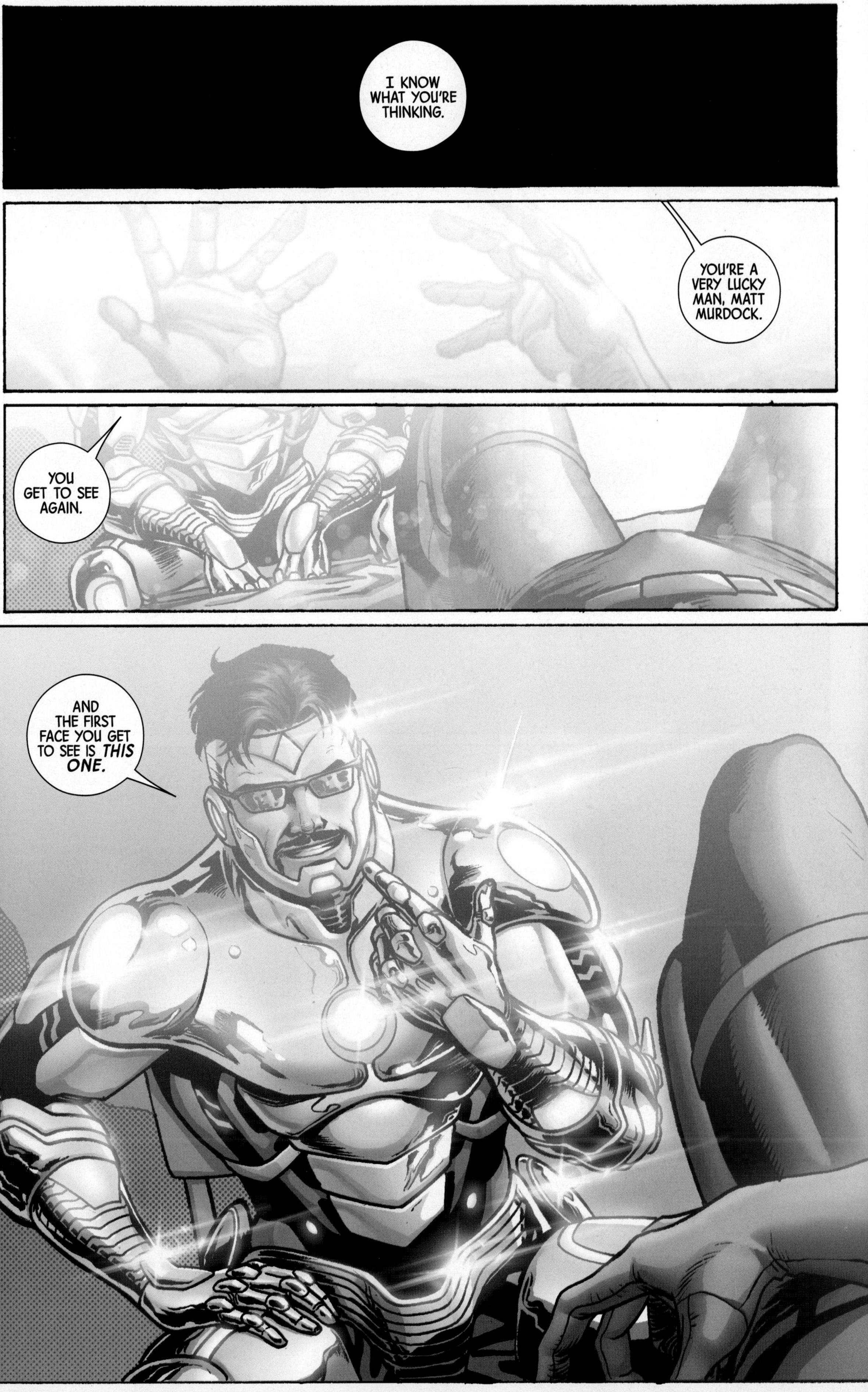
I KNOW WHAT YOU'RE THINKING.
YOU'RE A VERY LUCKY MAN, MATT MURDOCK.
YOU GET TO SEE AGAIN.
AND THE FIRST FACE YOU GET TO SEE IS *THIS ONE.*

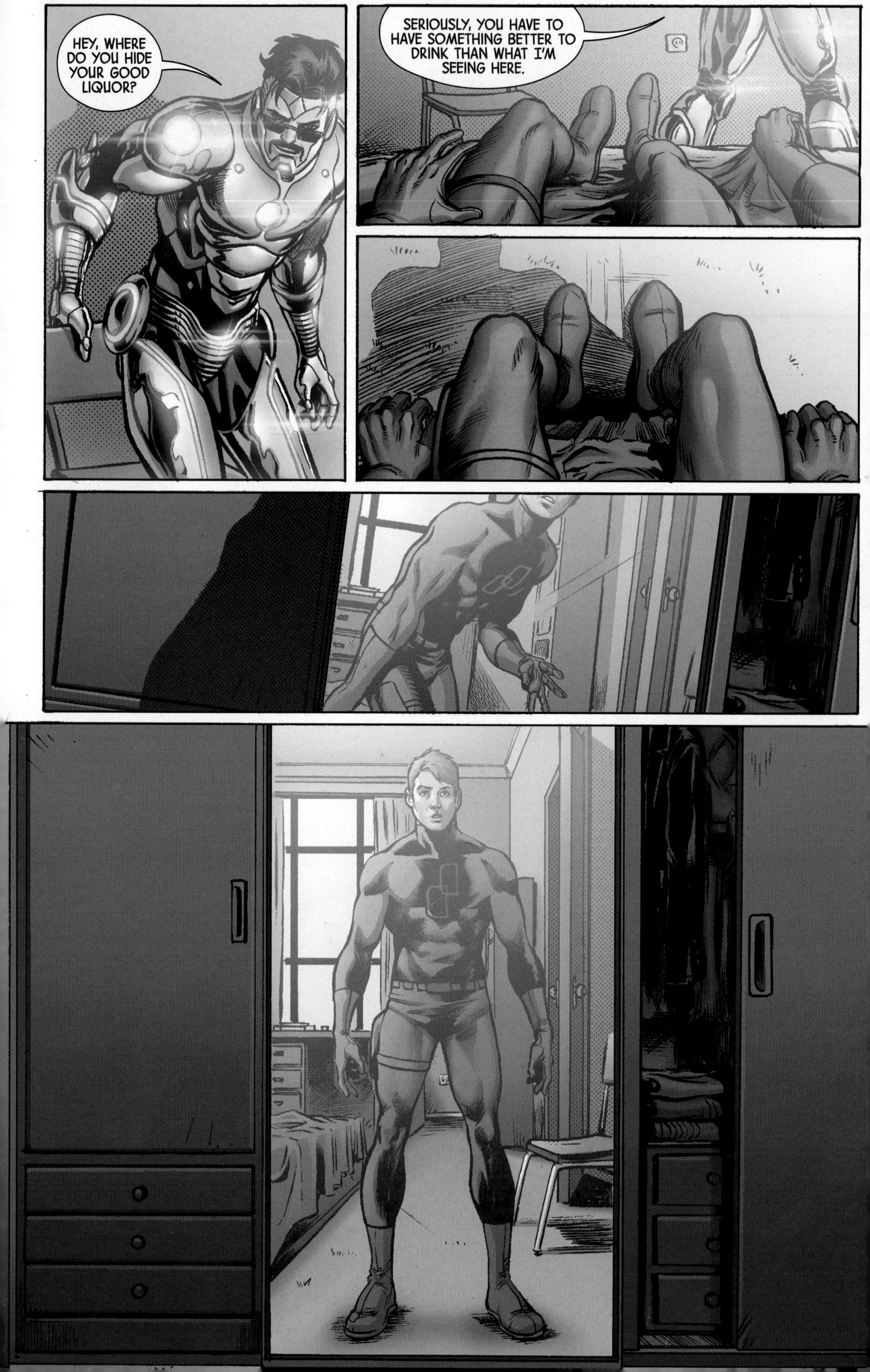
HEY, WHERE DO YOU HIDE YOUR GOOD LIQUOR?
SERIOUSLY, YOU HAVE TO HAVE SOMETHING BETTER TO DRINK THAN WHAT I'M SEEING HERE.

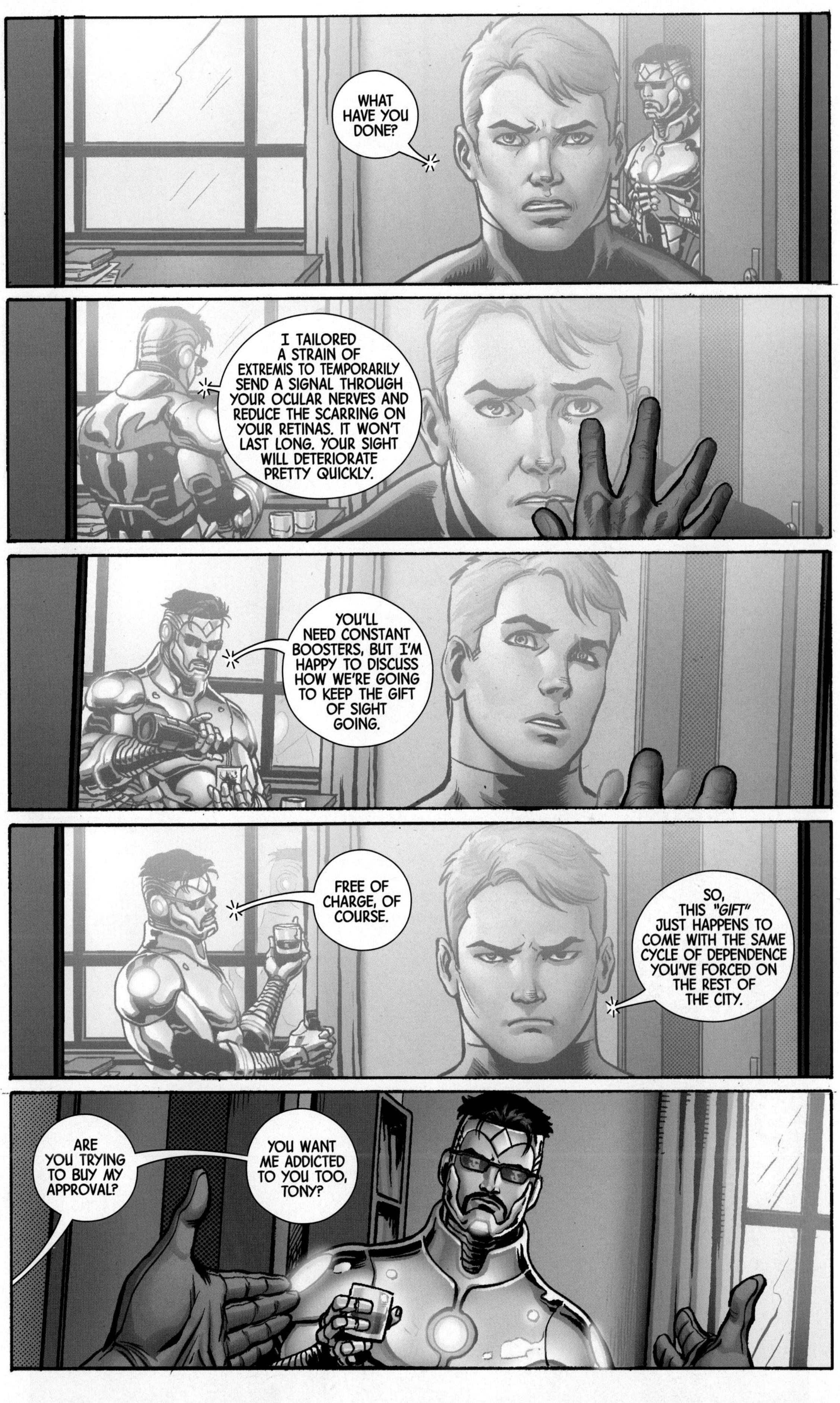
WHAT HAVE YOU DONE?
I TAILORED A STRAIN OF EXTREMIS TO TEMPORARILY SEND A SIGNAL THROUGH YOUR OCULAR NERVES AND REDUCE THE SCARRING ON YOUR RETINAS. IT WON'T LAST LONG. YOUR SIGHT WILL DETERIORATE PRETTY QUICKLY.
YOU'LL NEED CONSTANT BOOSTERS, BUT I'M HAPPY TO DISCUSS HOW WE'RE GOING TO KEEP THE GIFT OF SIGHT GOING.
FREE OF CHARGE, OF COURSE.
SO, THIS "GIFT" JUST HAPPENS TO COME WITH THE SAME CYCLE OF DEPENDENCE YOU'VE FORCED ON THE REST OF THE CITY.
ARE YOU TRYING TO BUY MY APPROVAL?
YOU WANT ME ADDICTED TO YOU TOO, TONY?

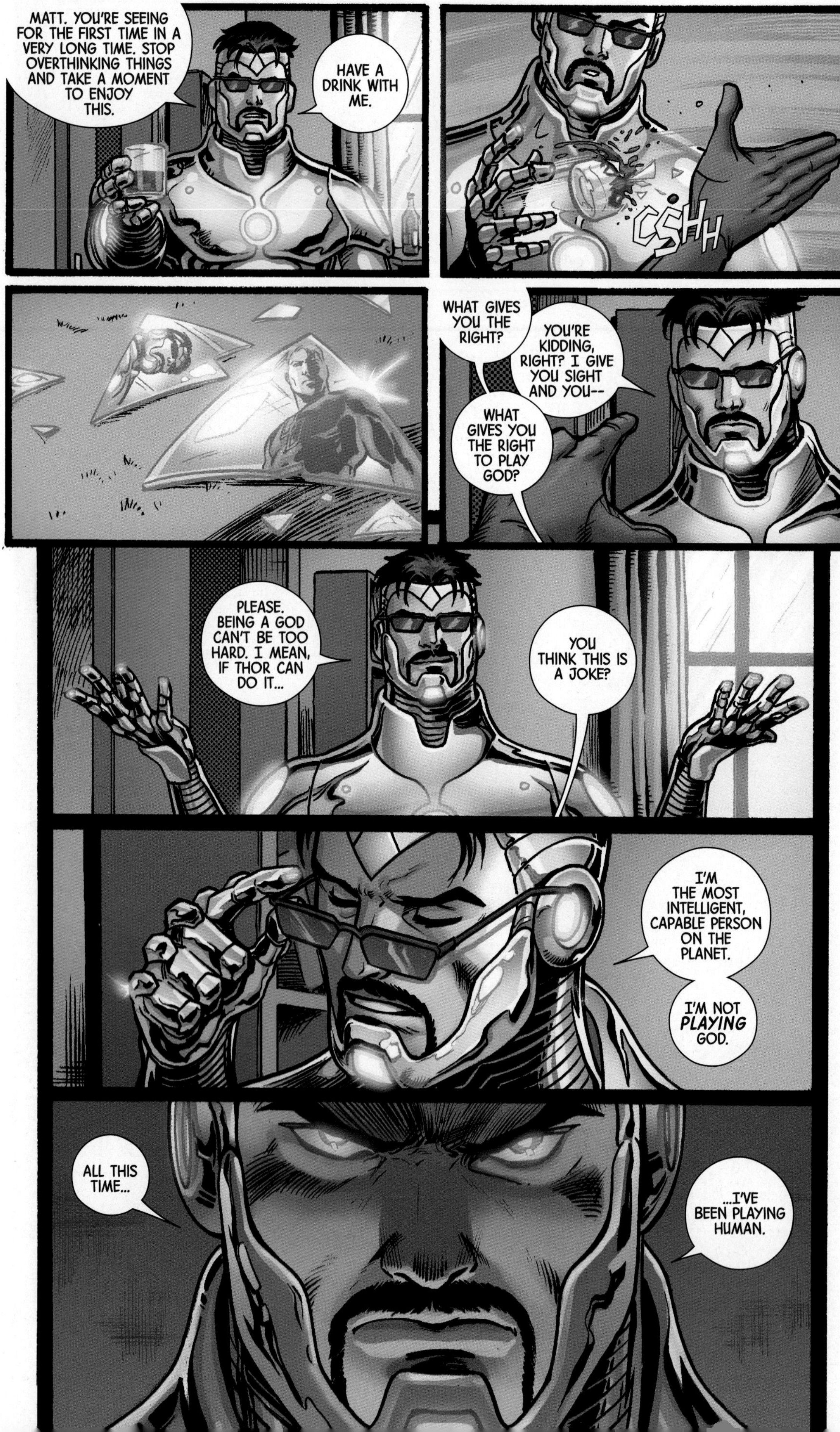
MATT. YOU'RE SEEING FOR THE FIRST TIME IN A VERY LONG TIME. STOP OVERTHINKING THINGS AND TAKE A MOMENT TO ENJOY THIS.
HAVE A DRINK WITH ME.
CSHH
WHAT GIVES YOU THE RIGHT?
YOU'RE KIDDING, RIGHT? I GIVE YOU SIGHT AND YOU--
WHAT GIVES YOU THE RIGHT TO PLAY GOD?
PLEASE. BEING A GOD CAN'T BE TOO HARD. I MEAN, IF THOR CAN DO IT...
YOU THINK THIS IS A JOKE?
I'M THE MOST INTELLIGENT, CAPABLE PERSON ON THE PLANET.
I'M NOT PLAYING GOD.
ALL THIS TIME...
...I'VE BEEN PLAYING HUMAN.

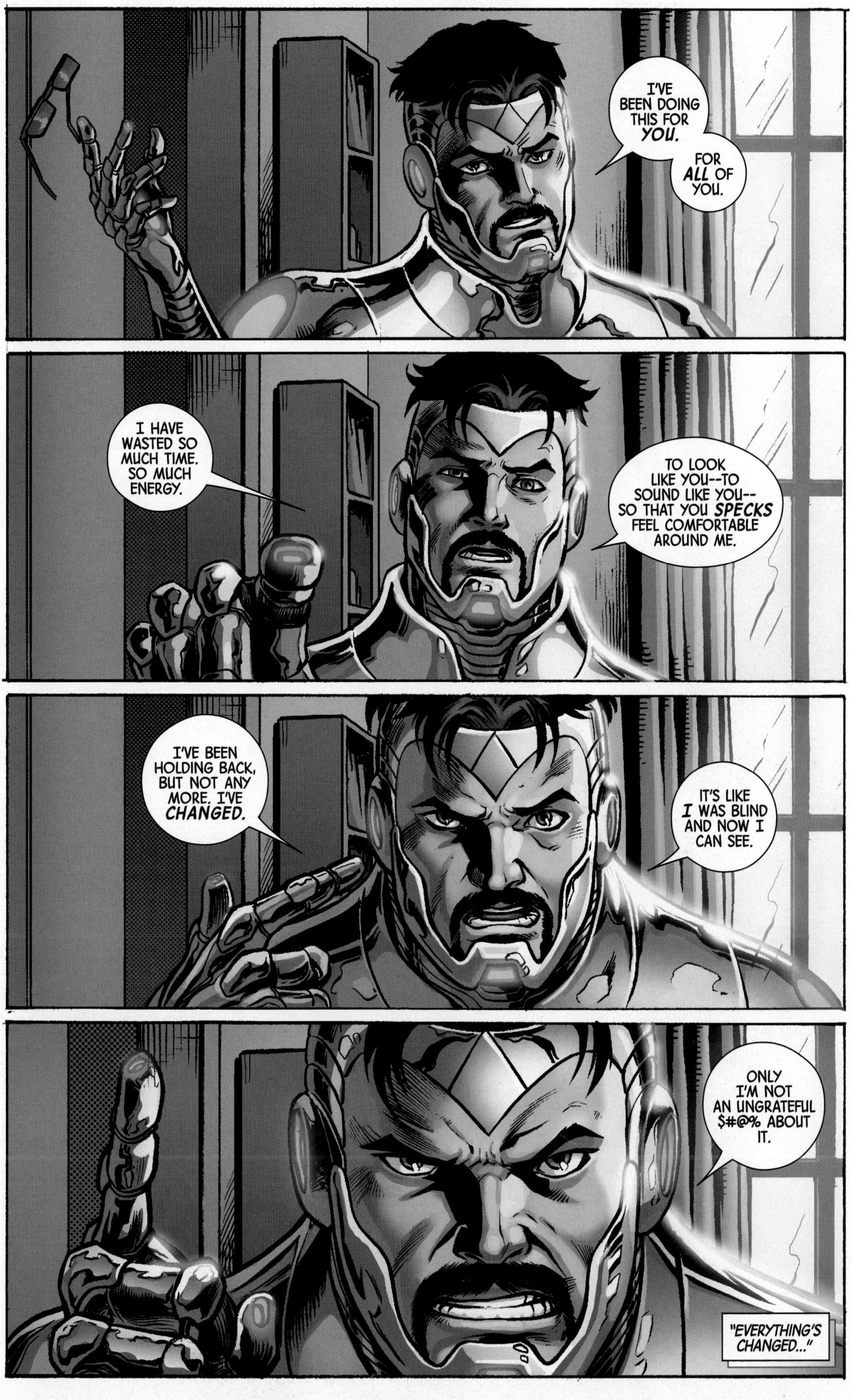
I'VE BEEN DOING THIS FOR YOU.
FOR ALL OF YOU.
I HAVE WASTED SO MUCH TIME. SO MUCH ENERGY.
TO LOOK LIKE YOU--TO SOUND LIKE YOU-- SO THAT YOU SPECKS FEEL COMFORTABLE AROUND ME.
I'VE BEEN HOLDING BACK, BUT NOT ANY MORE. I'VE CHANGED.
IT'S LIKE I WAS BLIND AND NOW I CAN SEE.
ONLY I'M NOT AN UNGRATEFUL $#@% ABOUT IT.
"EVERYTHING'S CHANGED..."

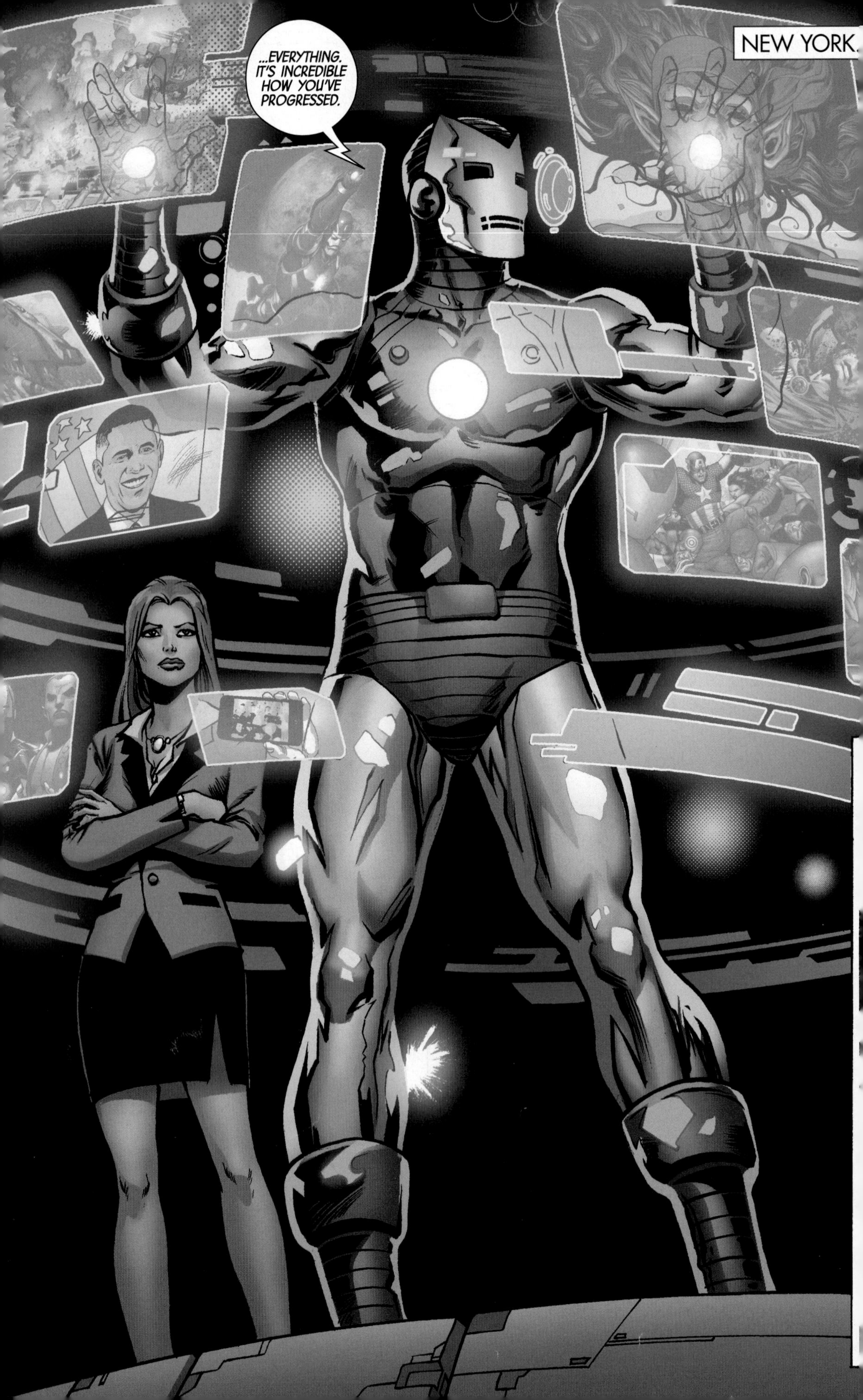

NEW YORK.
...EVERYTHING. IT'S INCREDIBLE HOW YOU'VE PROGRESSED.

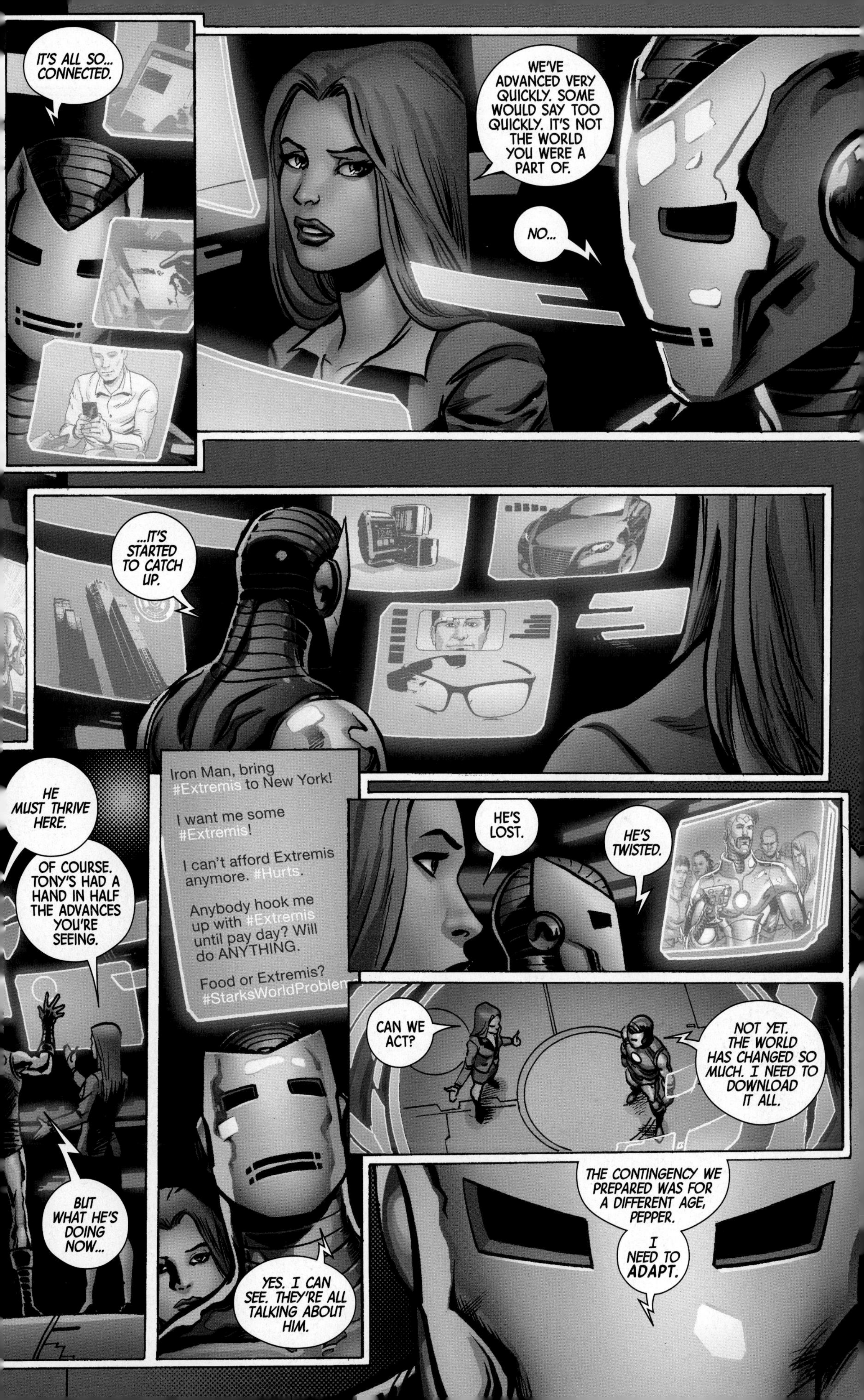
IT'S ALL SO... CONNECTED.
WE'VE ADVANCED VERY QUICKLY. SOME WOULD SAY TOO QUICKLY. IT'S NOT THE WORLD YOU WERE A PART OF.
NO...
...IT'S STARTED TO CATCH UP.
HE MUST THRIVE HERE.
OF COURSE. TONY'S HAD A HAND IN HALF THE ADVANCES YOU'RE SEEING.
BUT WHAT HE'S DOING NOW...
Iron Man, bring #Extremis to New York!
I want me some #Extremis!
I can't afford Extremis anymore. #Hurts.
Anybody hook me up with #Extremis until pay day? Will do ANYTHING.
Food or Extremis? #StarksWorldProblem
YES. I CAN SEE. THEY'RE ALL TALKING ABOUT HIM.
HE'S LOST.
HE'S TWISTED.
CAN WE ACT?
NOT YET. THE WORLD HAS CHANGED SO MUCH. I NEED TO DOWNLOAD IT ALL.
THE CONTINGENCY WE PREPARED WAS FOR A DIFFERENT AGE, PEPPER.
I NEED TO ADAPT.

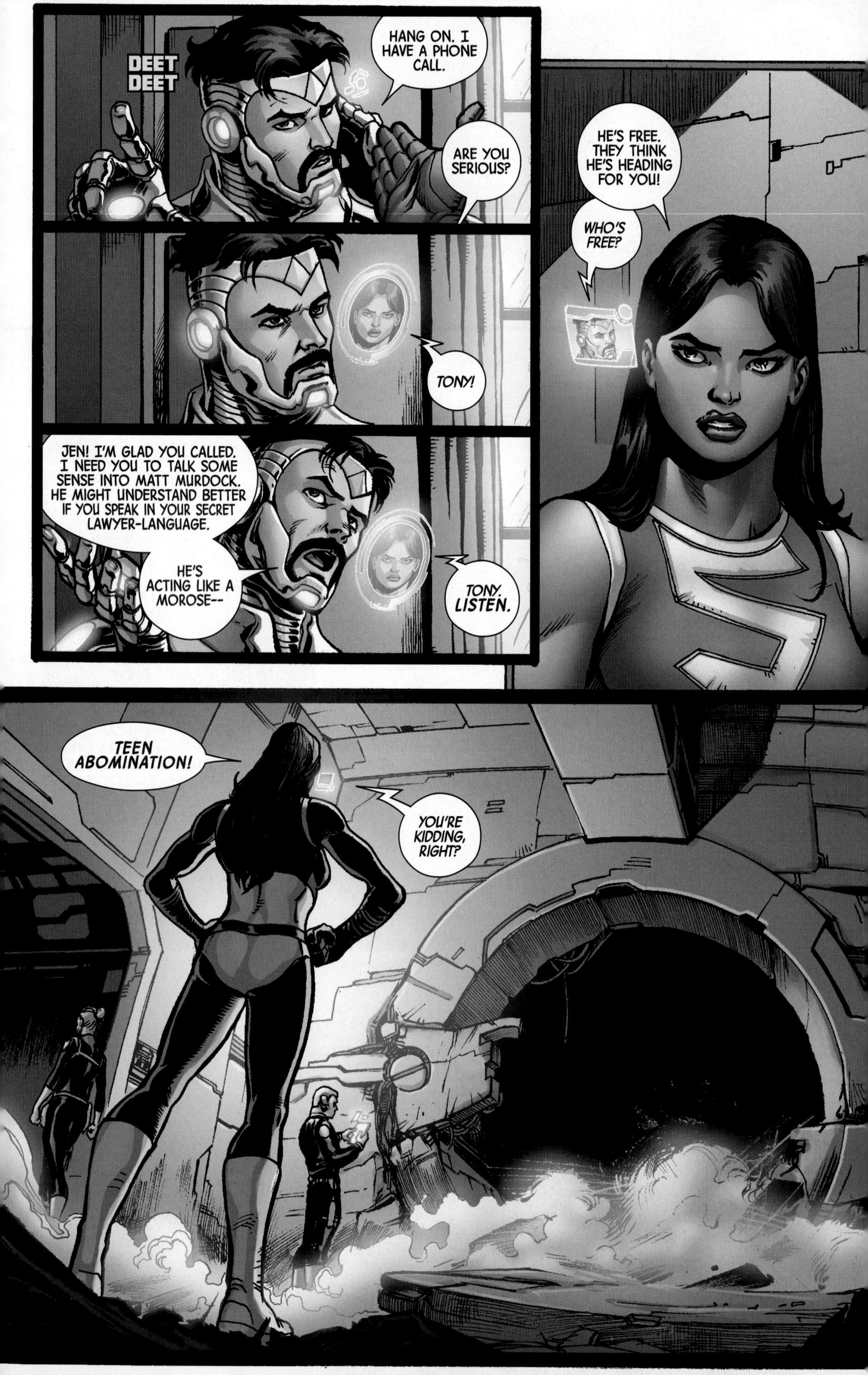
DEET DEET
HANG ON. I HAVE A PHONE CALL.
ARE YOU SERIOUS?
HE'S FREE. THEY THINK HE'S HEADING FOR YOU!
WHO'S FREE?
TONY!
JEN! I'M GLAD YOU CALLED. I NEED YOU TO TALK SOME SENSE INTO MATT MURDOCK. HE MIGHT UNDERSTAND BETTER IF YOU SPEAK IN YOUR SECRET LAWYER-LANGUAGE.
HE'S ACTING LIKE A MOROSE--
TONY. LISTEN.
TEEN ABOMINATION!
YOU'RE KIDDING, RIGHT?

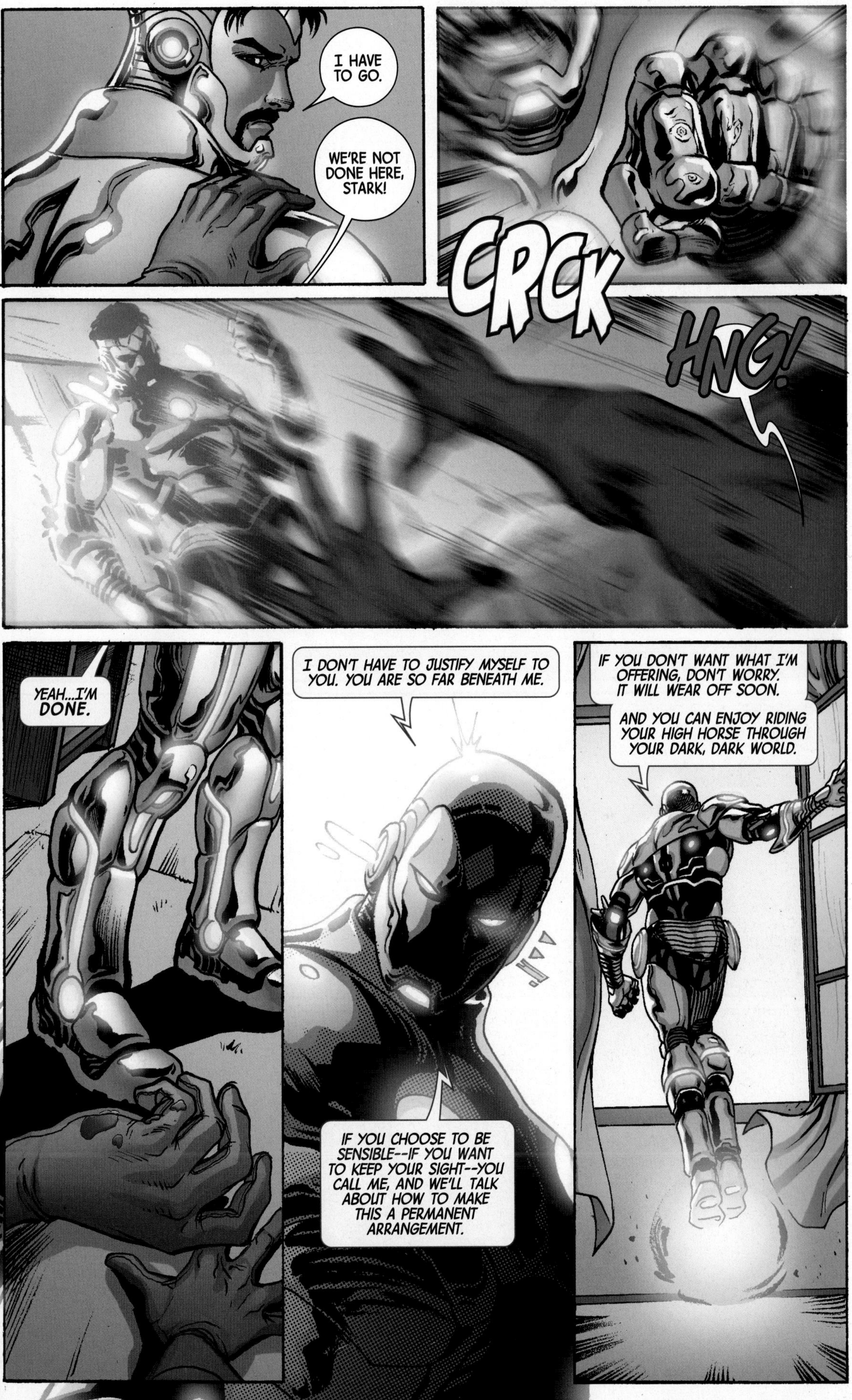
I HAVE TO GO.
WE'RE NOT DONE HERE, STARK!
CRCK
HNG!
YEAH...I'M DONE.
I DON'T HAVE TO JUSTIFY MYSELF TO YOU. YOU ARE SO FAR BENEATH ME.
IF YOU CHOOSE TO BE SENSIBLE--IF YOU WANT TO KEEP YOUR SIGHT--YOU CALL ME, AND WE'LL TALK ABOUT HOW TO MAKE THIS A PERMANENT ARRANGEMENT.
IF YOU DON'T WANT WHAT I'M OFFERING, DON'T WORRY. IT WILL WEAR OFF SOON.
AND YOU CAN ENJOY RIDING YOUR HIGH HORSE THROUGH YOUR DARK, DARK WORLD.

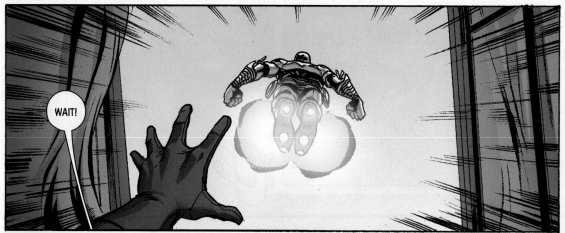

WAIT!

MY GOD.

DEET

MATT?

HI.

CAN WE MEET?

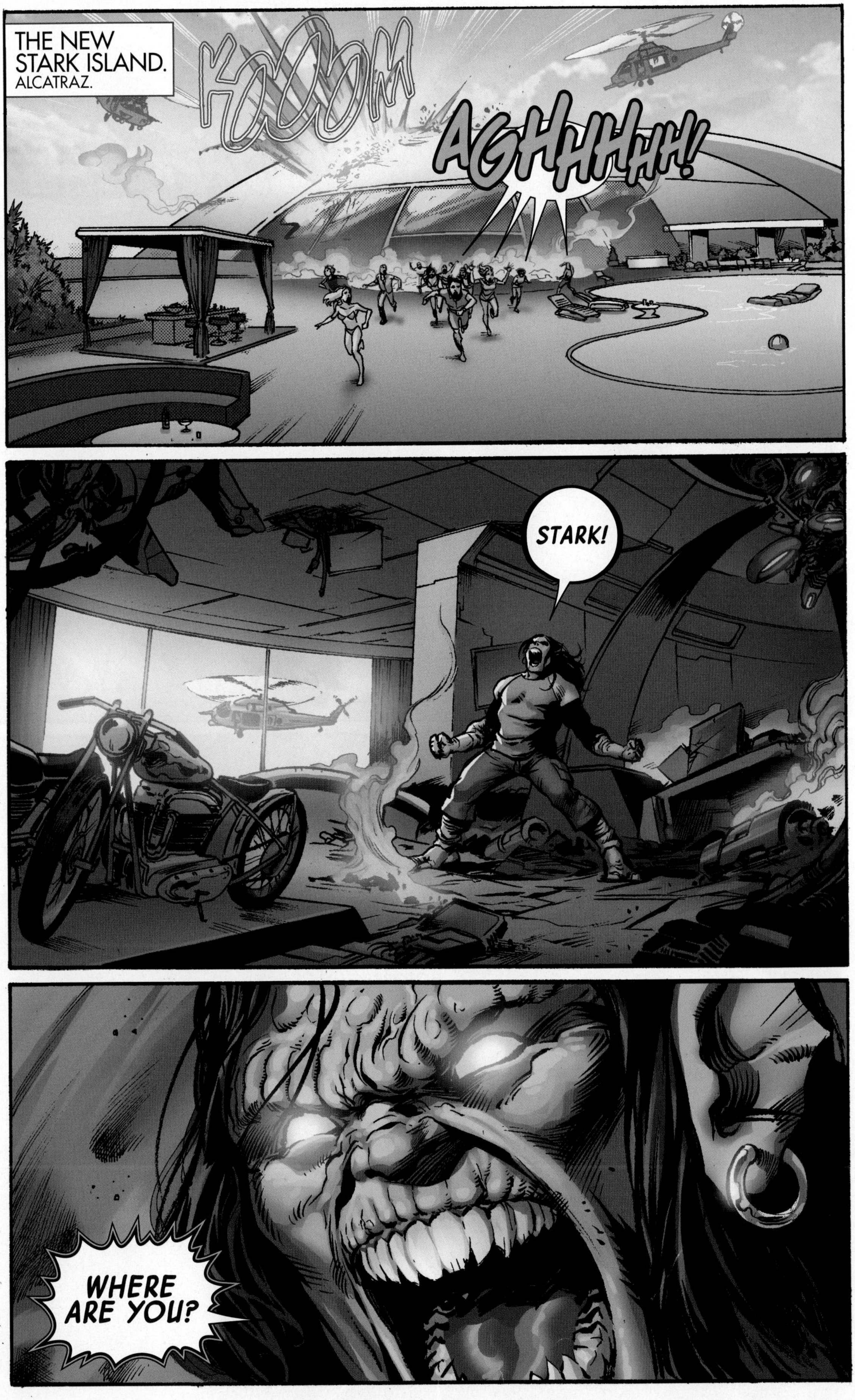

THE NEW STARK ISLAND. ALCATRAZ.
KOOOOM
AGHHHHH!
STARK!
WHERE ARE YOU?

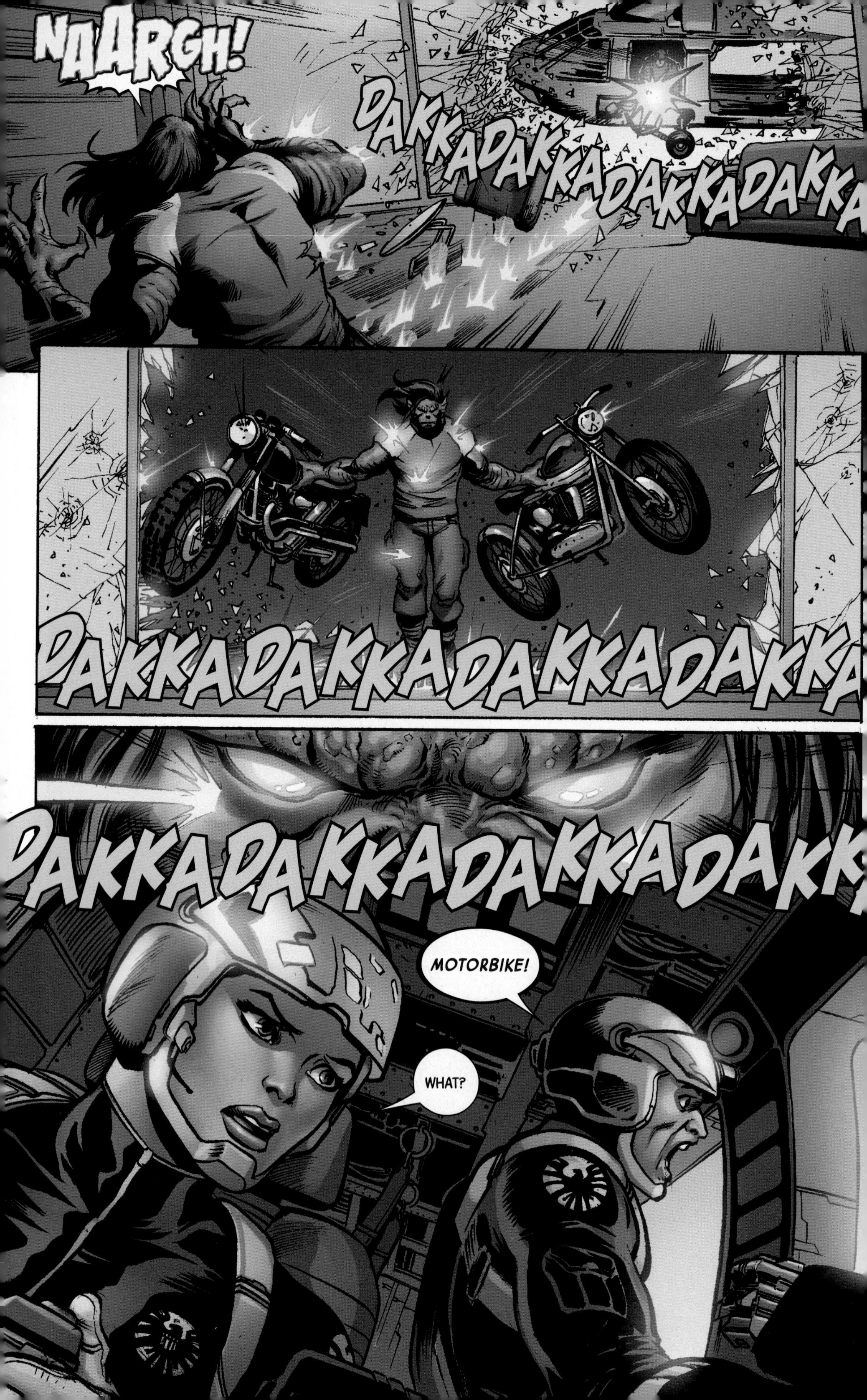
NAARGH!
DAKKADAKKADAKKADAKKA
DAKKADAKKADAKKADAKKA
DAKKADAKKADAKKADAKK
MOTORBIKE!
WHAT?

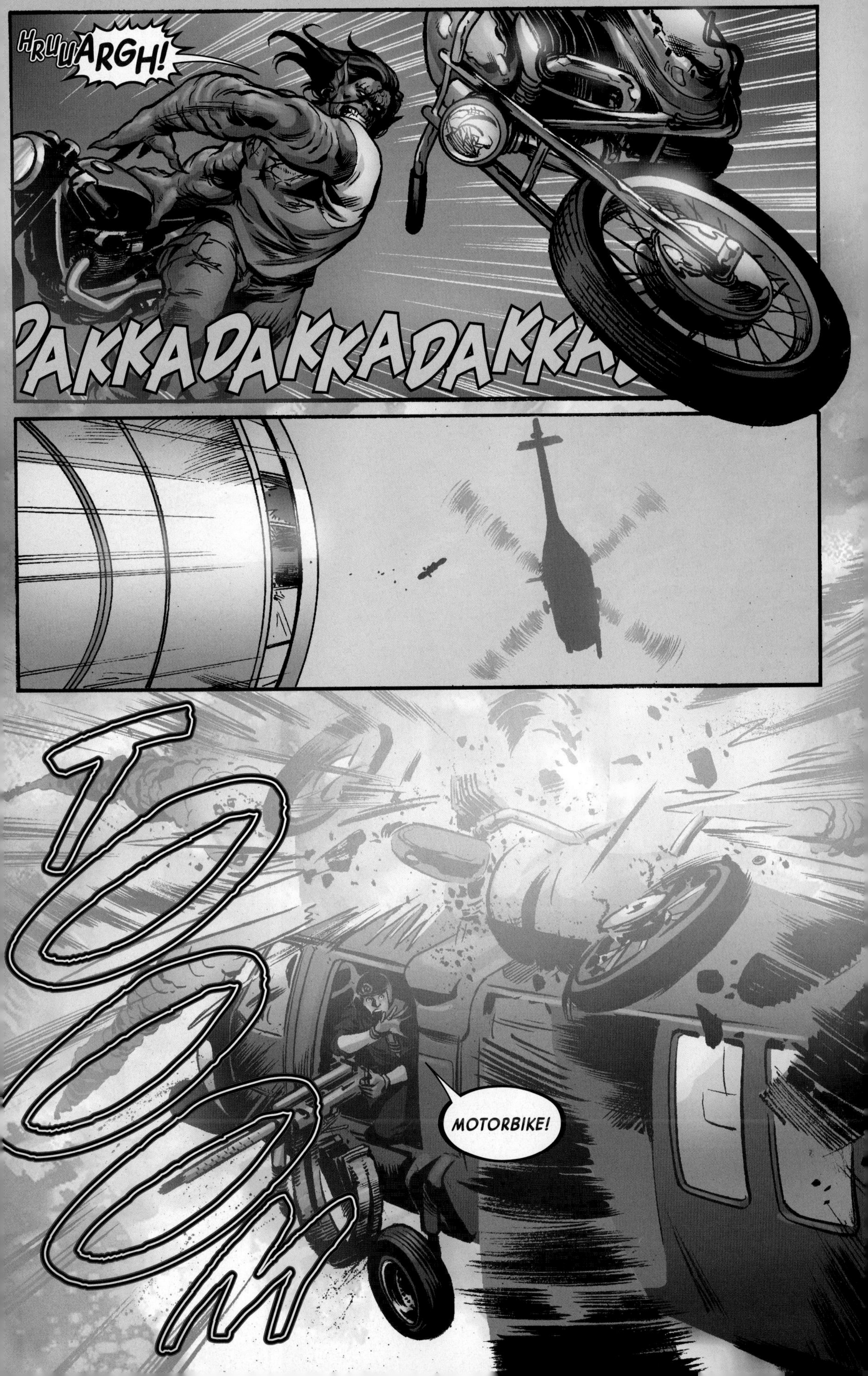
HRUUARGH!
DAKKADAKKADAKKA
TOOOM
MOTORBIKE!

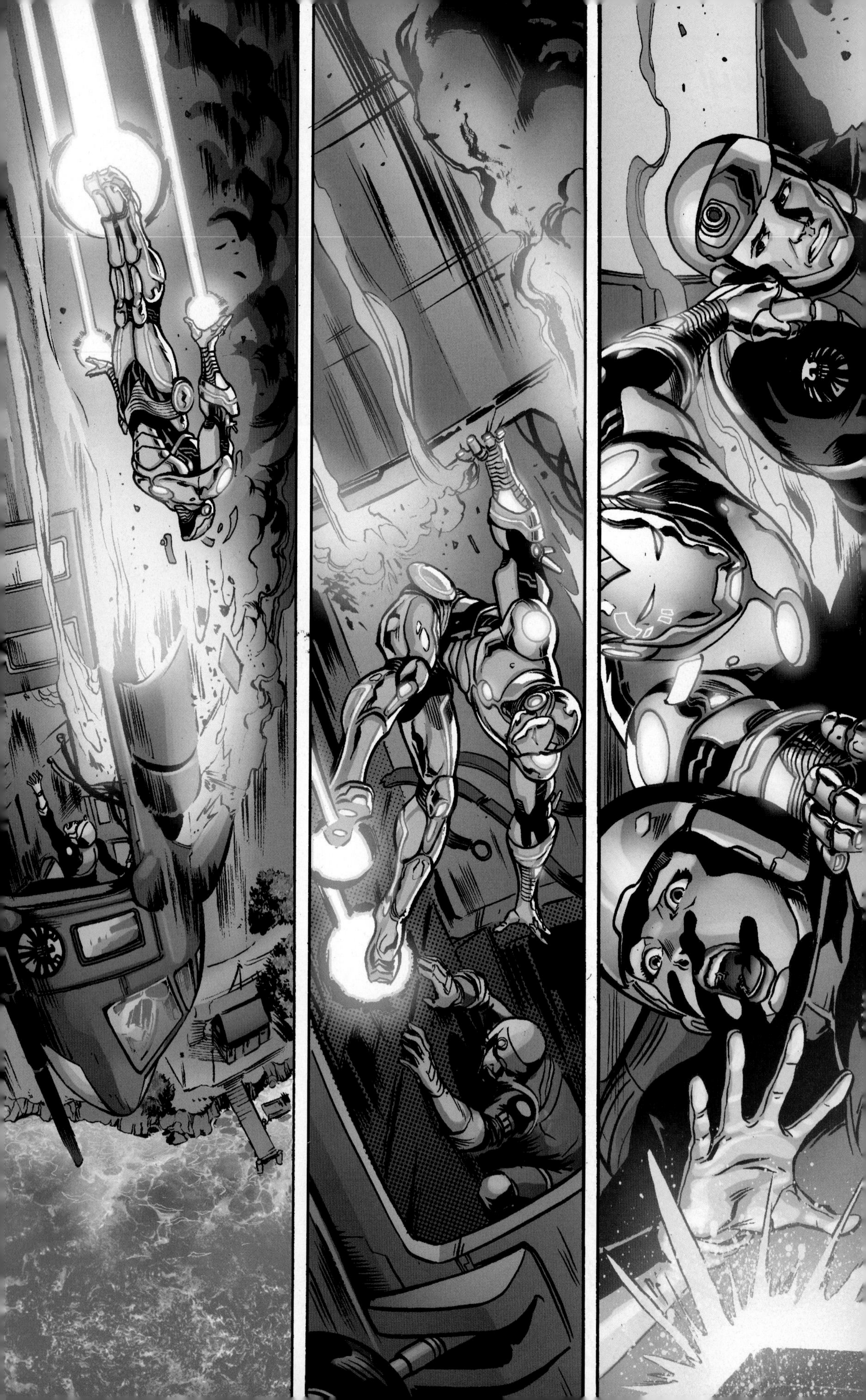

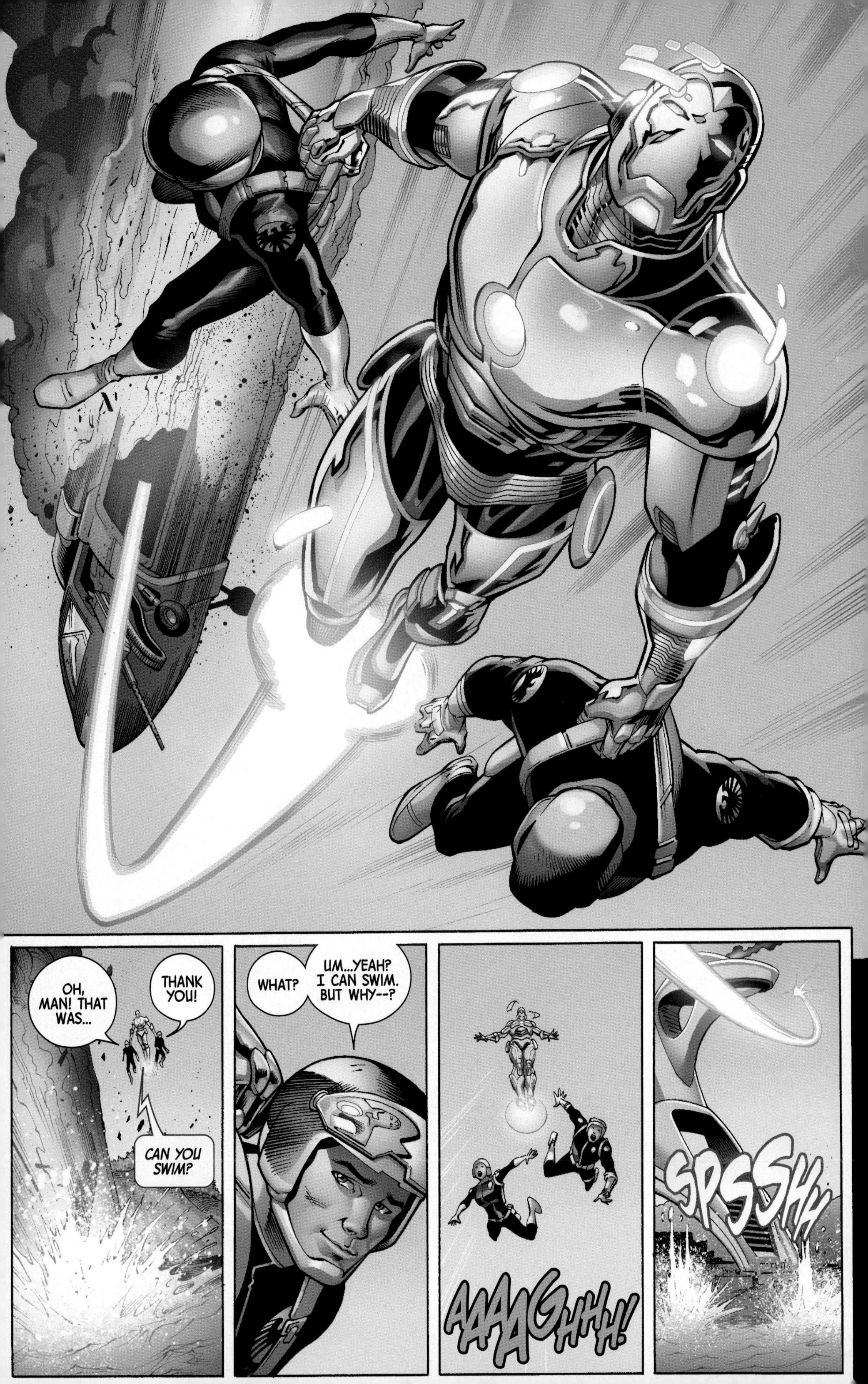
OH, MAN! THAT WAS...
THANK YOU!
CAN YOU SWIM?
WHAT?
UM...YEAH? I CAN SWIM. BUT WHY--?
AAAAGHHH!
SPSSHH

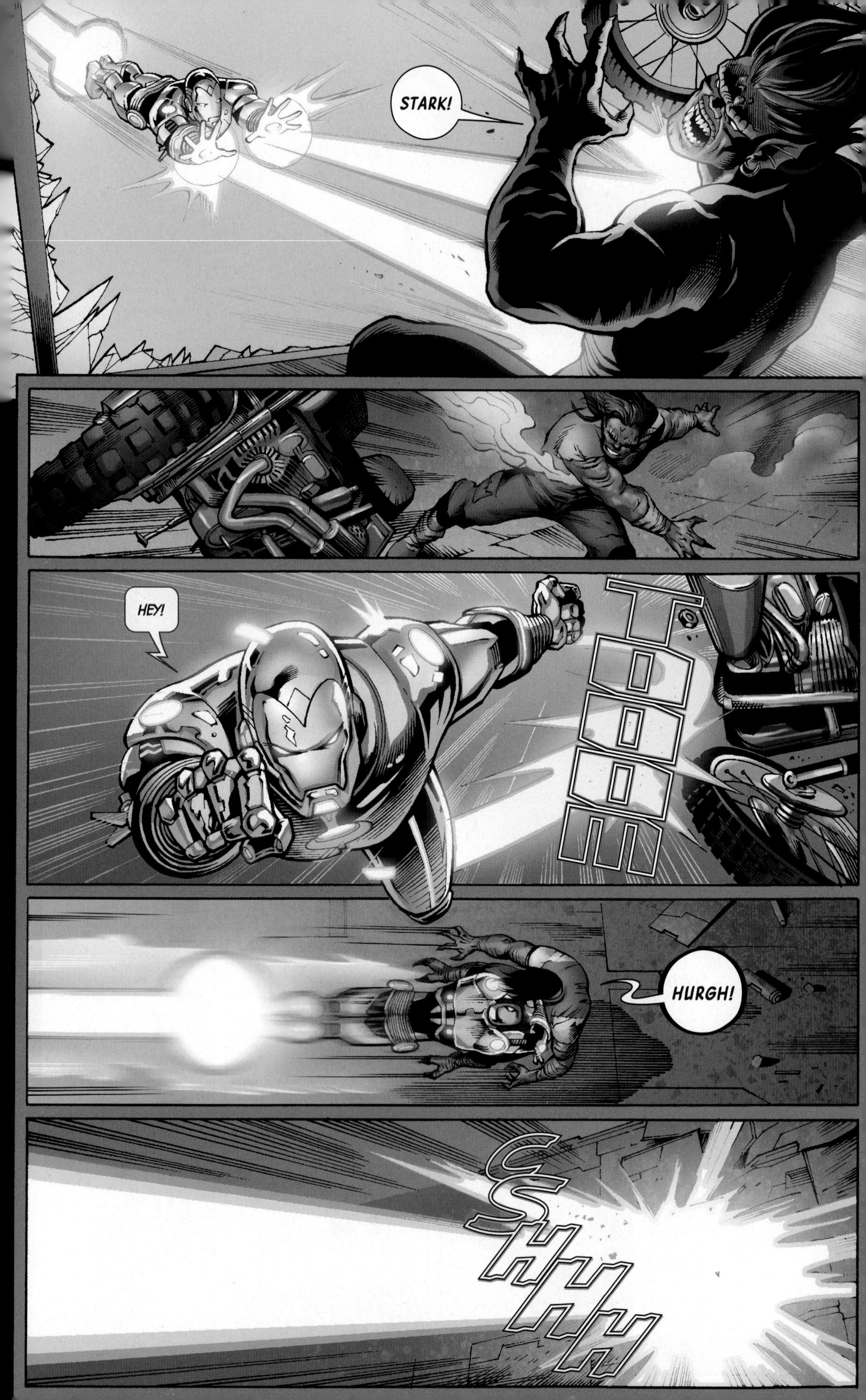
STARK!
HEY!
HURGH!

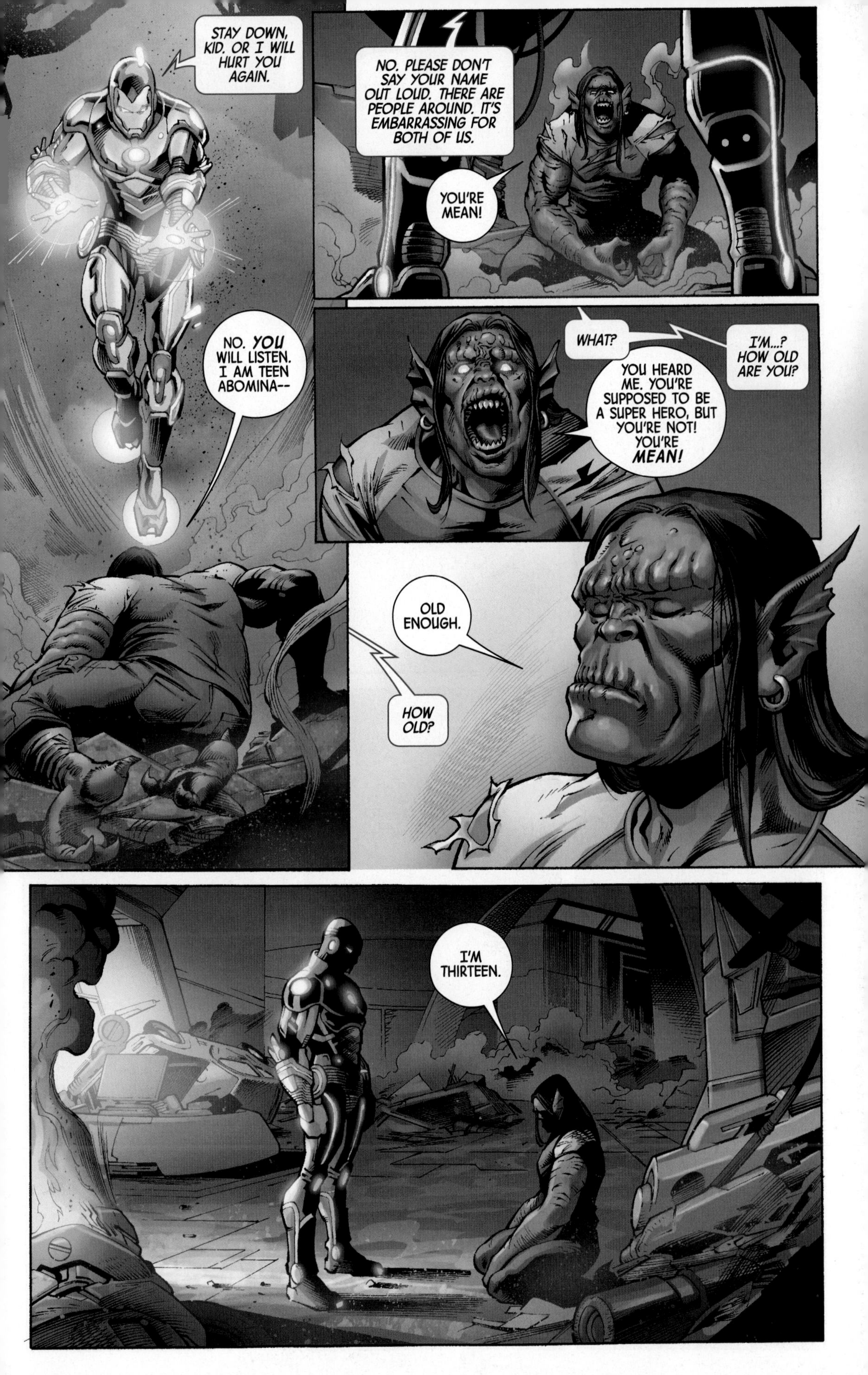
STAY DOWN, KID. OR I WILL HURT YOU AGAIN.
NO. YOU WILL LISTEN. I AM TEEN ABOMINA--
NO. PLEASE DON'T SAY YOUR NAME OUT LOUD. THERE ARE PEOPLE AROUND. IT'S EMBARRASSING FOR BOTH OF US.
YOU'RE MEAN!
WHAT?
YOU HEARD ME. YOU'RE SUPPOSED TO BE A SUPER HERO, BUT YOU'RE NOT! YOU'RE MEAN!
I'M...? HOW OLD ARE YOU?
OLD ENOUGH.
HOW OLD?
I'M THIRTEEN.

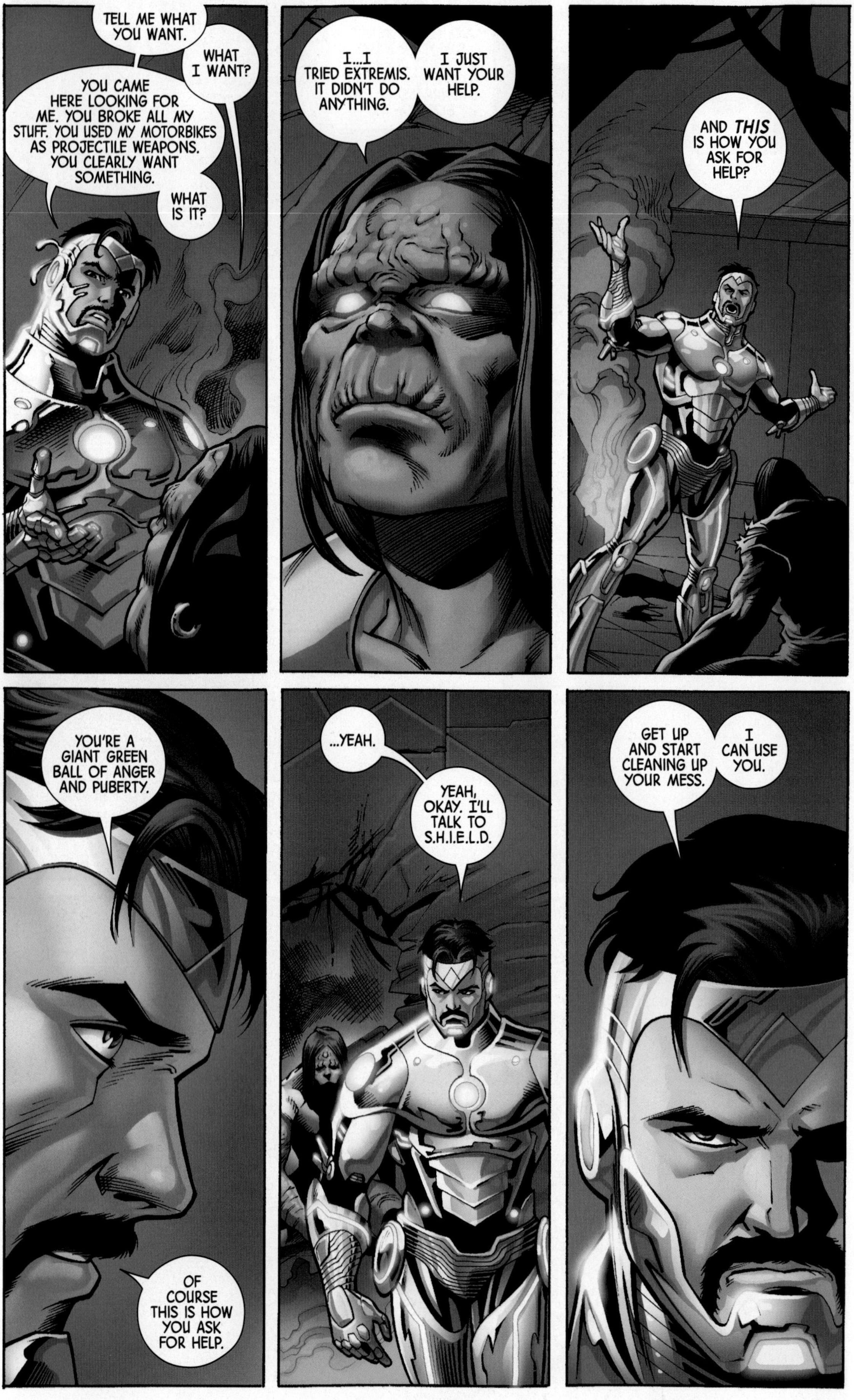
TELL ME WHAT YOU WANT.
WHAT I WANT?
YOU CAME HERE LOOKING FOR ME. YOU BROKE ALL MY STUFF. YOU USED MY MOTORBIKES AS PROJECTILE WEAPONS. YOU CLEARLY WANT SOMETHING.
WHAT IS IT?
I...I TRIED EXTREMIS. IT DIDN'T DO ANYTHING.
I JUST WANT YOUR HELP.
AND THIS IS HOW YOU ASK FOR HELP?
YOU'RE A GIANT GREEN BALL OF ANGER AND PUBERTY.
OF COURSE THIS IS HOW YOU ASK FOR HELP.
...YEAH.
YEAH, OKAY. I'LL TALK TO S.H.I.E.L.D.
GET UP AND START CLEANING UP YOUR MESS.
I CAN USE YOU.

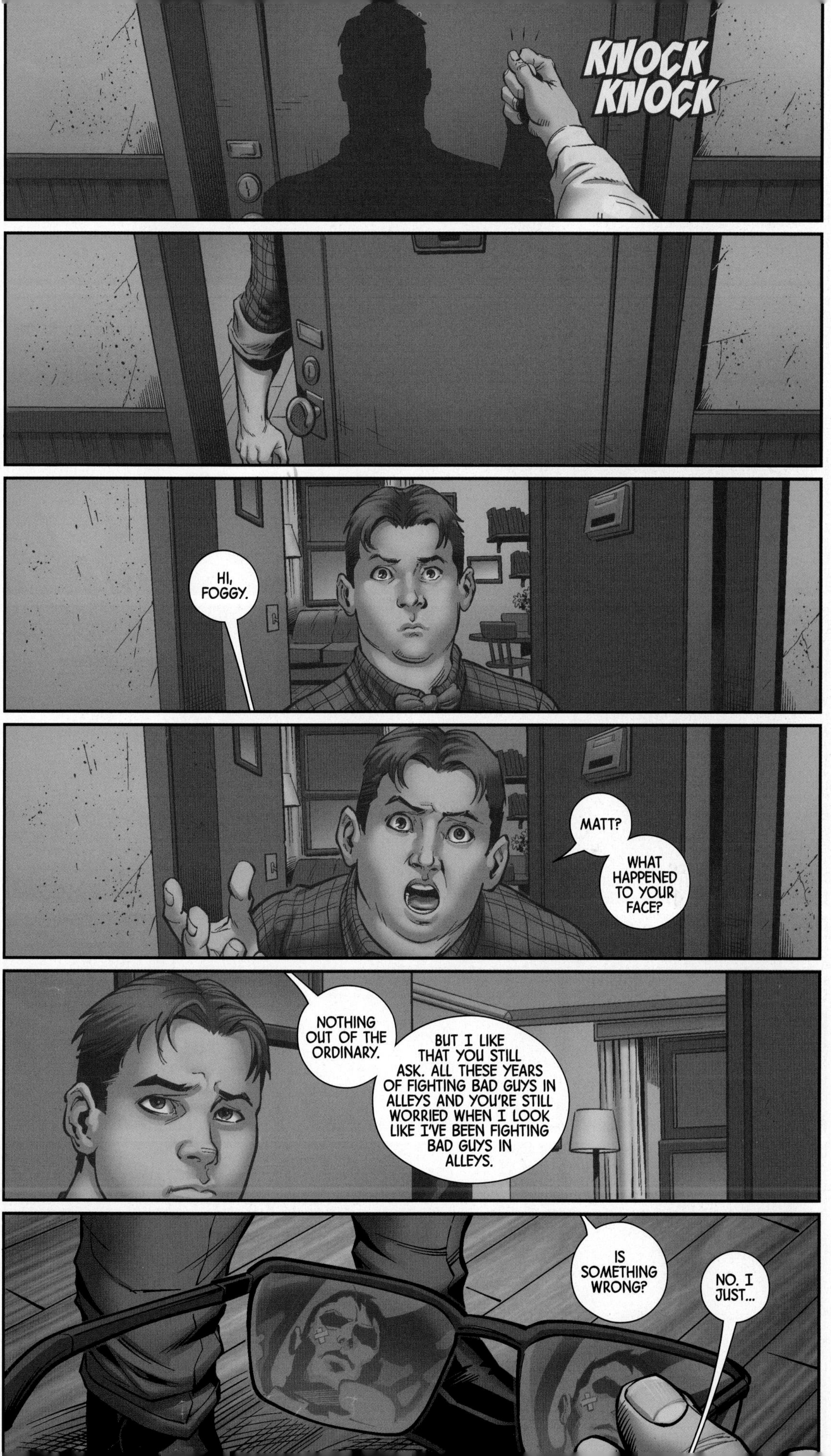
KNOCK KNOCK
HI, FOGGY.
MATT?
WHAT HAPPENED TO YOUR FACE?
NOTHING OUT OF THE ORDINARY.
BUT I LIKE THAT YOU STILL ASK. ALL THESE YEARS OF FIGHTING BAD GUYS IN ALLEYS AND YOU'RE STILL WORRIED WHEN I LOOK LIKE I'VE BEEN FIGHTING BAD GUYS IN ALLEYS.
IS SOMETHING WRONG?
NO. I JUST...

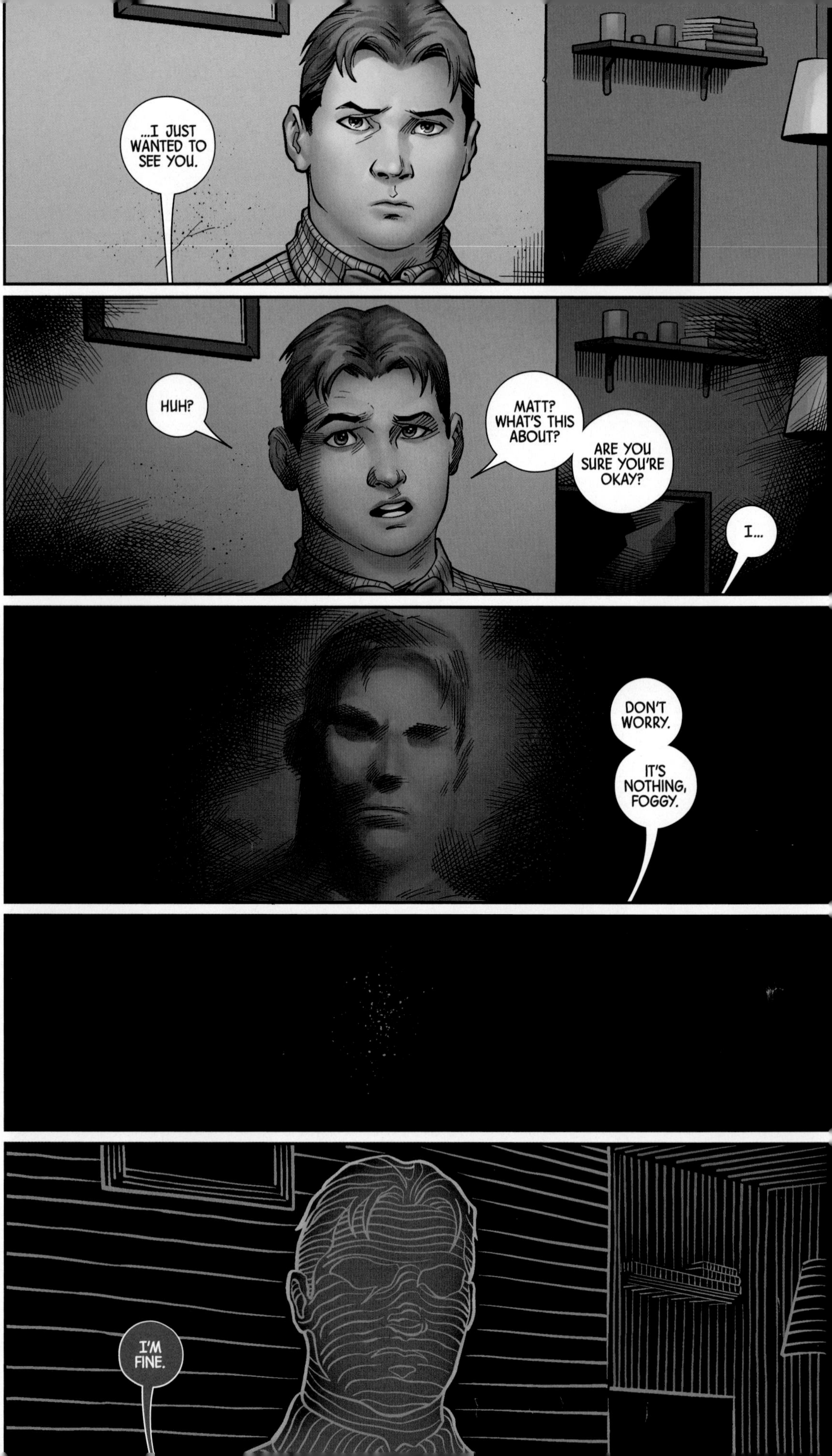
...I JUST WANTED TO SEE YOU.
HUH?
MATT? WHAT'S THIS ABOUT?
ARE YOU SURE YOU'RE OKAY?
I...
DON'T WORRY.
IT'S NOTHING, FOGGY.
I'M FINE.

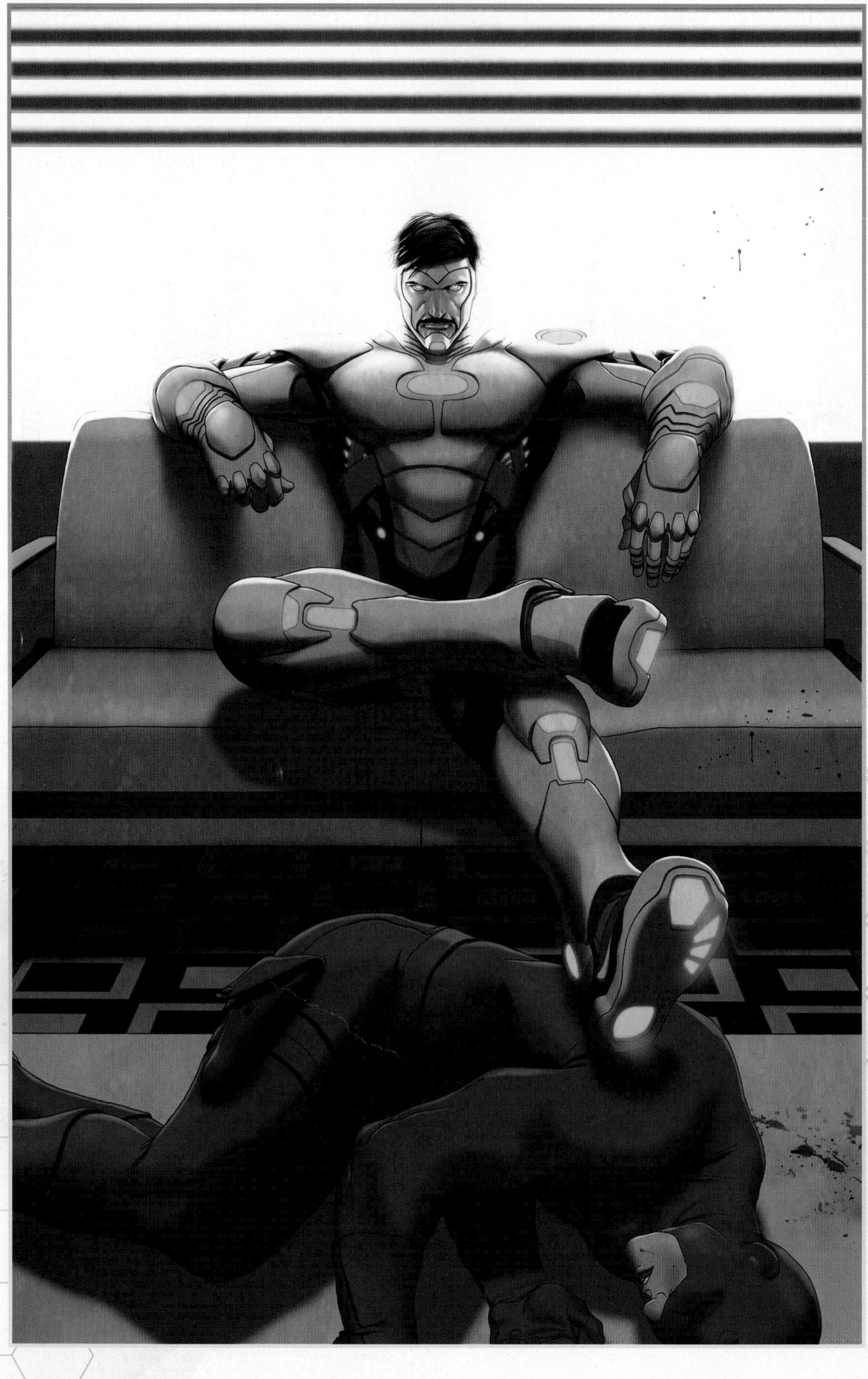

4: THE CHOICE

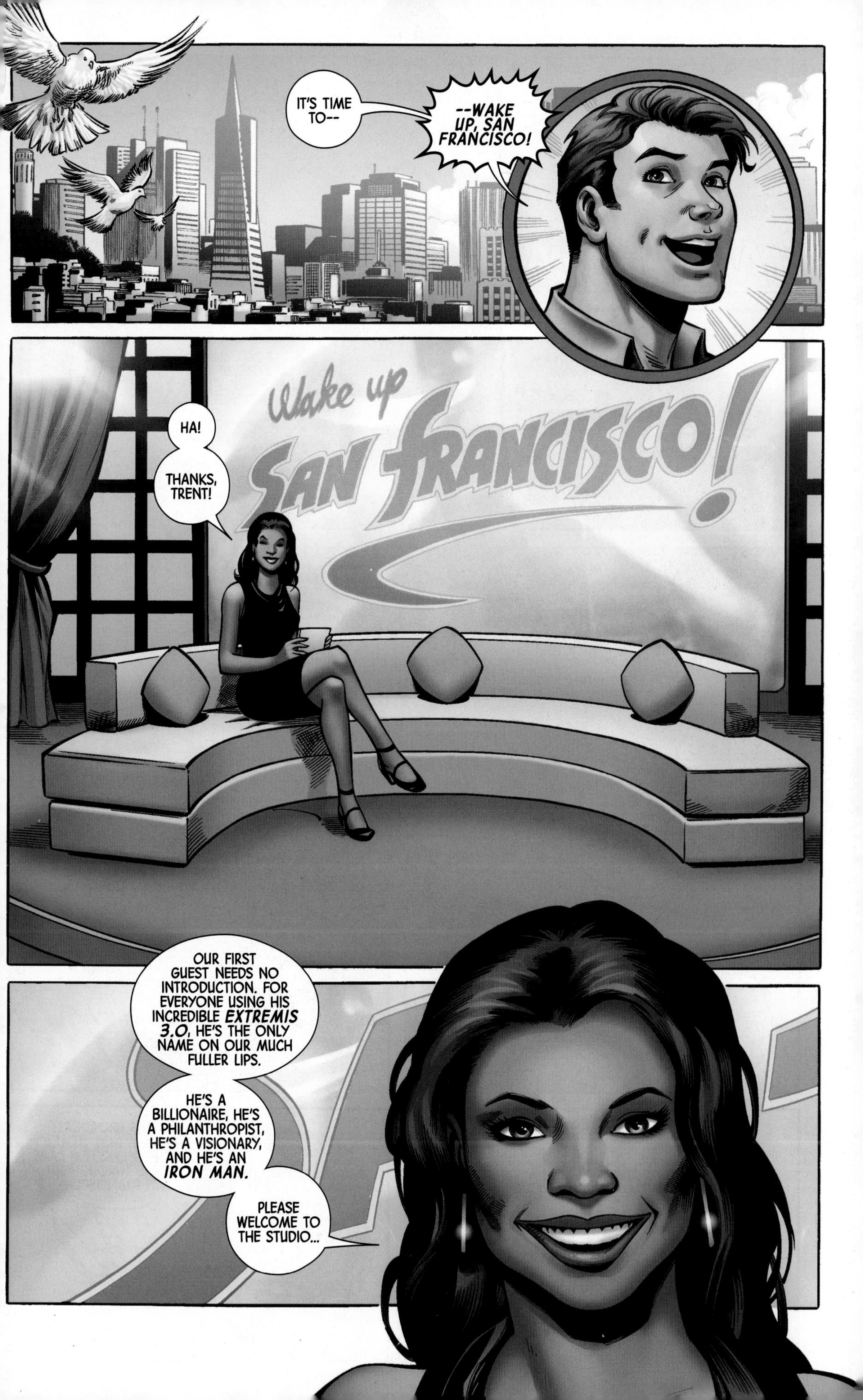
IT'S TIME TO--
--WAKE UP, SAN FRANCISCO!
Wake up SAN FRANCISCO!
HA!
THANKS, TRENT!
OUR FIRST GUEST NEEDS NO INTRODUCTION. FOR EVERYONE USING HIS INCREDIBLE EXTREMIS 3.0, HE'S THE ONLY NAME ON OUR MUCH FULLER LIPS.
HE'S A BILLIONAIRE, HE'S A PHILANTHROPIST, HE'S A VISIONARY, AND HE'S AN IRON MAN.
PLEASE WELCOME TO THE STUDIO...

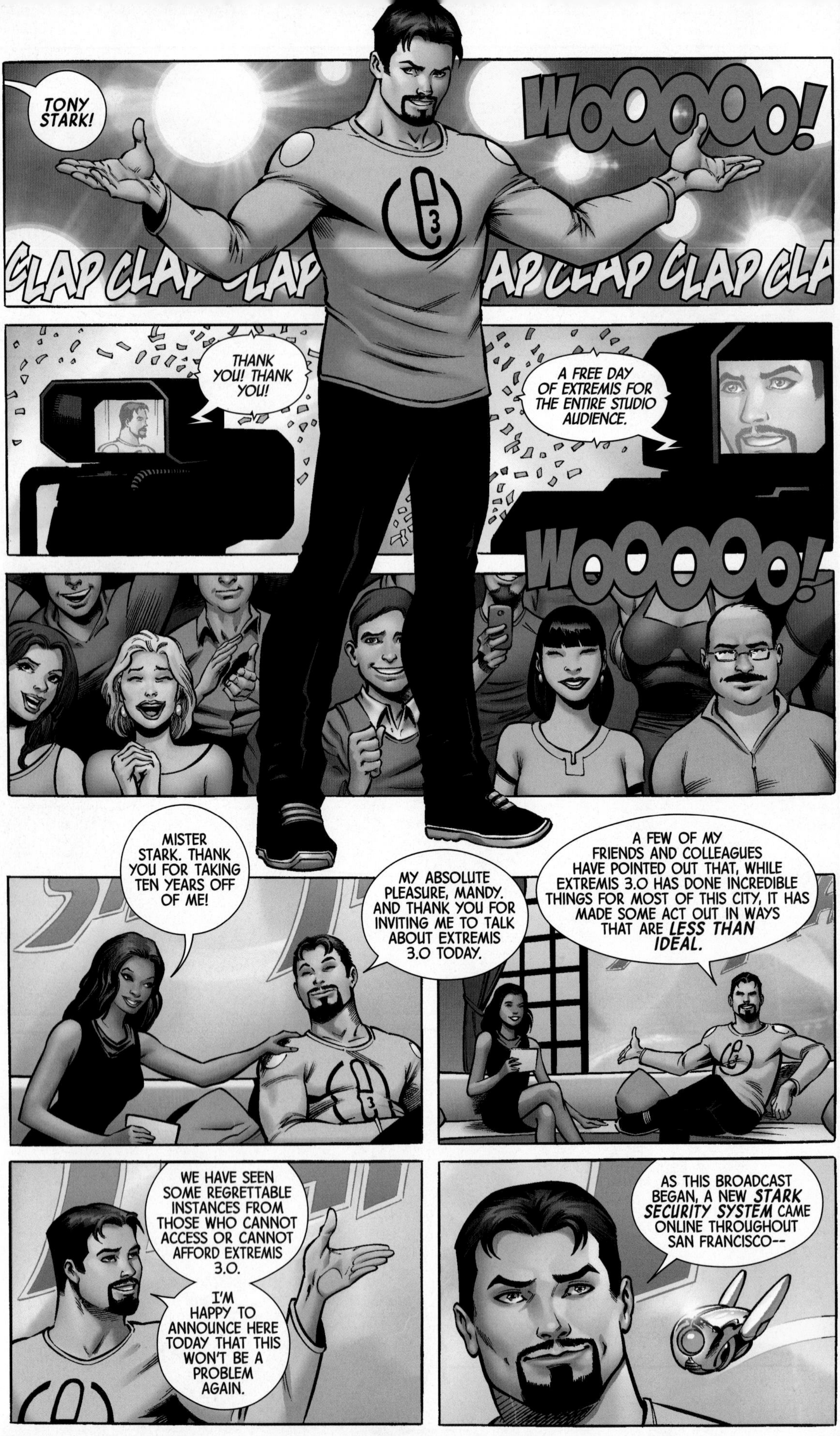
TONY STARK!
WOOOOO!
CLAP CLAP CLAP CLAP CLAP CLAP CLAP
THANK YOU! THANK YOU!
A FREE DAY OF EXTREMIS FOR THE ENTIRE STUDIO AUDIENCE.
WOOOOO!
MISTER STARK. THANK YOU FOR TAKING TEN YEARS OFF OF ME!
MY ABSOLUTE PLEASURE, MANDY. AND THANK YOU FOR INVITING ME TO TALK ABOUT EXTREMIS 3.0 TODAY.
A FEW OF MY FRIENDS AND COLLEAGUES HAVE POINTED OUT THAT, WHILE EXTREMIS 3.0 HAS DONE INCREDIBLE THINGS FOR MOST OF THIS CITY, IT HAS MADE SOME ACT OUT IN WAYS THAT ARE LESS THAN IDEAL.
WE HAVE SEEN SOME REGRETTABLE INSTANCES FROM THOSE WHO CANNOT ACCESS OR CANNOT AFFORD EXTREMIS 3.0.
I'M HAPPY TO ANNOUNCE HERE TODAY THAT THIS WON'T BE A PROBLEM AGAIN.
AS THIS BROADCAST BEGAN, A NEW STARK SECURITY SYSTEM CAME ONLINE THROUGHOUT SAN FRANCISCO--

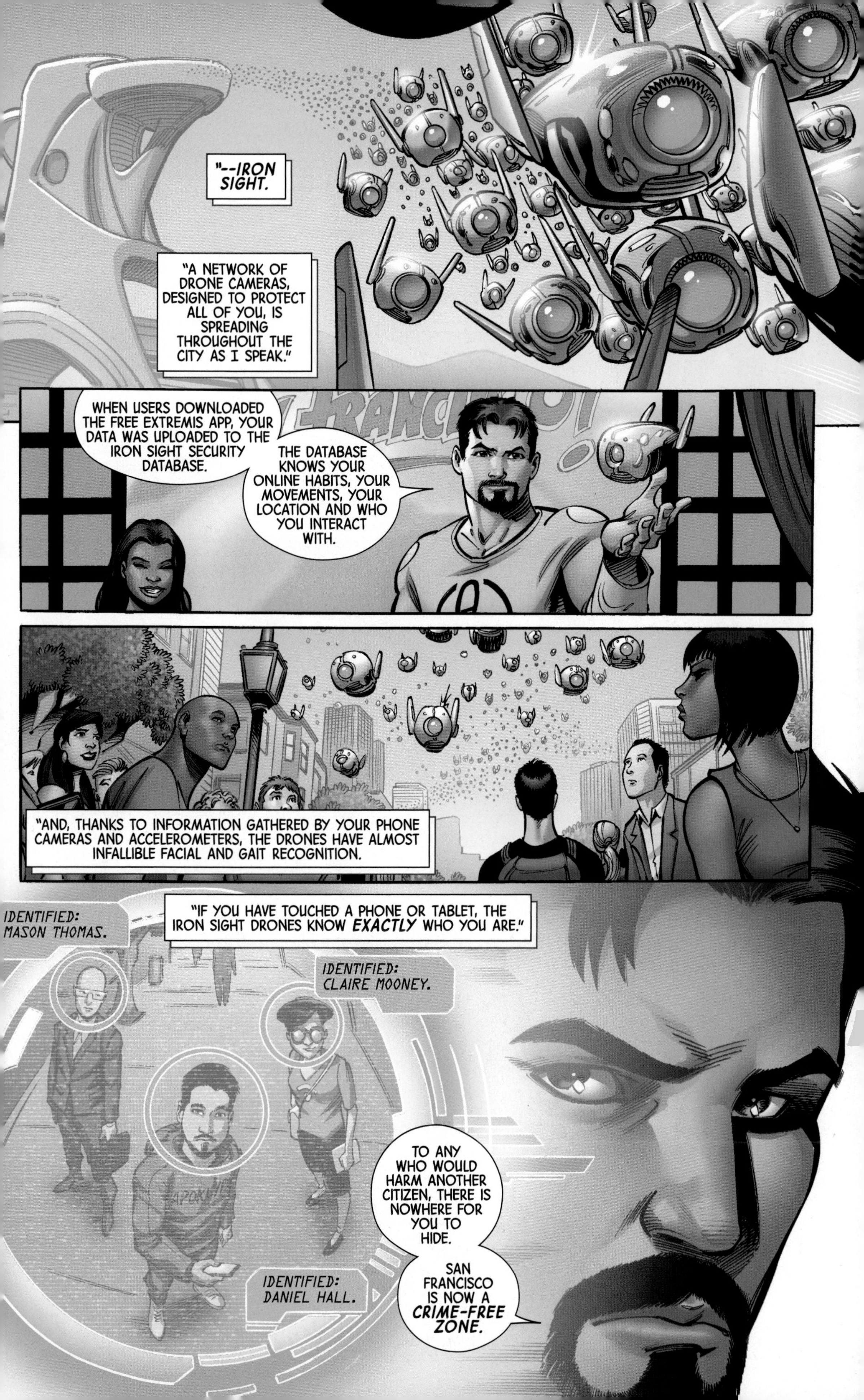
"--IRON SIGHT.
"A NETWORK OF DRONE CAMERAS, DESIGNED TO PROTECT ALL OF YOU, IS SPREADING THROUGHOUT THE CITY AS I SPEAK."
WHEN USERS DOWNLOADED THE FREE EXTREMIS APP, YOUR DATA WAS UPLOADED TO THE IRON SIGHT SECURITY DATABASE.
THE DATABASE KNOWS YOUR ONLINE HABITS, YOUR MOVEMENTS, YOUR LOCATION AND WHO YOU INTERACT WITH.
"AND, THANKS TO INFORMATION GATHERED BY YOUR PHONE CAMERAS AND ACCELEROMETERS, THE DRONES HAVE ALMOST INFALLIBLE FACIAL AND GAIT RECOGNITION.
IDENTIFIED: MASON THOMAS.
"IF YOU HAVE TOUCHED A PHONE OR TABLET, THE IRON SIGHT DRONES KNOW *EXACTLY* WHO YOU ARE."
IDENTIFIED: CLAIRE MOONEY.
TO ANY WHO WOULD HARM ANOTHER CITIZEN, THERE IS NOWHERE FOR YOU TO HIDE.
IDENTIFIED: DANIEL HALL.
SAN FRANCISCO IS NOW A ***CRIME-FREE ZONE.***

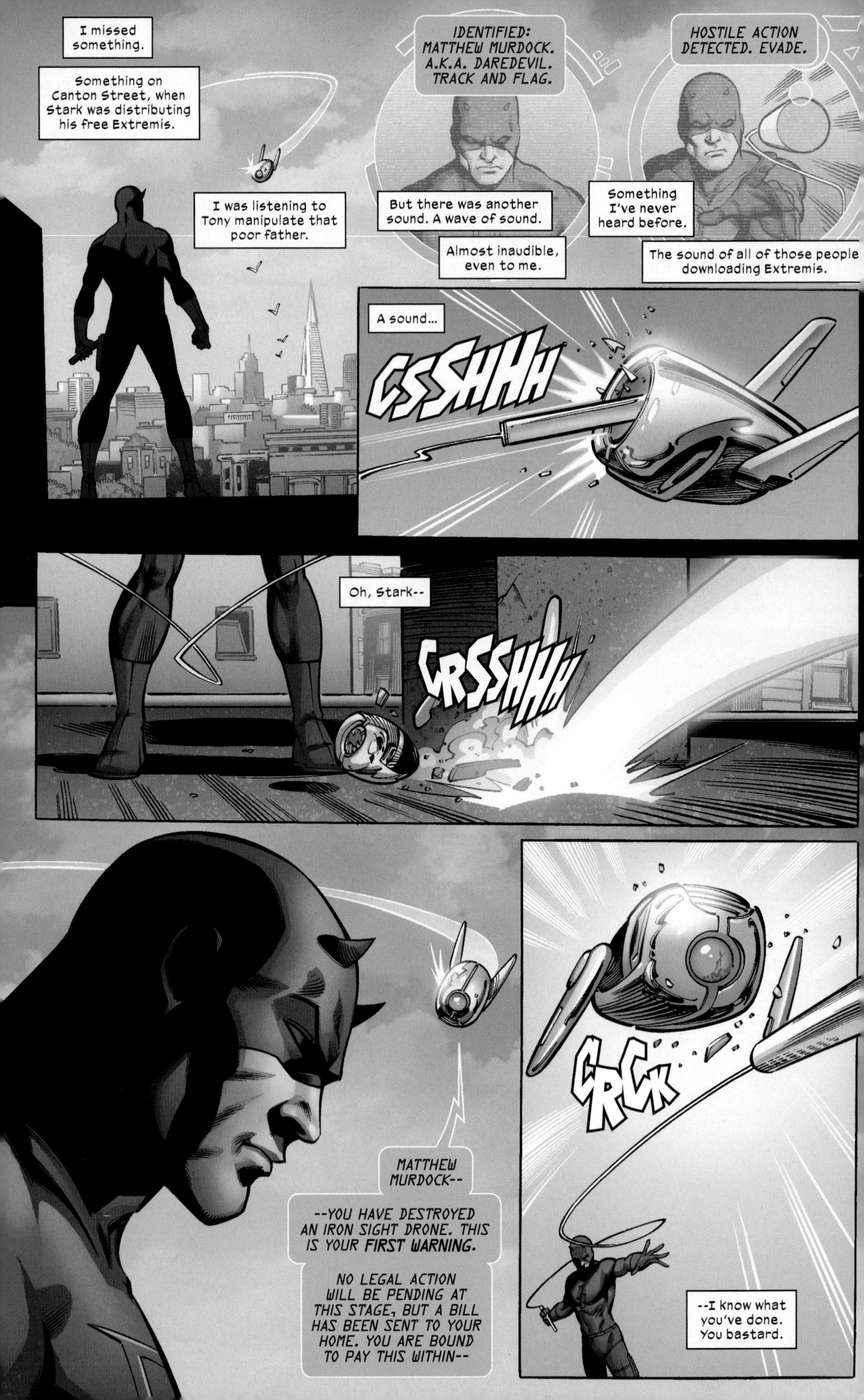

I missed something.
Something on Canton Street, when Stark was distributing his free Extremis.
IDENTIFIED: MATTHEW MURDOCK. A.K.A. DAREDEVIL. TRACK AND FLAG.
HOSTILE ACTION DETECTED. EVADE.
I was listening to Tony manipulate that poor father.
But there was another sound. A wave of sound.
Almost inaudible, even to me.
Something I've never heard before.
The sound of all of those people downloading Extremis.
A sound...
CSSHHH
Oh, Stark--
CRSSHHH
MATTHEW MURDOCK--
--YOU HAVE DESTROYED AN IRON SIGHT DRONE. THIS IS YOUR FIRST WARNING.
NO LEGAL ACTION WILL BE PENDING AT THIS STAGE, BUT A BILL HAS BEEN SENT TO YOUR HOME. YOU ARE BOUND TO PAY THIS WITHIN--
CRCK
--I know what you've done. You bastard.

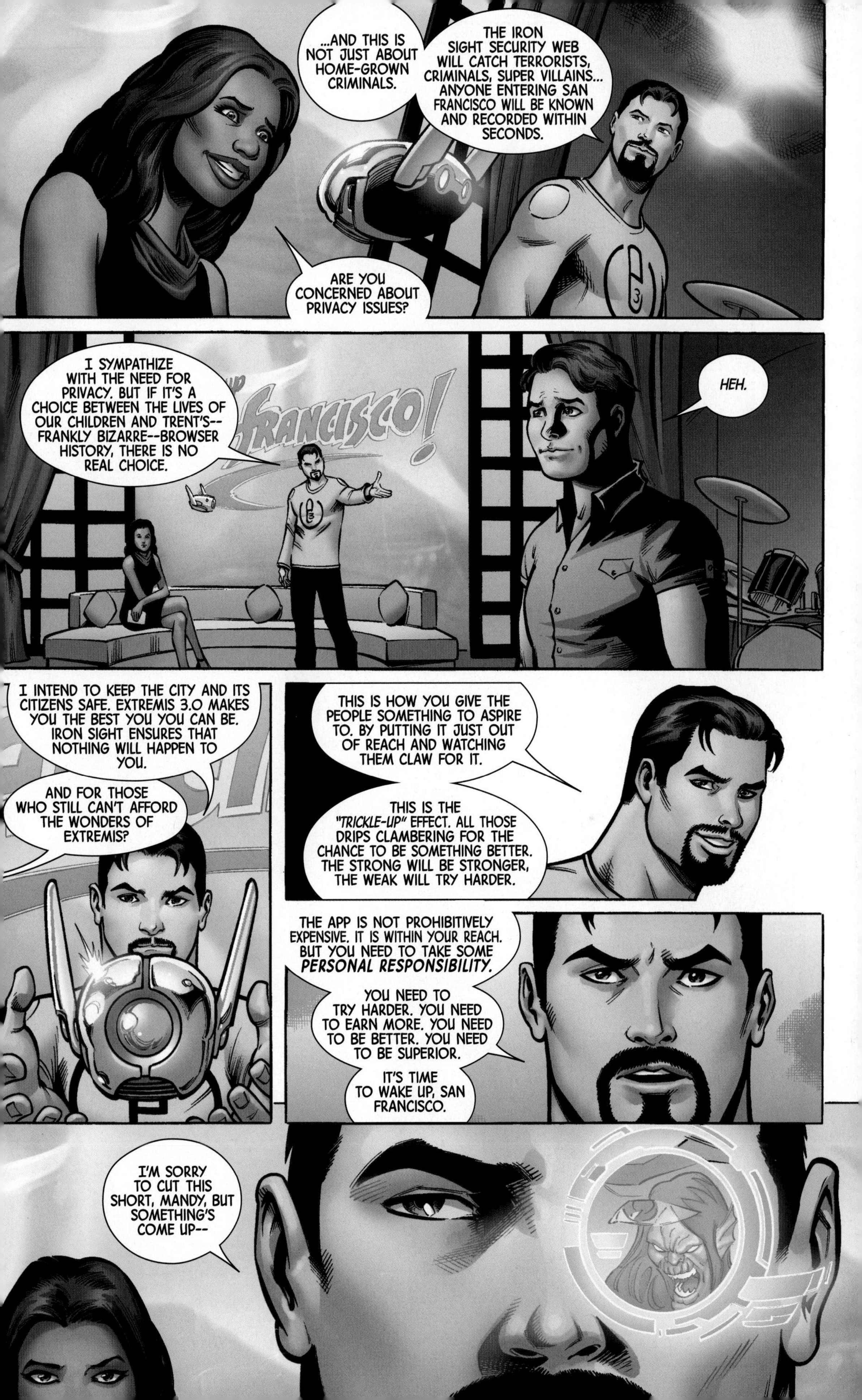
...AND THIS IS NOT JUST ABOUT HOME-GROWN CRIMINALS.
THE IRON SIGHT SECURITY WEB WILL CATCH TERRORISTS, CRIMINALS, SUPER VILLAINS... ANYONE ENTERING SAN FRANCISCO WILL BE KNOWN AND RECORDED WITHIN SECONDS.
ARE YOU CONCERNED ABOUT PRIVACY ISSUES?
I SYMPATHIZE WITH THE NEED FOR PRIVACY. BUT IF IT'S A CHOICE BETWEEN THE LIVES OF OUR CHILDREN AND TRENT'S--FRANKLY BIZARRE--BROWSER HISTORY, THERE IS NO REAL CHOICE.
HEH.
FRANCISCO!
I INTEND TO KEEP THE CITY AND ITS CITIZENS SAFE. EXTREMIS 3.0 MAKES YOU THE BEST YOU YOU CAN BE. IRON SIGHT ENSURES THAT NOTHING WILL HAPPEN TO YOU.
AND FOR THOSE WHO STILL CAN'T AFFORD THE WONDERS OF EXTREMIS?
THIS IS HOW YOU GIVE THE PEOPLE SOMETHING TO ASPIRE TO. BY PUTTING IT JUST OUT OF REACH AND WATCHING THEM CLAW FOR IT.
THIS IS THE "TRICKLE-UP" EFFECT. ALL THOSE DRIPS CLAMBERING FOR THE CHANCE TO BE SOMETHING BETTER. THE STRONG WILL BE STRONGER, THE WEAK WILL TRY HARDER.
THE APP IS NOT PROHIBITIVELY EXPENSIVE. IT IS WITHIN YOUR REACH. BUT YOU NEED TO TAKE SOME PERSONAL RESPONSIBILITY.
YOU NEED TO TRY HARDER. YOU NEED TO EARN MORE. YOU NEED TO BE BETTER. YOU NEED TO BE SUPERIOR.
IT'S TIME TO WAKE UP, SAN FRANCISCO.
I'M SORRY TO CUT THIS SHORT, MANDY, BUT SOMETHING'S COME UP--

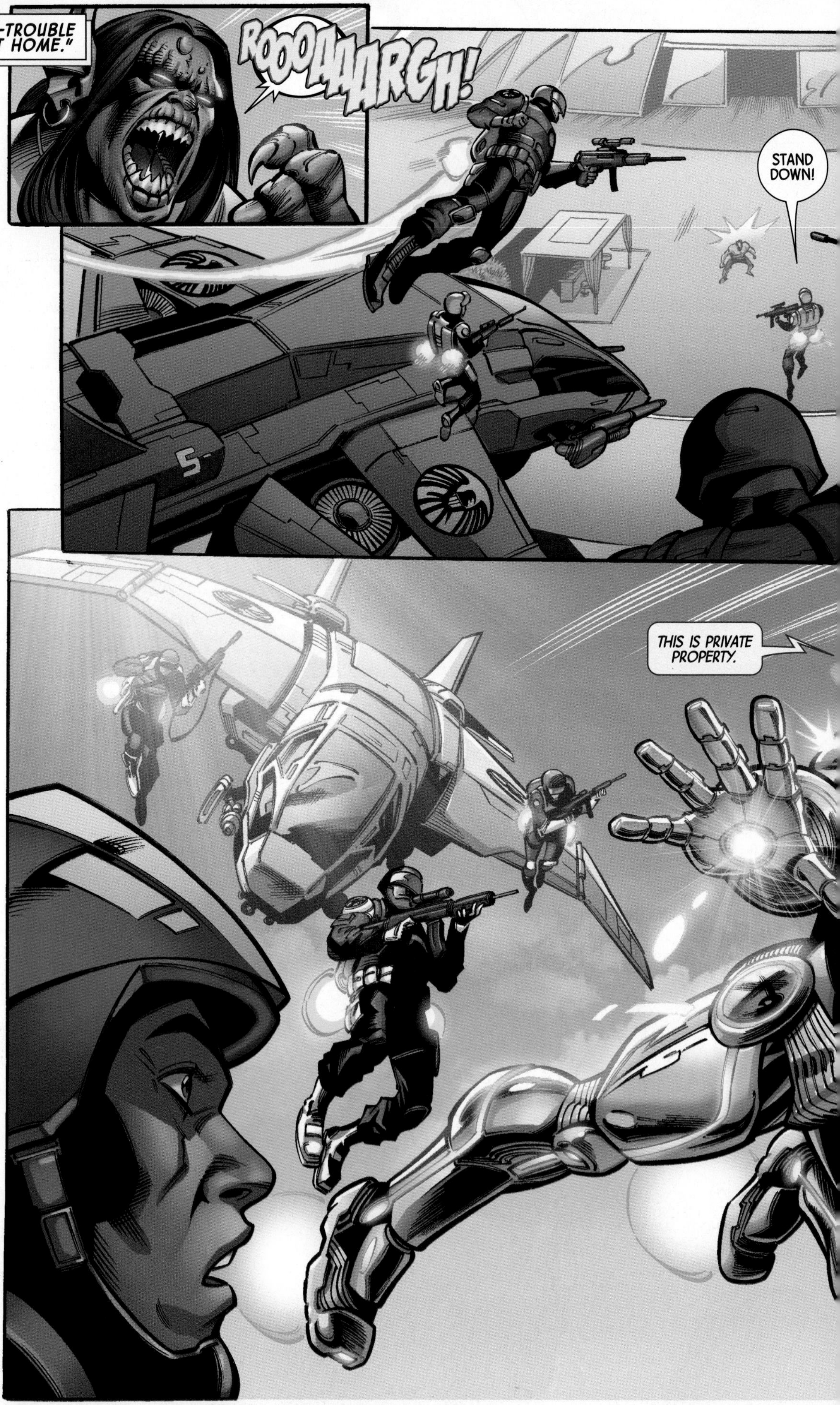
"--TROUBLE AT HOME."
ROOOAAARGH!
STAND DOWN!
THIS IS PRIVATE PROPERTY.

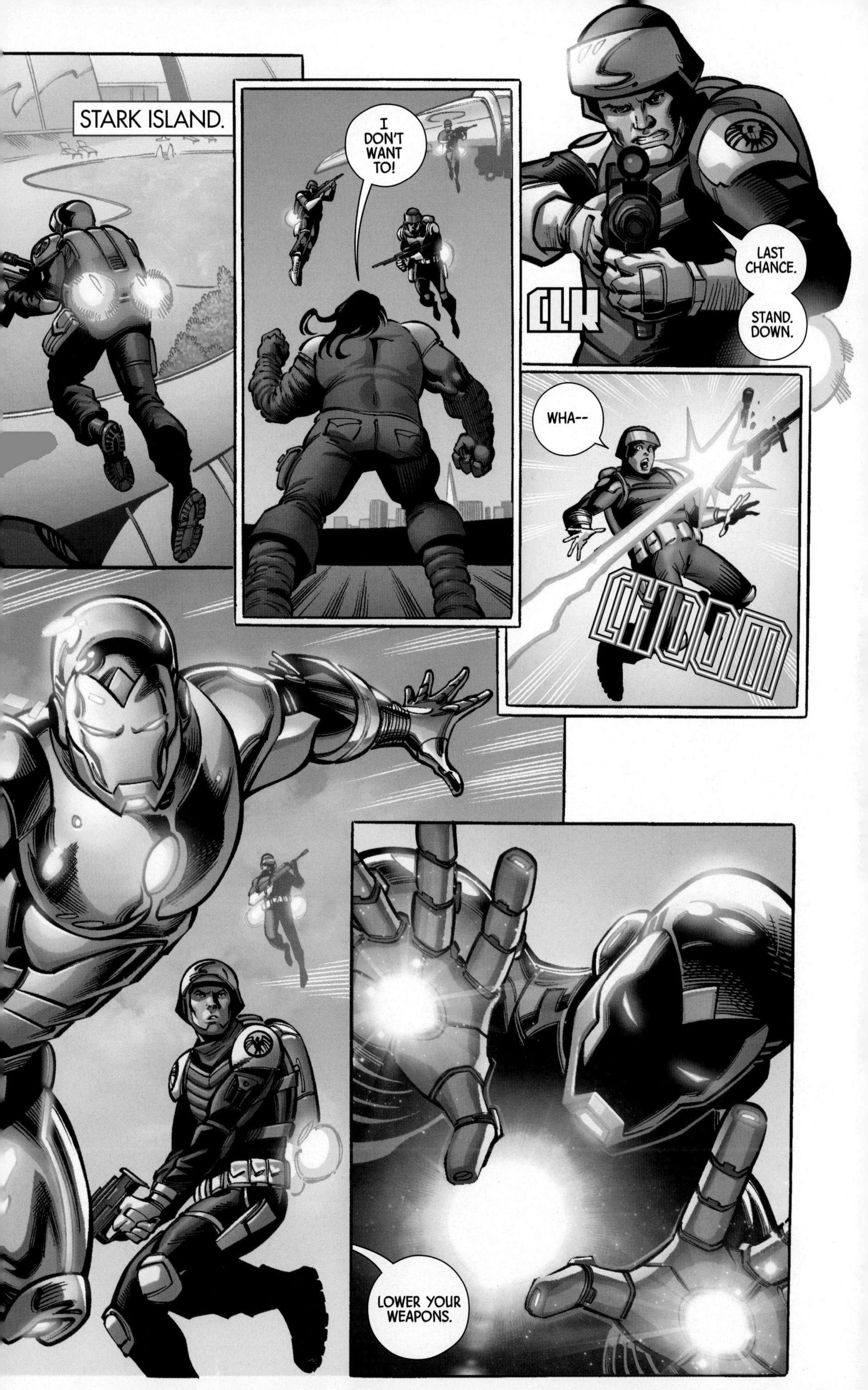
STARK ISLAND.
I DON'T WANT TO!
CLK
LAST CHANCE.
STAND. DOWN.
WHA--
CHOOM
LOWER YOUR WEAPONS.

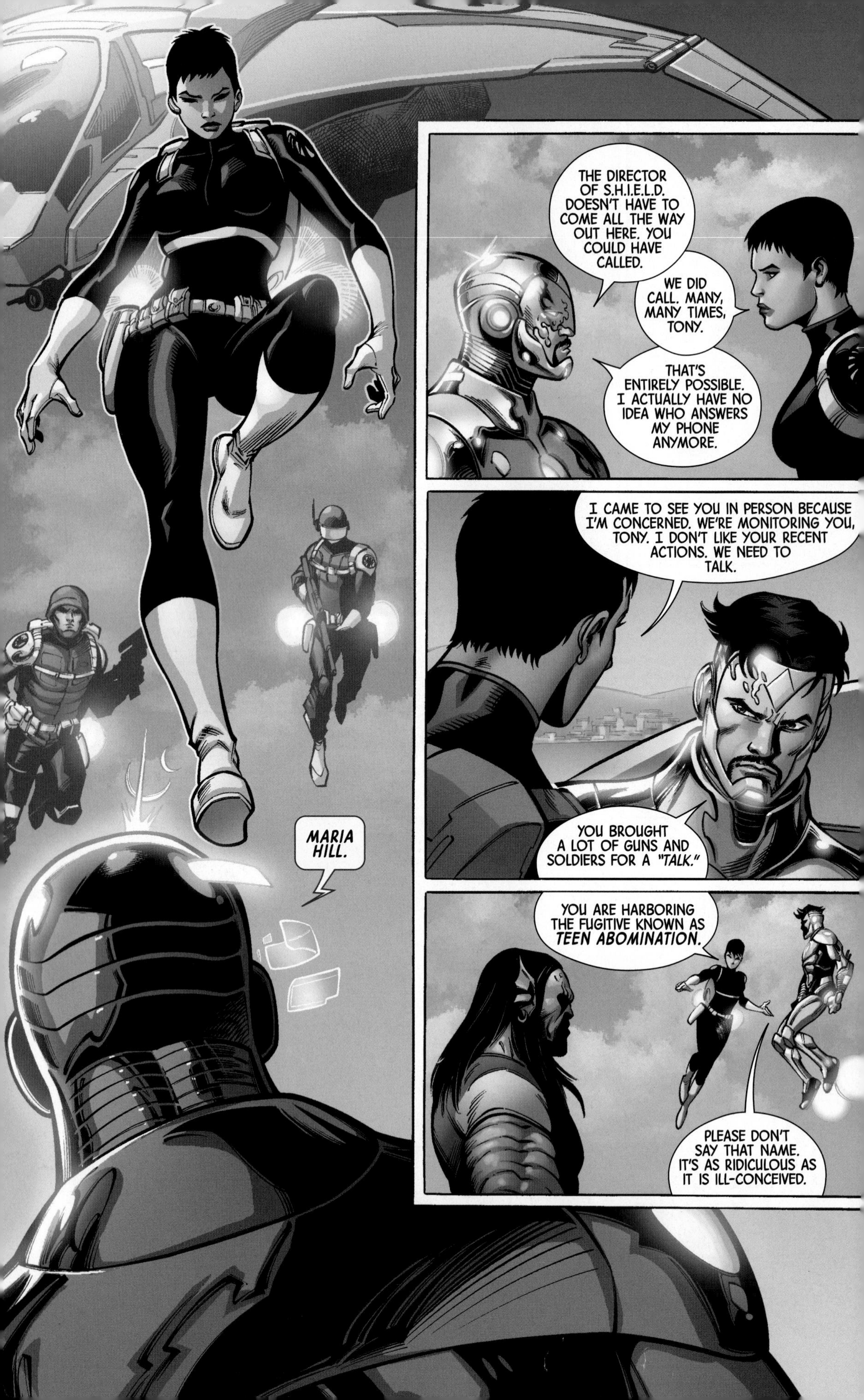
MARIA HILL.
THE DIRECTOR OF S.H.I.E.L.D. DOESN'T HAVE TO COME ALL THE WAY OUT HERE. YOU COULD HAVE CALLED.
WE DID CALL. MANY, MANY TIMES, TONY.
THAT'S ENTIRELY POSSIBLE. I ACTUALLY HAVE NO IDEA WHO ANSWERS MY PHONE ANYMORE.
I CAME TO SEE YOU IN PERSON BECAUSE I'M CONCERNED. WE'RE MONITORING YOU, TONY. I DON'T LIKE YOUR RECENT ACTIONS. WE NEED TO TALK.
YOU BROUGHT A LOT OF GUNS AND SOLDIERS FOR A "TALK."
YOU ARE HARBORING THE FUGITIVE KNOWN AS TEEN ABOMINATION.
PLEASE DON'T SAY THAT NAME. IT'S AS RIDICULOUS AS IT IS ILL-CONCEIVED.

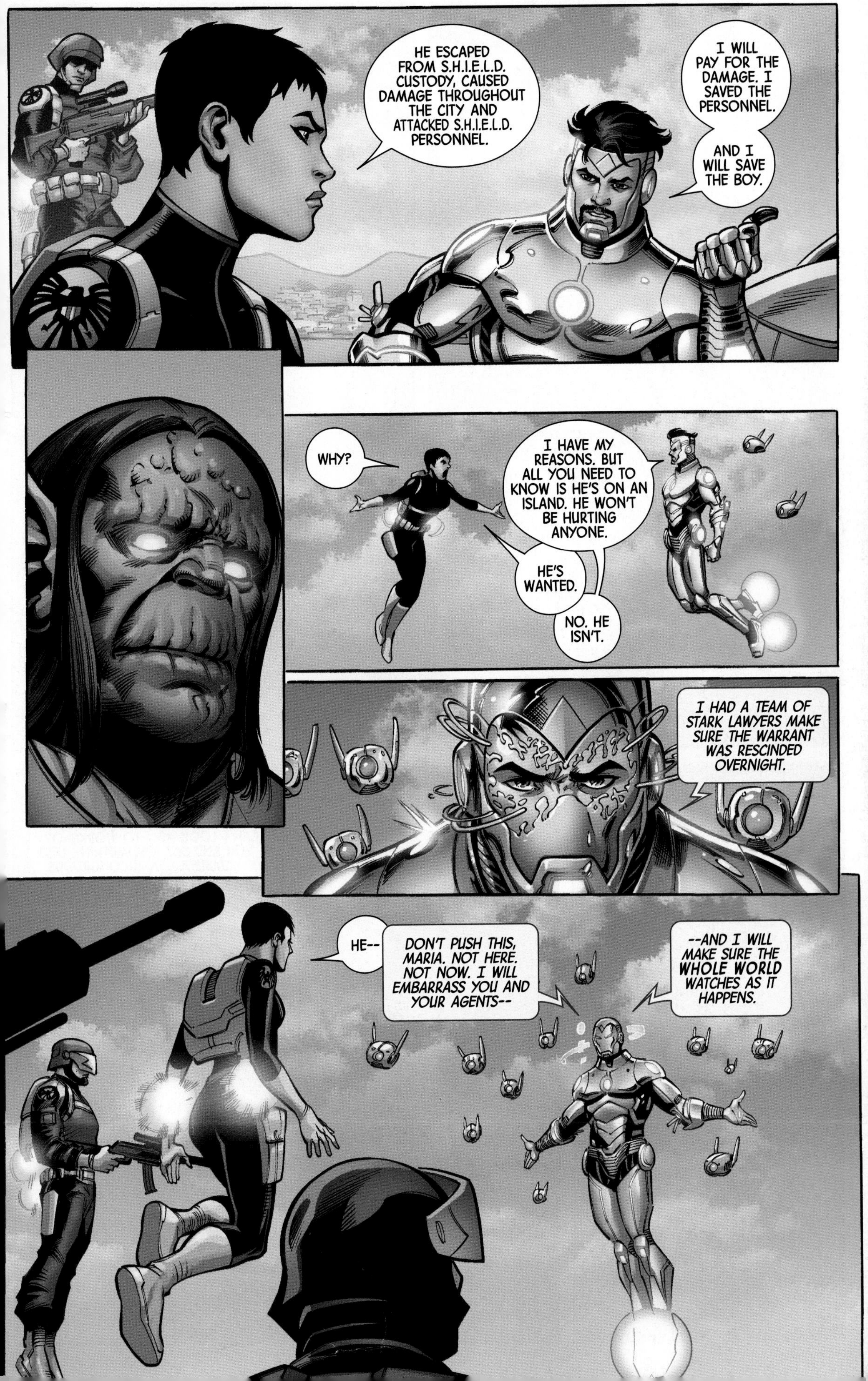
HE ESCAPED FROM S.H.I.E.L.D. CUSTODY, CAUSED DAMAGE THROUGHOUT THE CITY AND ATTACKED S.H.I.E.L.D. PERSONNEL.
I WILL PAY FOR THE DAMAGE. I SAVED THE PERSONNEL.
AND I WILL SAVE THE BOY.
WHY?
I HAVE MY REASONS. BUT ALL YOU NEED TO KNOW IS HE'S ON AN ISLAND. HE WON'T BE HURTING ANYONE.
HE'S WANTED.
NO. HE ISN'T.
I HAD A TEAM OF STARK LAWYERS MAKE SURE THE WARRANT WAS RESCINDED OVERNIGHT.
HE--
DON'T PUSH THIS, MARIA. NOT HERE. NOT NOW. I WILL EMBARRASS YOU AND YOUR AGENTS--
--AND I WILL MAKE SURE THE WHOLE WORLD WATCHES AS IT HAPPENS.

STARK TOWER.

WELL... THAT WAS TENSE.

THEY SHOULD LEAVE YOU ALONE NOW.

NOW, IF YOU'RE STAYING HERE, THERE ARE SOME HOUSE RULES.

RULE ONE. NO TOUCHING.

WHAT?

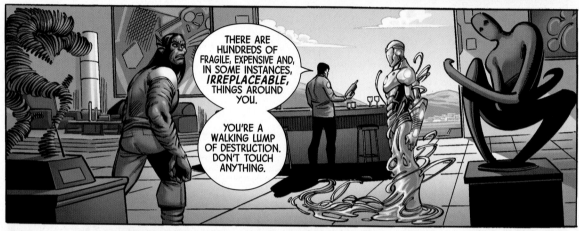

THERE ARE HUNDREDS OF FRAGILE, EXPENSIVE AND, IN SOME INSTANCES, *IRREPLACEABLE*, THINGS AROUND YOU.

YOU'RE A WALKING LUMP OF DESTRUCTION. DON'T TOUCH ANYTHING.

RULE TWO. NO MORE RAGE-FIGHTS. THAT ONE'S PRETTY SELF-EXPLANATORY.

RULE THREE. THERE WILL BE NO *"TEEN ABOMINATION"* IN THIS TOWER.

WHAT'S YOUR REAL NAME?

JAMIE.

YES.

REALLY?

NO. I CAN'T LOOK AT YOU AND SAY *"JAMIE."*

WE'LL HAVE TO WORKSHOP SOMETHING LESS INCONGRUOUS.

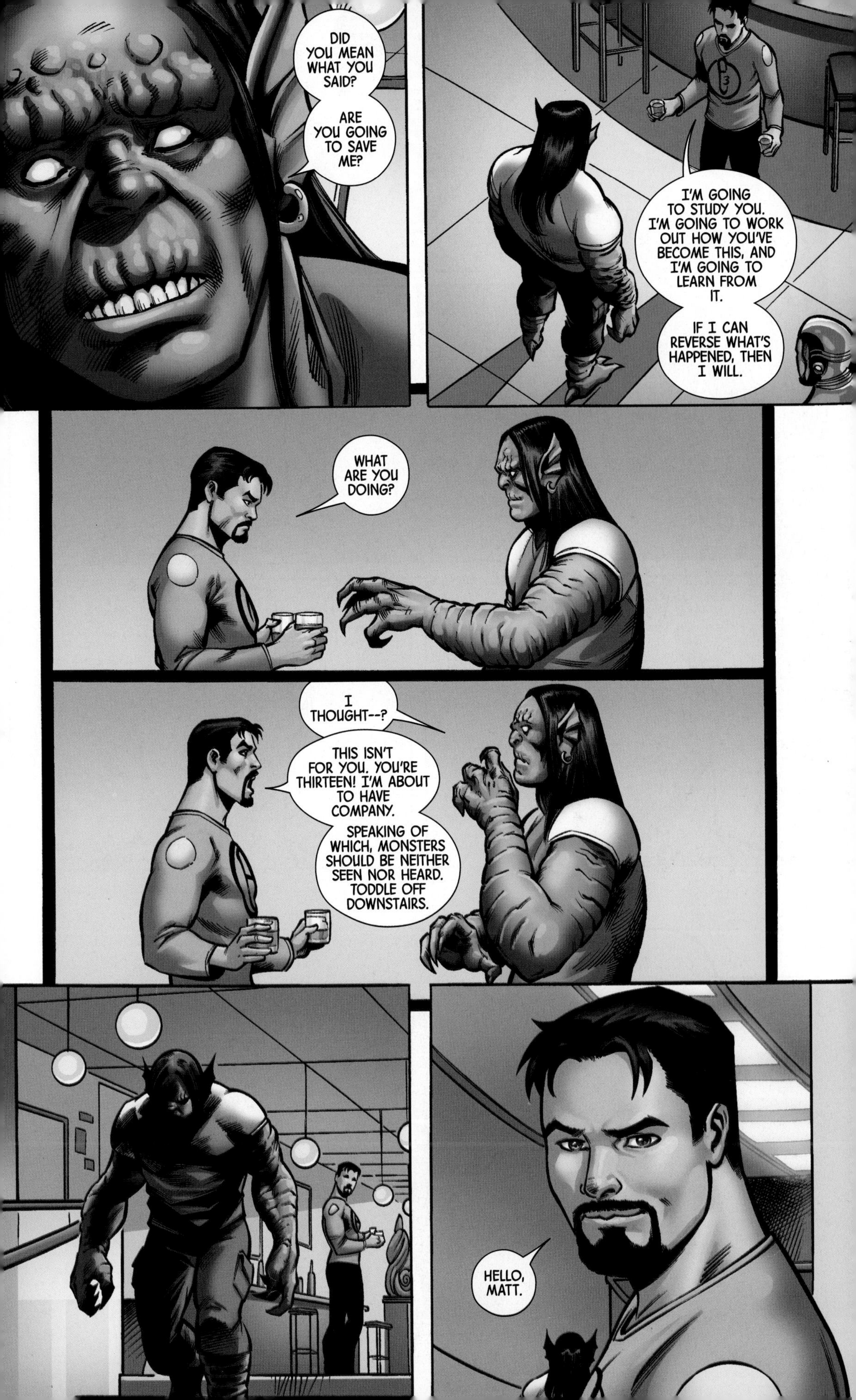
DID YOU MEAN WHAT YOU SAID?
ARE YOU GOING TO SAVE ME?
I'M GOING TO STUDY YOU. I'M GOING TO WORK OUT HOW YOU'VE BECOME THIS, AND I'M GOING TO LEARN FROM IT.
IF I CAN REVERSE WHAT'S HAPPENED, THEN I WILL.
WHAT ARE YOU DOING?
I THOUGHT--?
THIS ISN'T FOR YOU. YOU'RE THIRTEEN! I'M ABOUT TO HAVE COMPANY.
SPEAKING OF WHICH, MONSTERS SHOULD BE NEITHER SEEN NOR HEARD. TODDLE OFF DOWNSTAIRS.
HELLO, MATT.

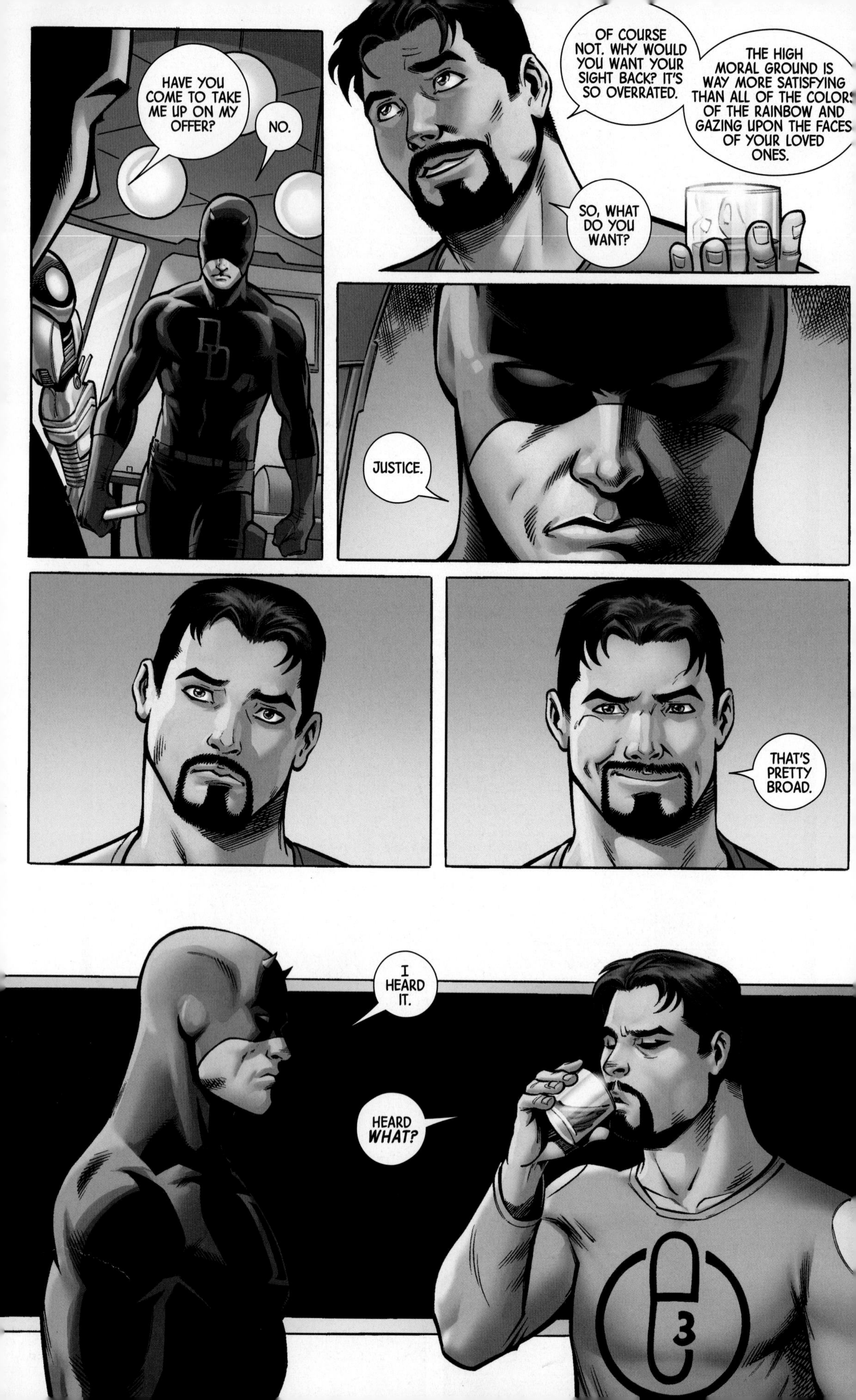
HAVE YOU COME TO TAKE ME UP ON MY OFFER?
NO.
OF COURSE NOT. WHY WOULD YOU WANT YOUR SIGHT BACK? IT'S SO OVERRATED.
THE HIGH MORAL GROUND IS WAY MORE SATISFYING THAN ALL OF THE COLORS OF THE RAINBOW AND GAZING UPON THE FACES OF YOUR LOVED ONES.
SO, WHAT DO YOU WANT?
JUSTICE.
THAT'S PRETTY BROAD.
I HEARD IT.
HEARD *WHAT?*

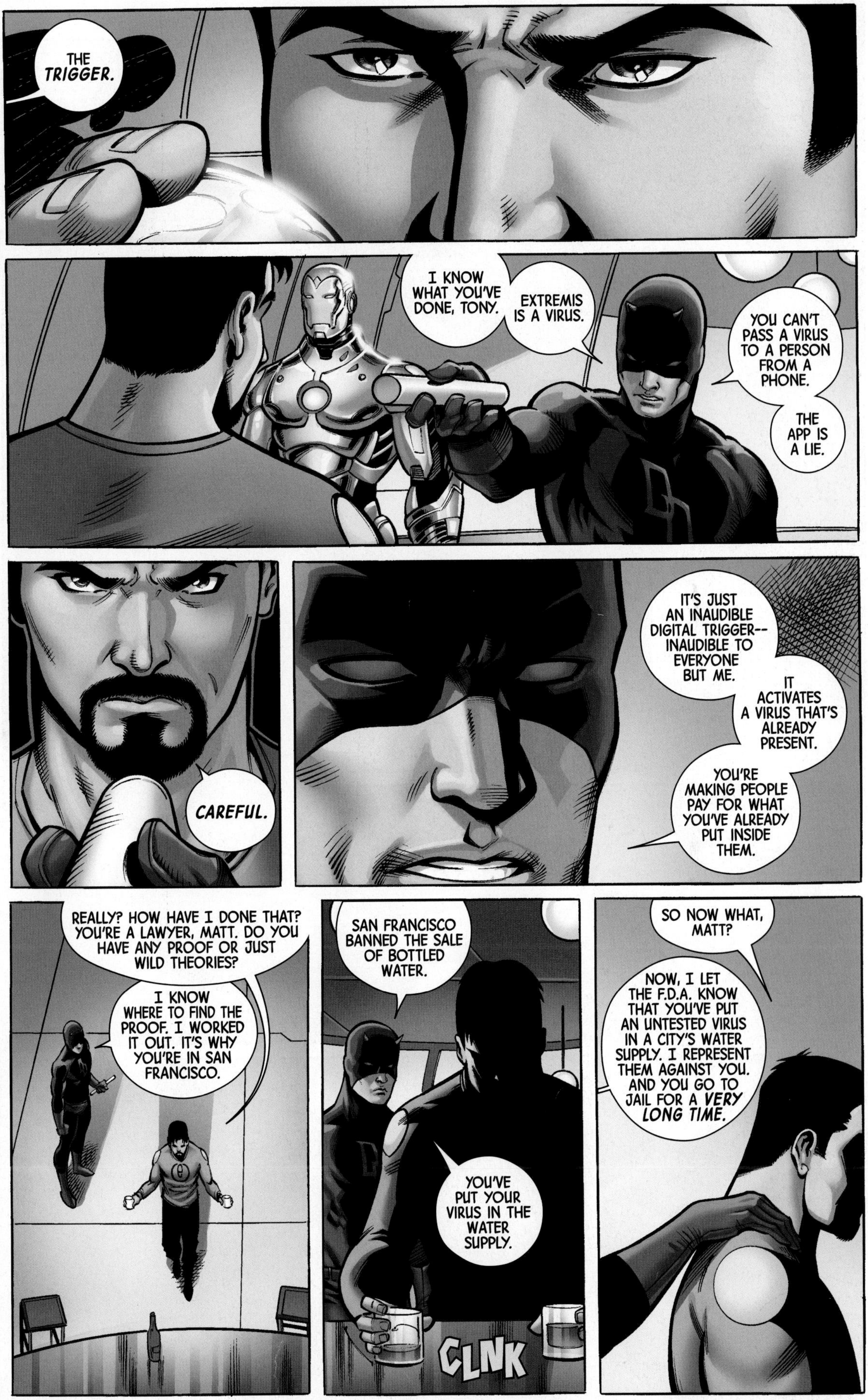
THE TRIGGER.
I KNOW WHAT YOU'VE DONE, TONY.
EXTREMIS IS A VIRUS.
YOU CAN'T PASS A VIRUS TO A PERSON FROM A PHONE.
THE APP IS A LIE.
CAREFUL.
IT'S JUST AN INAUDIBLE DIGITAL TRIGGER-- INAUDIBLE TO EVERYONE BUT ME.
IT ACTIVATES A VIRUS THAT'S ALREADY PRESENT.
YOU'RE MAKING PEOPLE PAY FOR WHAT YOU'VE ALREADY PUT INSIDE THEM.
REALLY? HOW HAVE I DONE THAT? YOU'RE A LAWYER, MATT. DO YOU HAVE ANY PROOF OR JUST WILD THEORIES?
I KNOW WHERE TO FIND THE PROOF. I WORKED IT OUT. IT'S WHY YOU'RE IN SAN FRANCISCO.
SAN FRANCISCO BANNED THE SALE OF BOTTLED WATER.
YOU'VE PUT YOUR VIRUS IN THE WATER SUPPLY.
CLNK
SO NOW WHAT, MATT?
NOW, I LET THE F.D.A. KNOW THAT YOU'VE PUT AN UNTESTED VIRUS IN A CITY'S WATER SUPPLY. I REPRESENT THEM AGAINST YOU. AND YOU GO TO JAIL FOR A VERY LONG TIME.

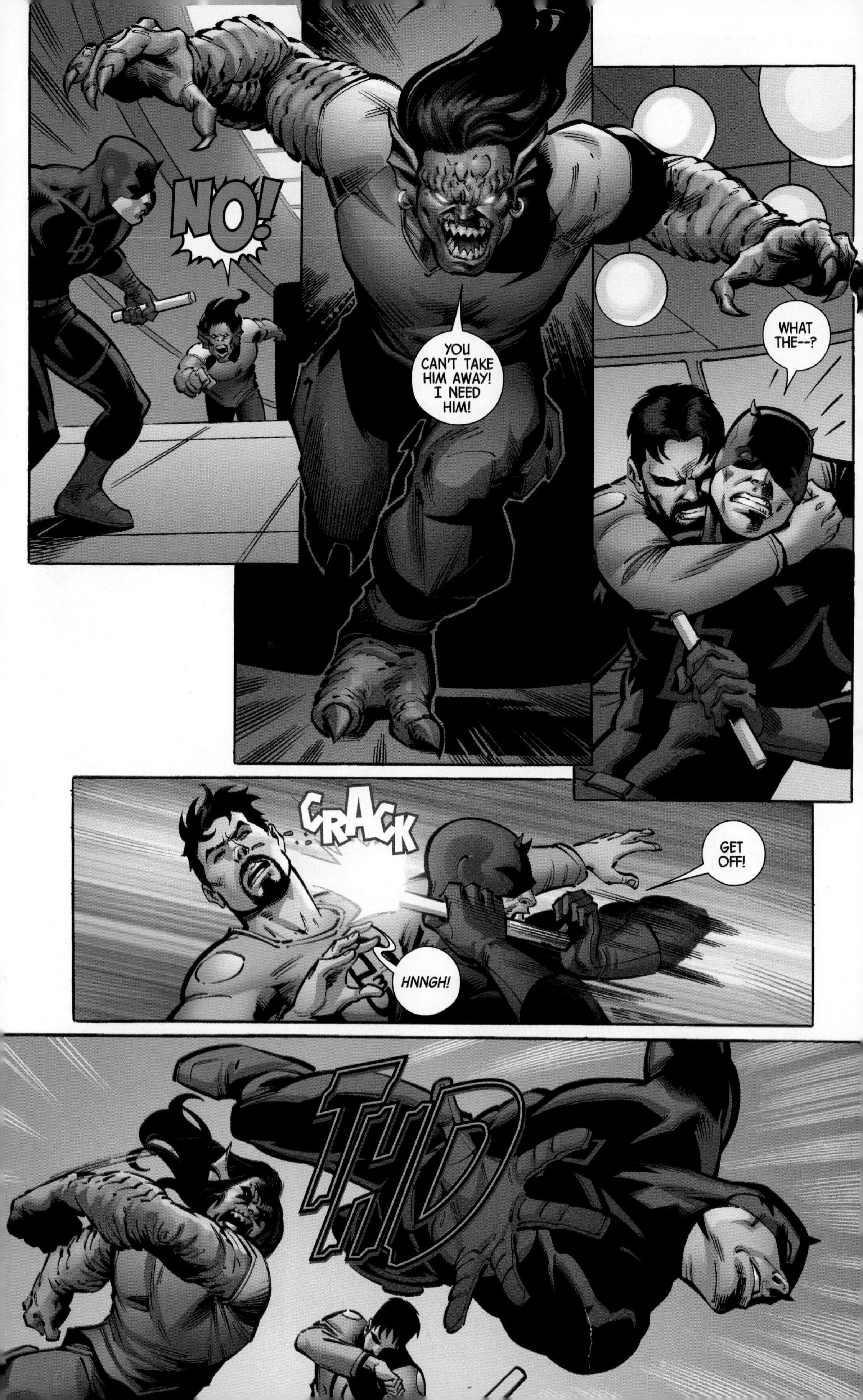
NO!
YOU CAN'T TAKE HIM AWAY! I NEED HIM!
WHAT THE--?
CRACK
GET OFF!
HNNGH!
THD

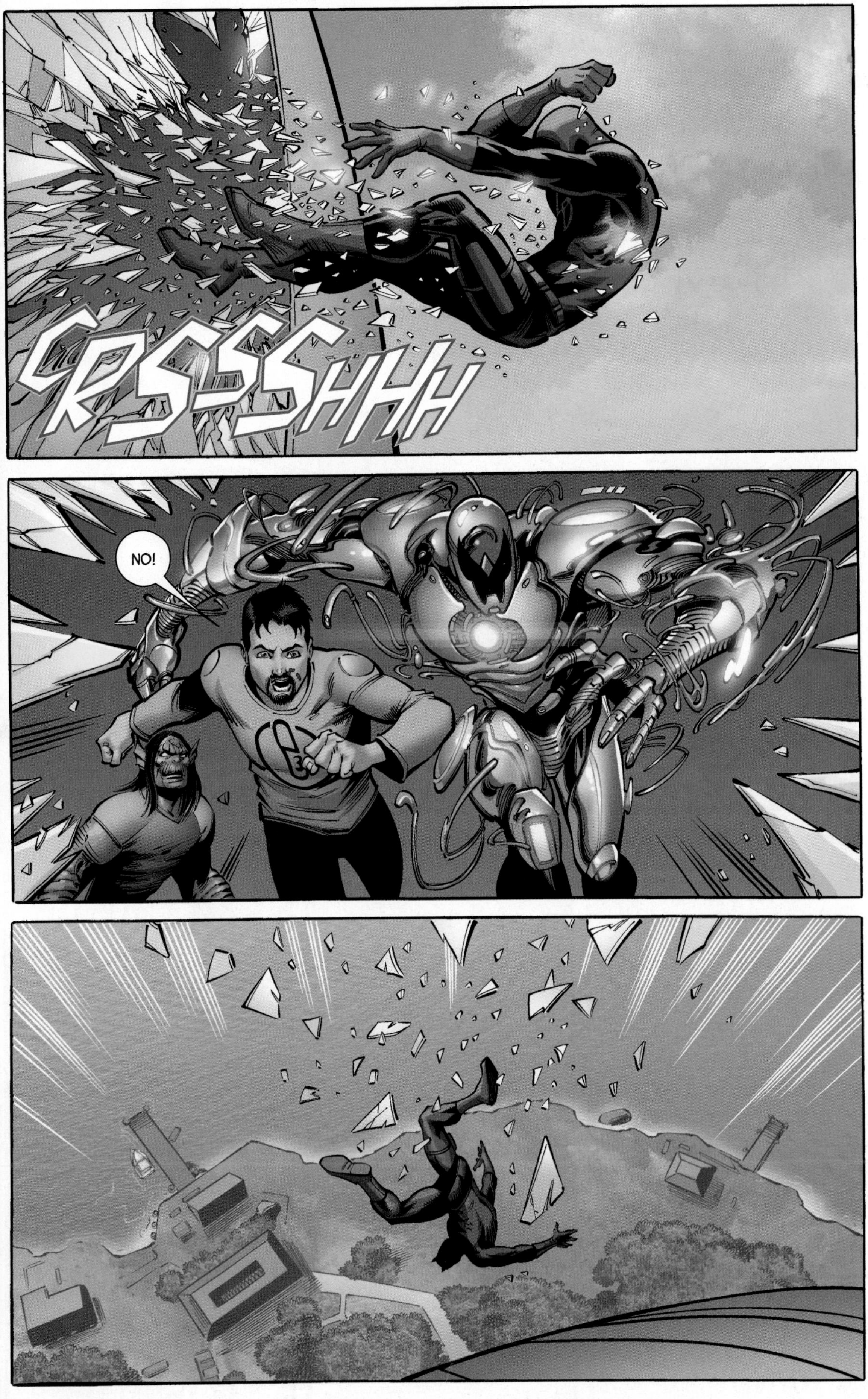
CRSSSHHH
NO!

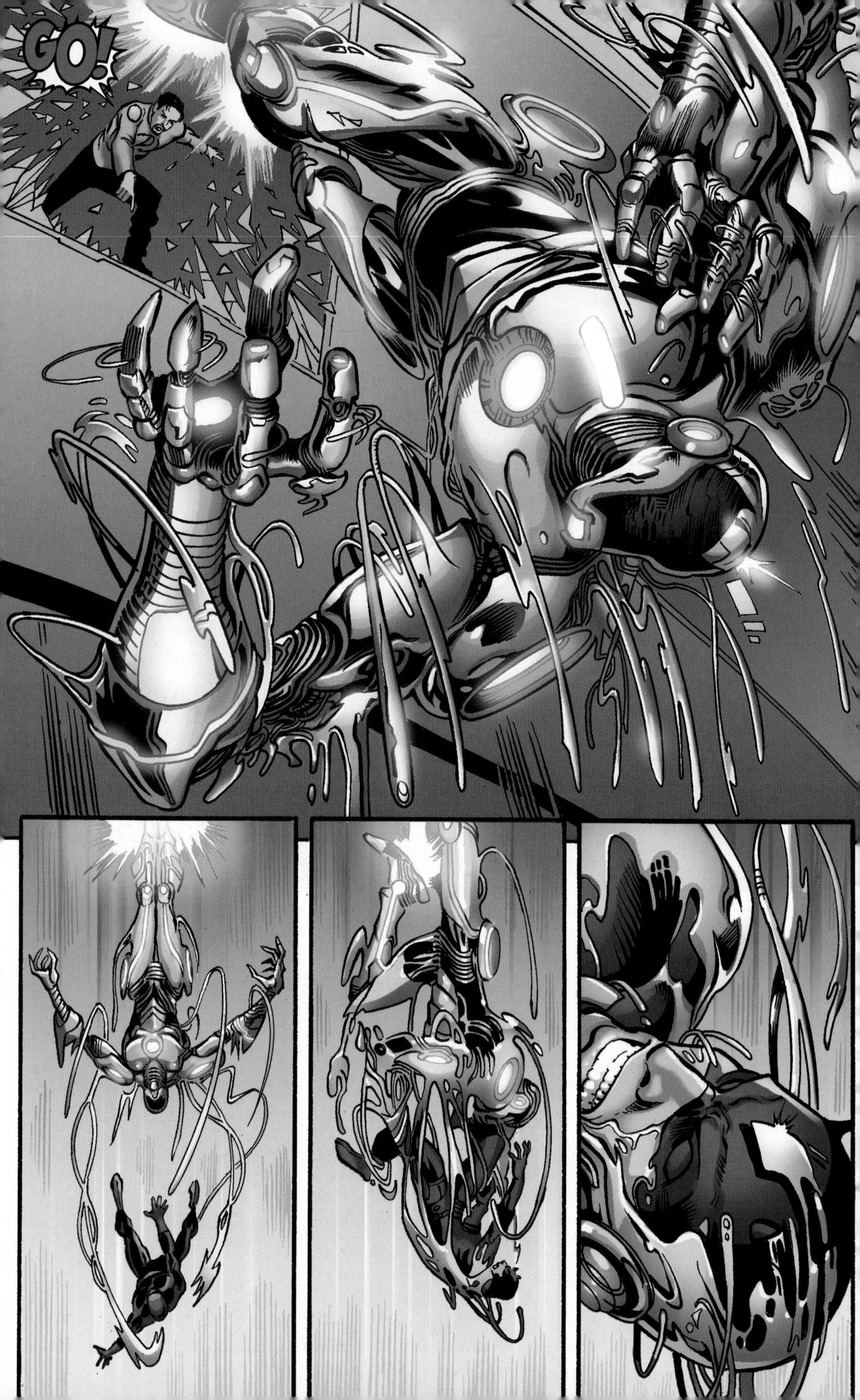
GO!

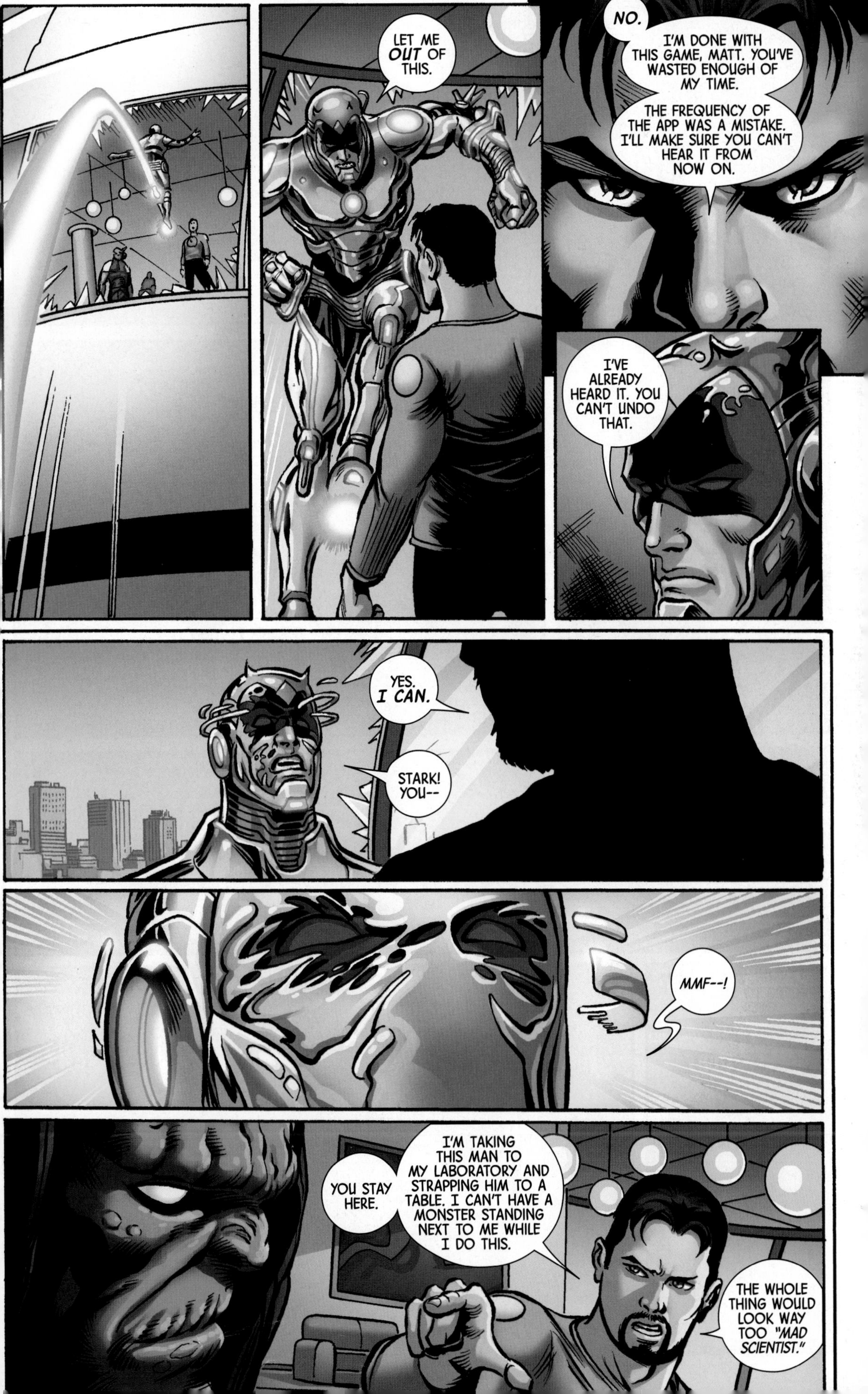
LET ME OUT OF THIS.
NO.
I'M DONE WITH THIS GAME, MATT. YOU'VE WASTED ENOUGH OF MY TIME.
THE FREQUENCY OF THE APP WAS A MISTAKE. I'LL MAKE SURE YOU CAN'T HEAR IT FROM NOW ON.
I'VE ALREADY HEARD IT. YOU CAN'T UNDO THAT.
YES. I CAN.
STARK! YOU--
MMF--!
YOU STAY HERE.
I'M TAKING THIS MAN TO MY LABORATORY AND STRAPPING HIM TO A TABLE. I CAN'T HAVE A MONSTER STANDING NEXT TO ME WHILE I DO THIS.
THE WHOLE THING WOULD LOOK WAY TOO "MAD SCIENTIST."

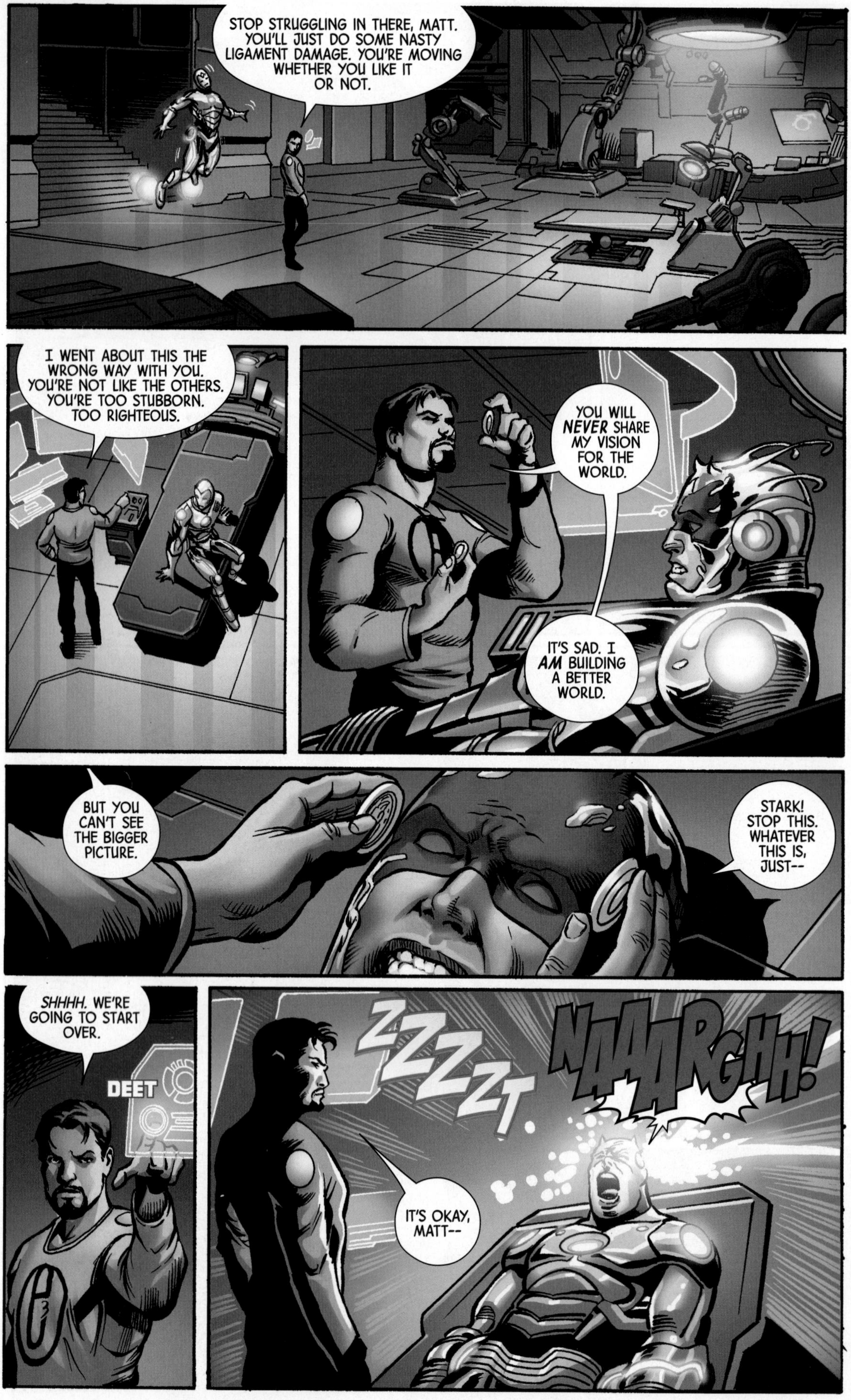
STOP STRUGGLING IN THERE, MATT. YOU'LL JUST DO SOME NASTY LIGAMENT DAMAGE. YOU'RE MOVING WHETHER YOU LIKE IT OR NOT.
I WENT ABOUT THIS THE WRONG WAY WITH YOU. YOU'RE NOT LIKE THE OTHERS. YOU'RE TOO STUBBORN. TOO RIGHTEOUS.
YOU WILL NEVER SHARE MY VISION FOR THE WORLD.
IT'S SAD. I AM BUILDING A BETTER WORLD.
BUT YOU CAN'T SEE THE BIGGER PICTURE.
STARK! STOP THIS. WHATEVER THIS IS, JUST--
SHHHH. WE'RE GOING TO START OVER.
DEET
ZZZZT
NAAARGHH!
IT'S OKAY, MATT--

"--THIS NEVER HAPPENED."

HE'S COMING AROUND, MISTER STARK.

MATT? MATT, CAN YOU HEAR ME?

TONY...? IS THAT YOU?

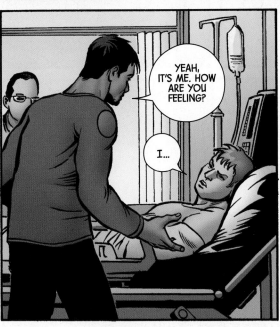

YEAH, IT'S ME. HOW ARE YOU FEELING?

I...

WHAT HAPPENED?

YOU DON'T REMEMBER?

I... I DON'T REMEMBER ANYTHING.

YOU GAVE US A BIT OF A SCARE. WE WERE FIGHTING A MONSTER. YOU TOOK A NASTY HIT.

WHAT MONSTER? DID IT...?

HE LIVES AT MY PLACE NOW. IT'S A LONG STORY. WE'LL TALK ABOUT IT LATER.

HOW LONG HAVE I BEEN OUT?

A FEW DAYS. KIRSTEN'S BARELY LEFT YOUR--

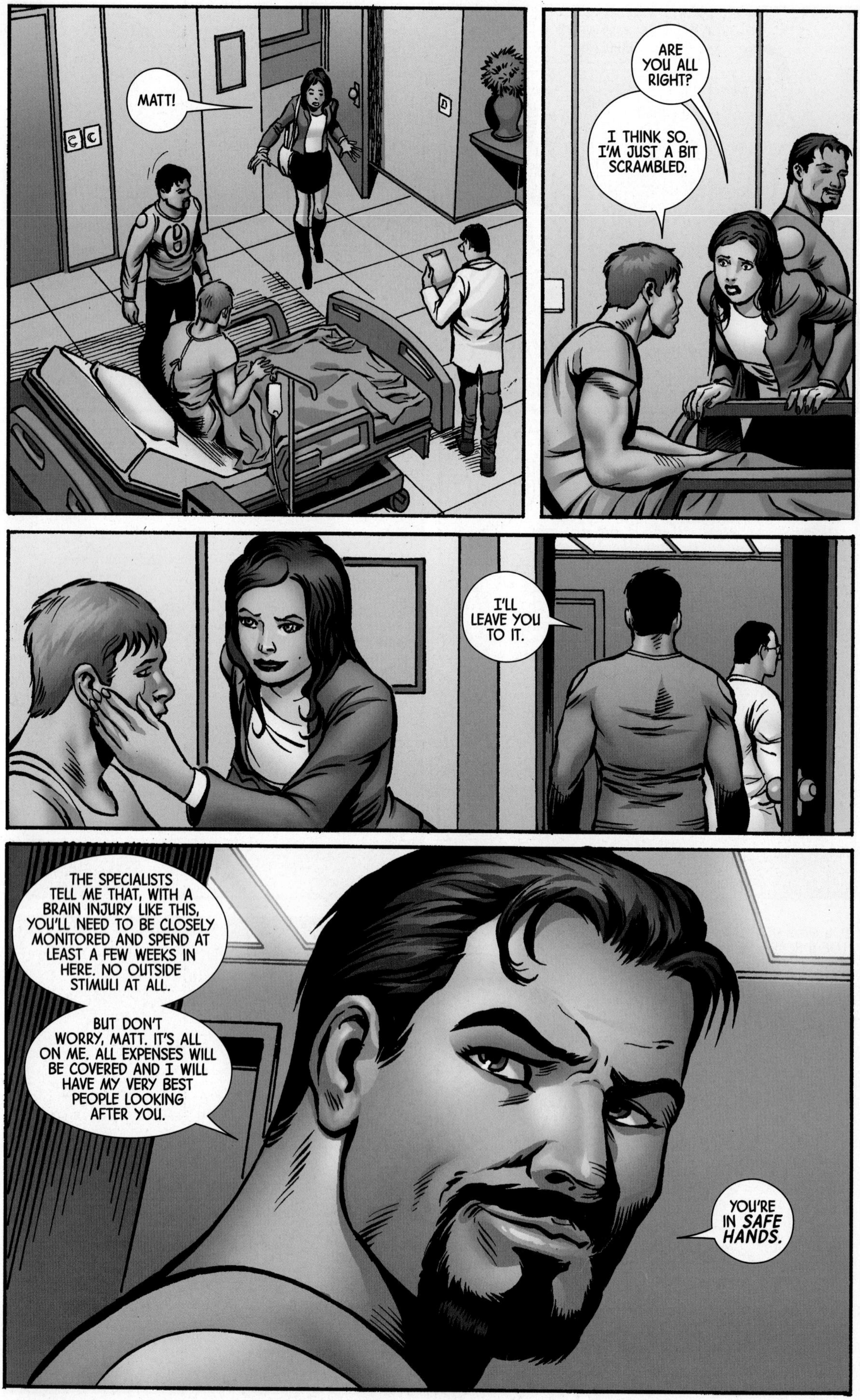

MATT!
ARE YOU ALL RIGHT?
I THINK SO. I'M JUST A BIT SCRAMBLED.
I'LL LEAVE YOU TO IT.
THE SPECIALISTS TELL ME THAT, WITH A BRAIN INJURY LIKE THIS, YOU'LL NEED TO BE CLOSELY MONITORED AND SPEND AT LEAST A FEW WEEKS IN HERE. NO OUTSIDE STIMULI AT ALL.
BUT DON'T WORRY, MATT. IT'S ALL ON ME. ALL EXPENSES WILL BE COVERED AND I WILL HAVE MY VERY BEST PEOPLE LOOKING AFTER YOU.
YOU'RE IN *SAFE HANDS.*

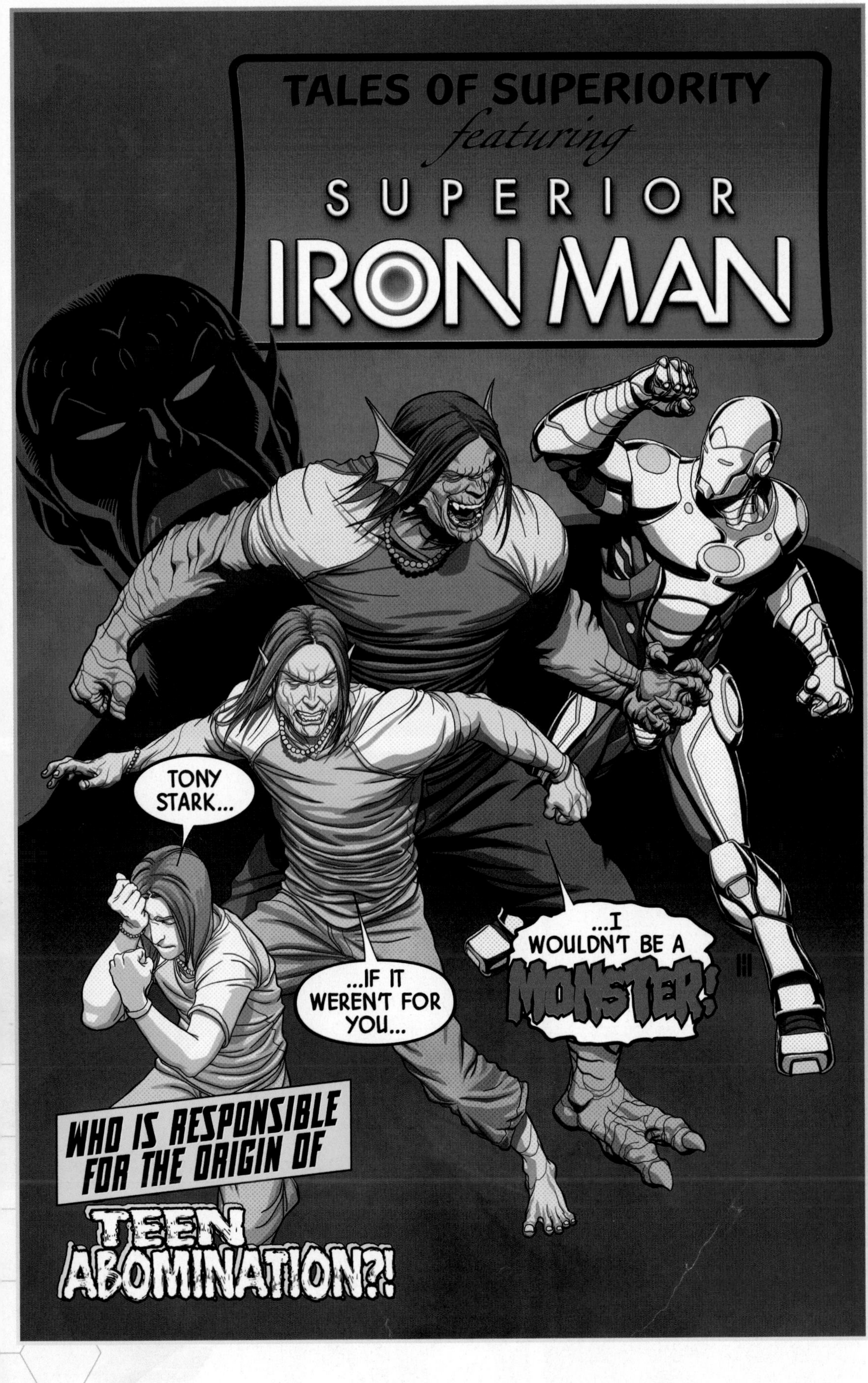
TALES OF SUPERIORITY
featuring
SUPERIOR
IRON MAN
TONY STARK...
...IF IT WEREN'T FOR YOU...
...I WOULDN'T BE A MONSTER!
WHO IS RESPONSIBLE FOR THE ORIGIN OF
TEEN ABOMINATION?!

5: THE ORIGIN OF TEEN ABOMINATION

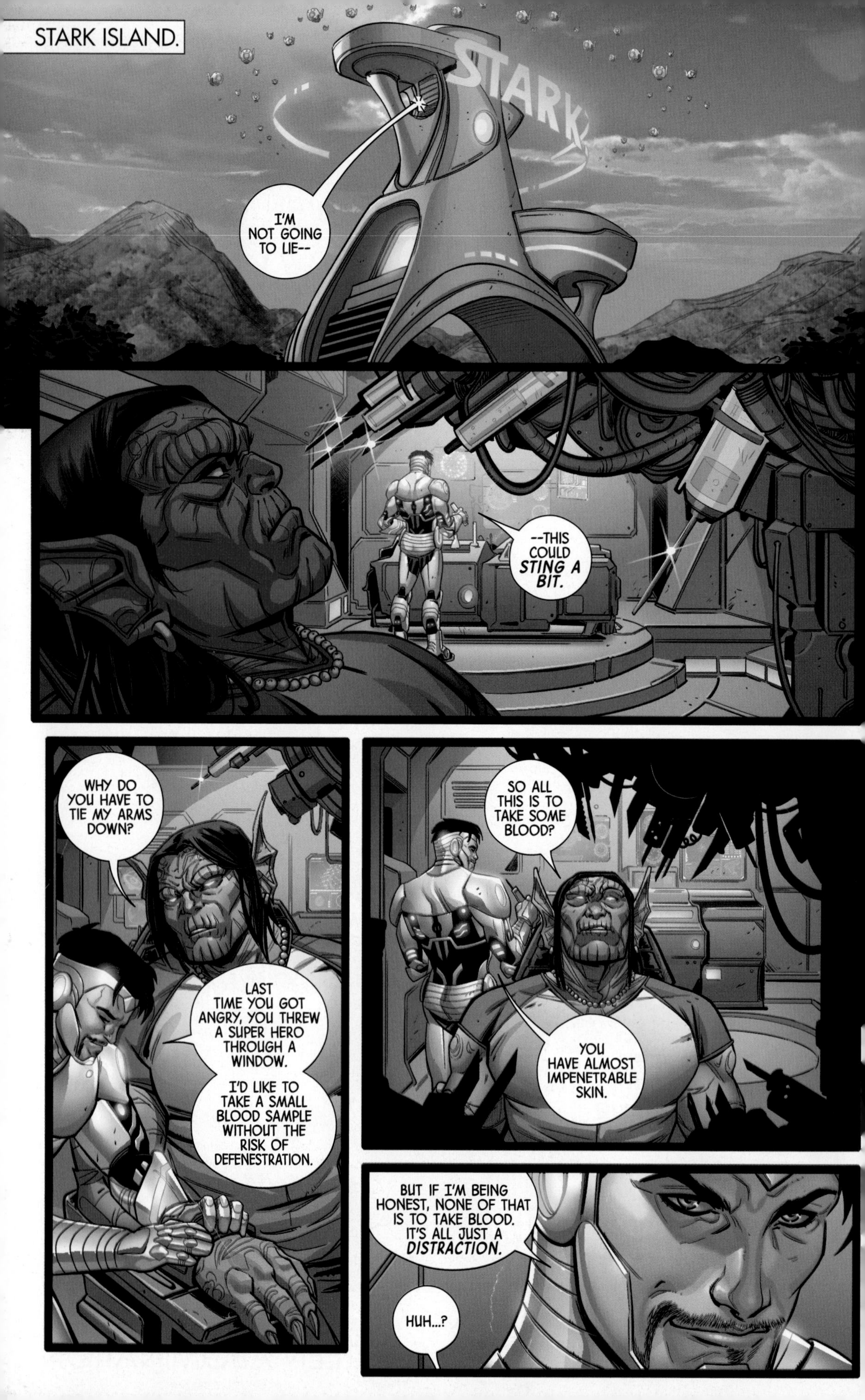
STARK ISLAND.
STARK
I'M NOT GOING TO LIE--
--THIS COULD *STING A BIT.*
WHY DO YOU HAVE TO TIE MY ARMS DOWN?
LAST TIME YOU GOT ANGRY, YOU THREW A SUPER HERO THROUGH A WINDOW.
I'D LIKE TO TAKE A SMALL BLOOD SAMPLE WITHOUT THE RISK OF DEFENESTRATION.
SO ALL THIS IS TO TAKE SOME BLOOD?
YOU HAVE ALMOST IMPENETRABLE SKIN.
BUT IF I'M BEING HONEST, NONE OF THAT IS TO TAKE BLOOD. IT'S ALL JUST A *DISTRACTION.*
HUH...?

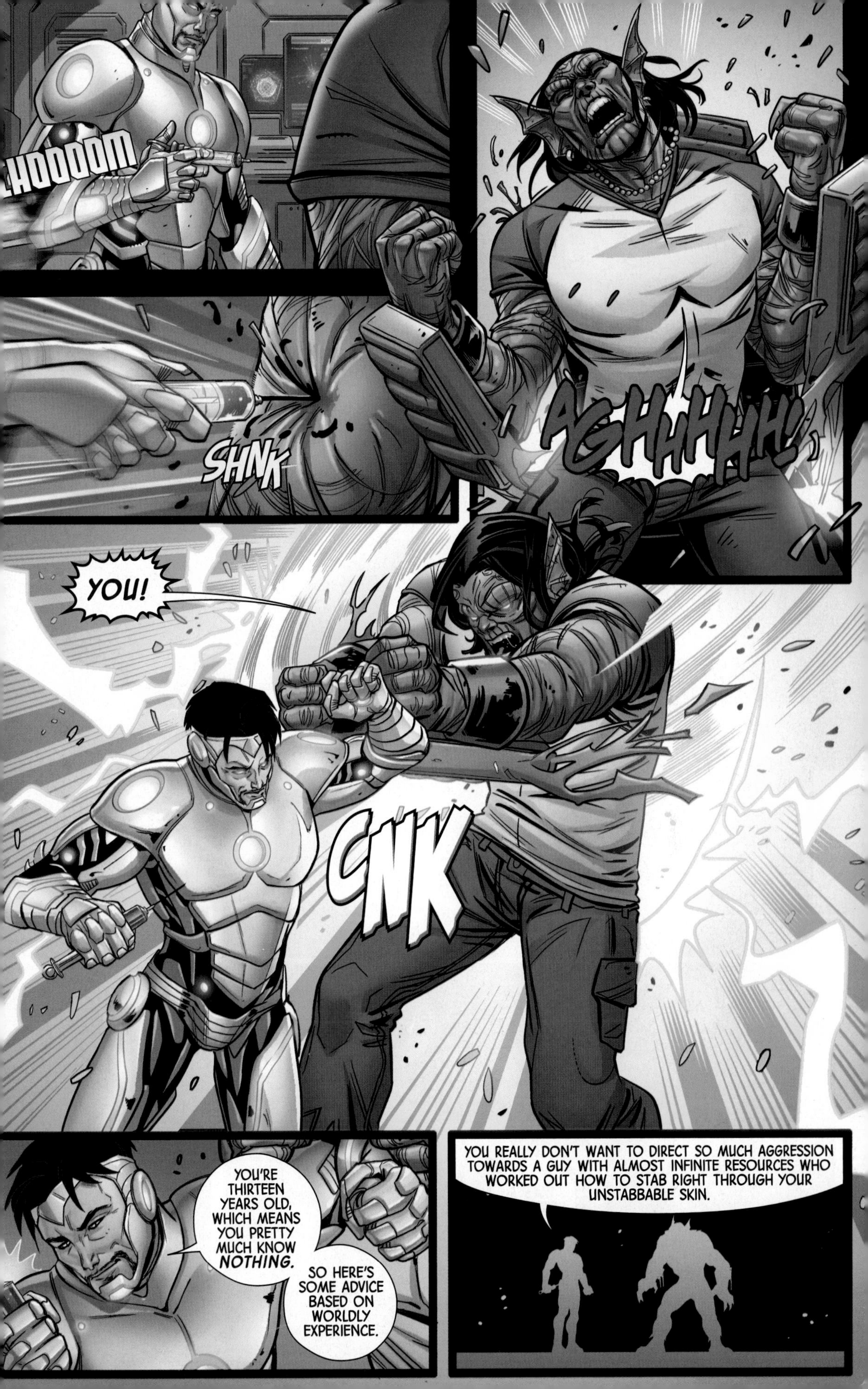

HOOOOM
SHNK
AGHHHHH!
YOU!
CNK
YOU'RE THIRTEEN YEARS OLD, WHICH MEANS YOU PRETTY MUCH KNOW NOTHING.
SO HERE'S SOME ADVICE BASED ON WORLDLY EXPERIENCE.
YOU REALLY DON'T WANT TO DIRECT SO MUCH AGGRESSION TOWARDS A GUY WITH ALMOST INFINITE RESOURCES WHO WORKED OUT HOW TO STAB RIGHT THROUGH YOUR UNSTABBABLE SKIN.

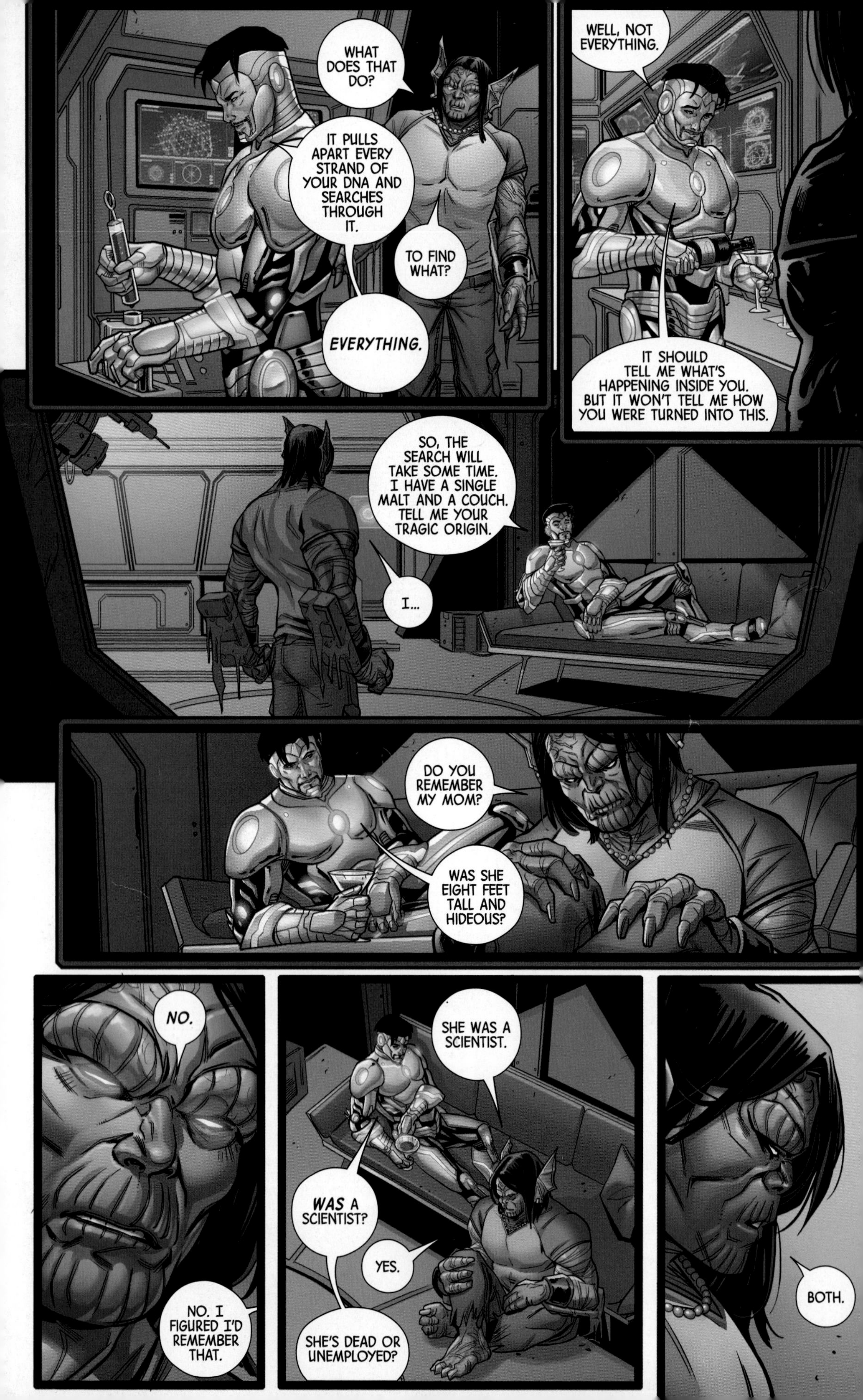
WHAT DOES THAT DO?
IT PULLS APART EVERY STRAND OF YOUR DNA AND SEARCHES THROUGH IT.
TO FIND WHAT?
EVERYTHING.
WELL, NOT EVERYTHING.
IT SHOULD TELL ME WHAT'S HAPPENING INSIDE YOU. BUT IT WON'T TELL ME HOW YOU WERE TURNED INTO THIS.
SO, THE SEARCH WILL TAKE SOME TIME. I HAVE A SINGLE MALT AND A COUCH. TELL ME YOUR TRAGIC ORIGIN.
I...
DO YOU REMEMBER MY MOM?
WAS SHE EIGHT FEET TALL AND HIDEOUS?
NO.
NO. I FIGURED I'D REMEMBER THAT.
SHE WAS A SCIENTIST.
WAS A SCIENTIST?
YES.
SHE'S DEAD OR UNEMPLOYED?
BOTH.

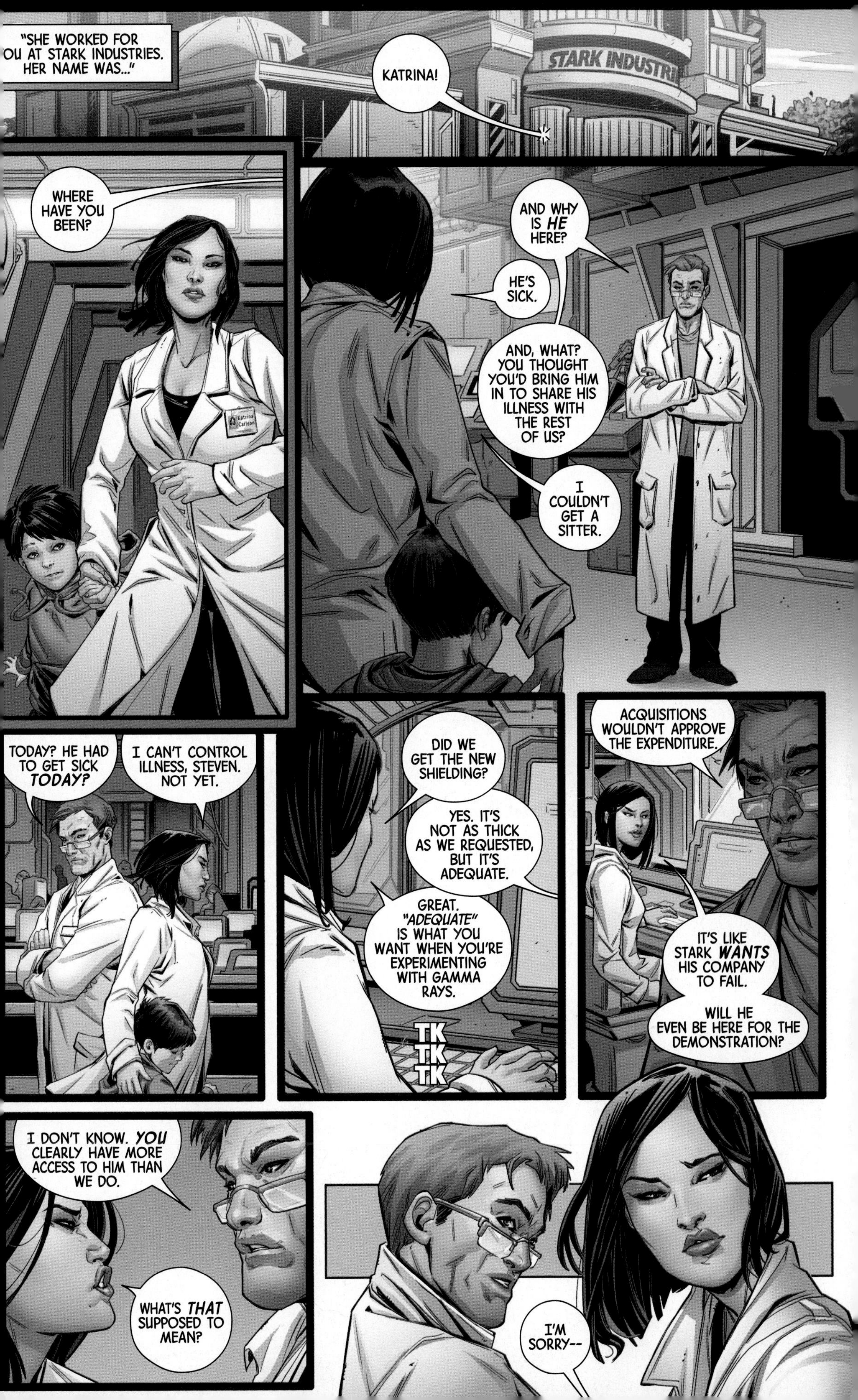

"SHE WORKED FOR
OU AT STARK INDUSTRIES.
HER NAME WAS..."
STARK INDUSTRI
KATRINA!
WHERE HAVE YOU BEEN?
Katrina Carlson
AND WHY IS HE HERE?
HE'S SICK.
AND, WHAT? YOU THOUGHT YOU'D BRING HIM IN TO SHARE HIS ILLNESS WITH THE REST OF US?
I COULDN'T GET A SITTER.
TODAY? HE HAD TO GET SICK TODAY?
I CAN'T CONTROL ILLNESS, STEVEN. NOT YET.
DID WE GET THE NEW SHIELDING?
YES. IT'S NOT AS THICK AS WE REQUESTED, BUT IT'S ADEQUATE.
GREAT. "ADEQUATE" IS WHAT YOU WANT WHEN YOU'RE EXPERIMENTING WITH GAMMA RAYS.
TK TK TK
ACQUISITIONS WOULDN'T APPROVE THE EXPENDITURE.
IT'S LIKE STARK WANTS HIS COMPANY TO FAIL.
WILL HE EVEN BE HERE FOR THE DEMONSTRATION?
I DON'T KNOW. YOU CLEARLY HAVE MORE ACCESS TO HIM THAN WE DO.
WHAT'S THAT SUPPOSED TO MEAN?
I'M SORRY--

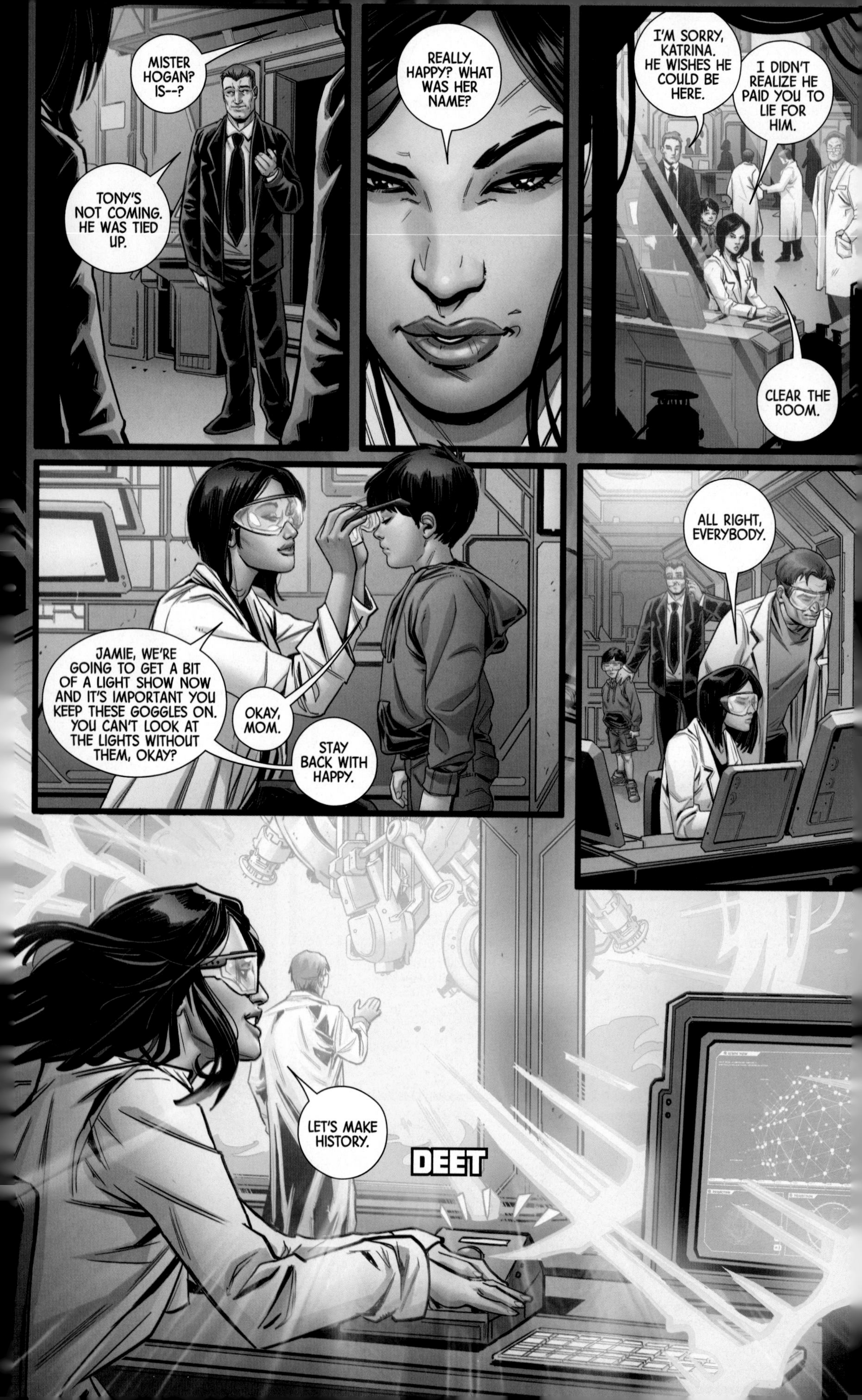

MISTER HOGAN? IS--?
TONY'S NOT COMING. HE WAS TIED UP.
REALLY, HAPPY? WHAT WAS HER NAME?
I'M SORRY, KATRINA. HE WISHES HE COULD BE HERE.
I DIDN'T REALIZE HE PAID YOU TO LIE FOR HIM.
CLEAR THE ROOM.
JAMIE, WE'RE GOING TO GET A BIT OF A LIGHT SHOW NOW AND IT'S IMPORTANT YOU KEEP THESE GOGGLES ON. YOU CAN'T LOOK AT THE LIGHTS WITHOUT THEM, OKAY?
OKAY, MOM.
STAY BACK WITH HAPPY.
ALL RIGHT, EVERYBODY.
LET'S MAKE HISTORY.
DEET

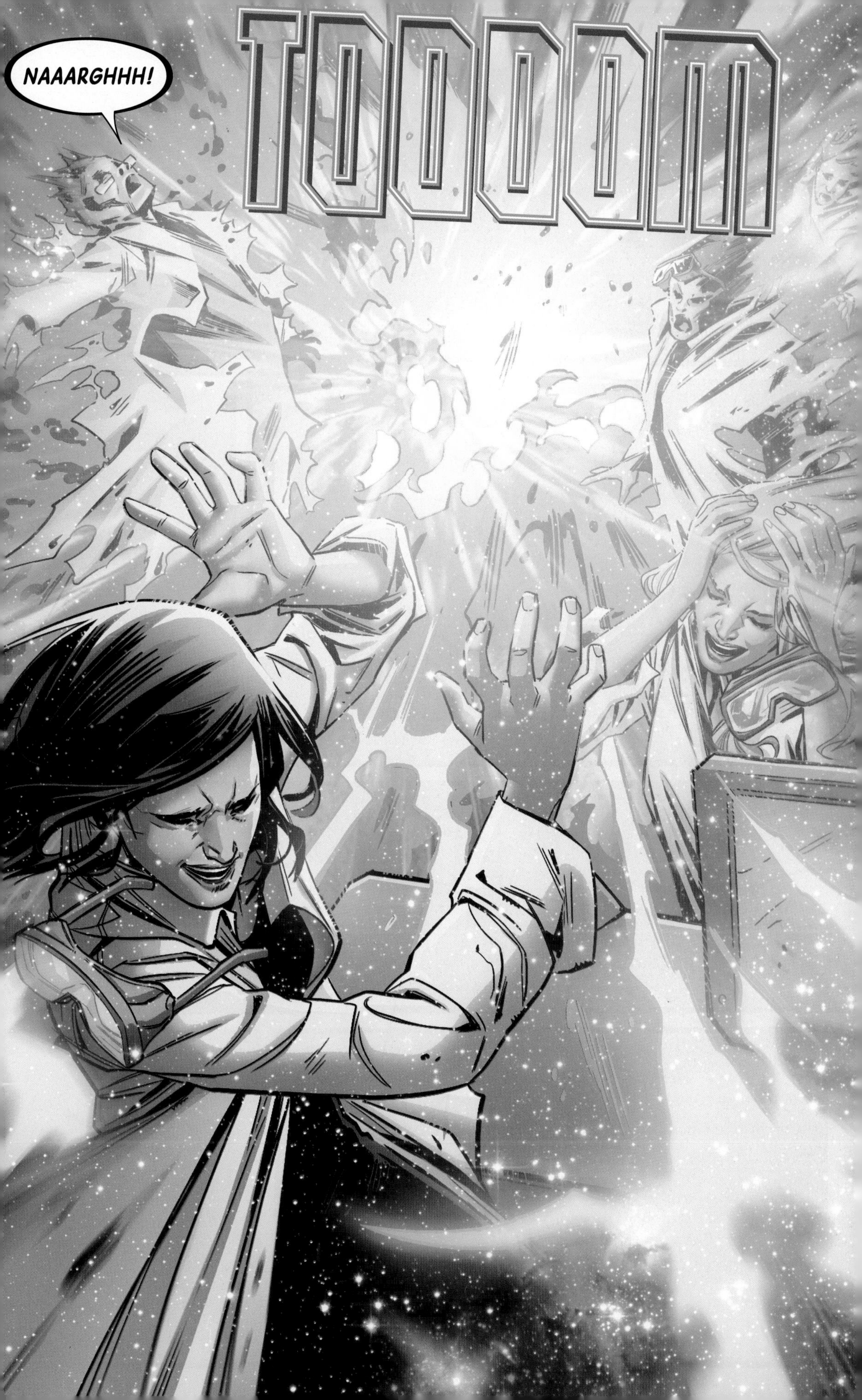
NAAARGHHH!
TOOOOM

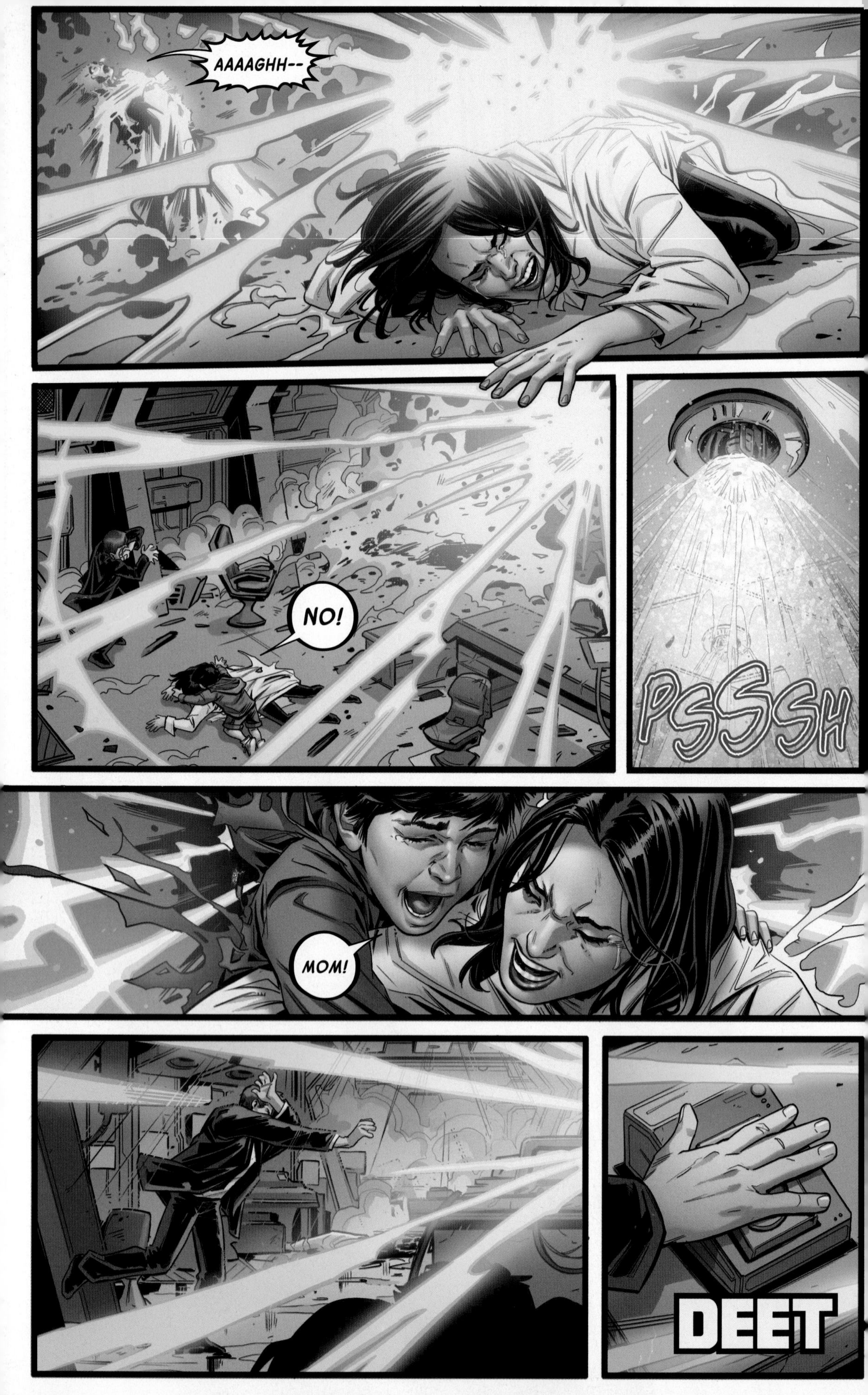
AAAAGHH--
NO!
PSSSH
MOM!
DEET

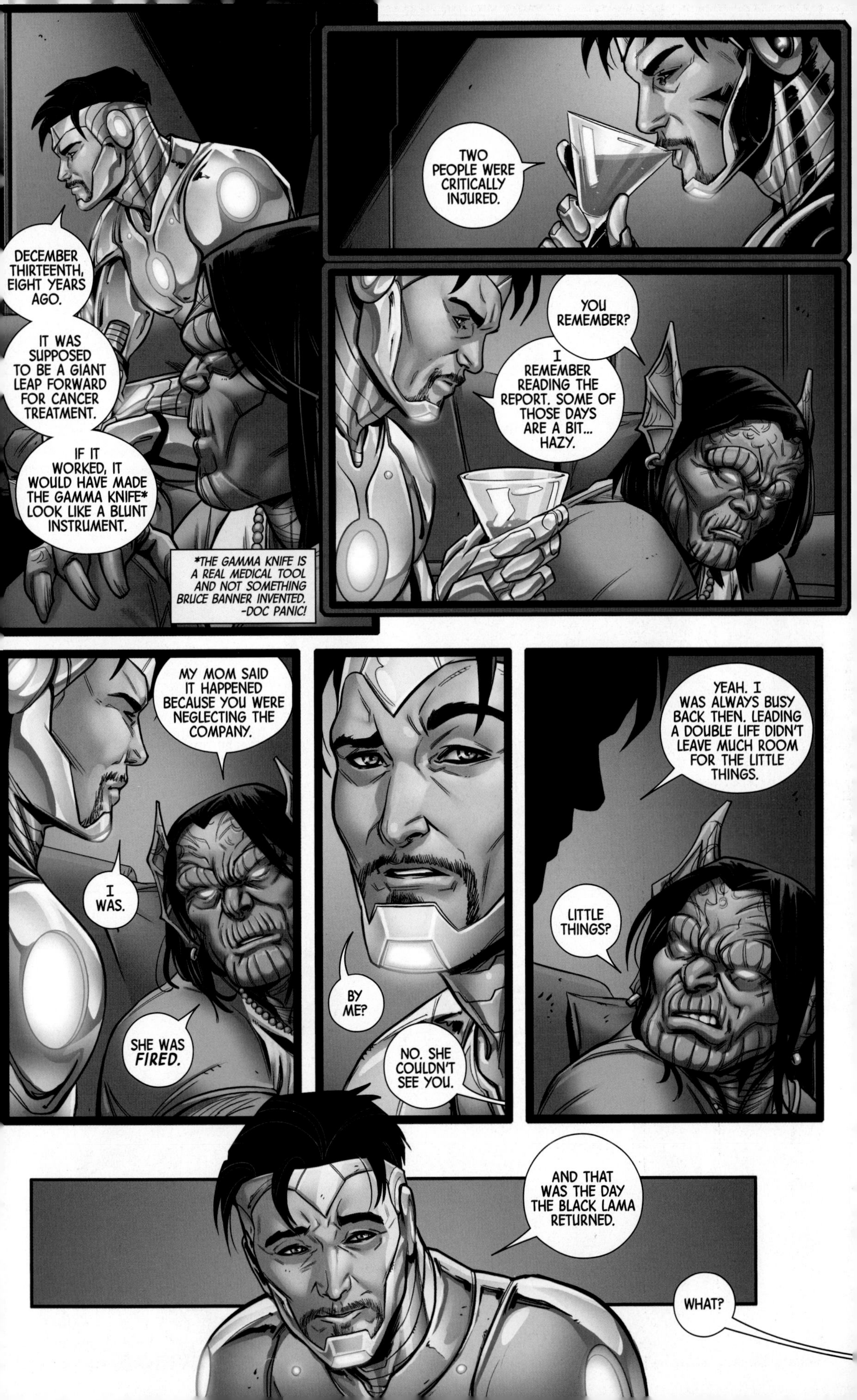
DECEMBER THIRTEENTH, EIGHT YEARS AGO.
IT WAS SUPPOSED TO BE A GIANT LEAP FORWARD FOR CANCER TREATMENT.
IF IT WORKED, IT WOULD HAVE MADE THE GAMMA KNIFE* LOOK LIKE A BLUNT INSTRUMENT.
*THE GAMMA KNIFE IS A REAL MEDICAL TOOL AND NOT SOMETHING BRUCE BANNER INVENTED. -DOC PANIC!
TWO PEOPLE WERE CRITICALLY INJURED.
YOU REMEMBER?
I REMEMBER READING THE REPORT. SOME OF THOSE DAYS ARE A BIT... HAZY.
MY MOM SAID IT HAPPENED BECAUSE YOU WERE NEGLECTING THE COMPANY.
I WAS.
SHE WAS *FIRED.*
BY ME?
NO. SHE COULDN'T SEE YOU.
YEAH. I WAS ALWAYS BUSY BACK THEN. LEADING A DOUBLE LIFE DIDN'T LEAVE MUCH ROOM FOR THE LITTLE THINGS.
LITTLE THINGS?
AND THAT WAS THE DAY THE BLACK LAMA RETURNED.
WHAT?

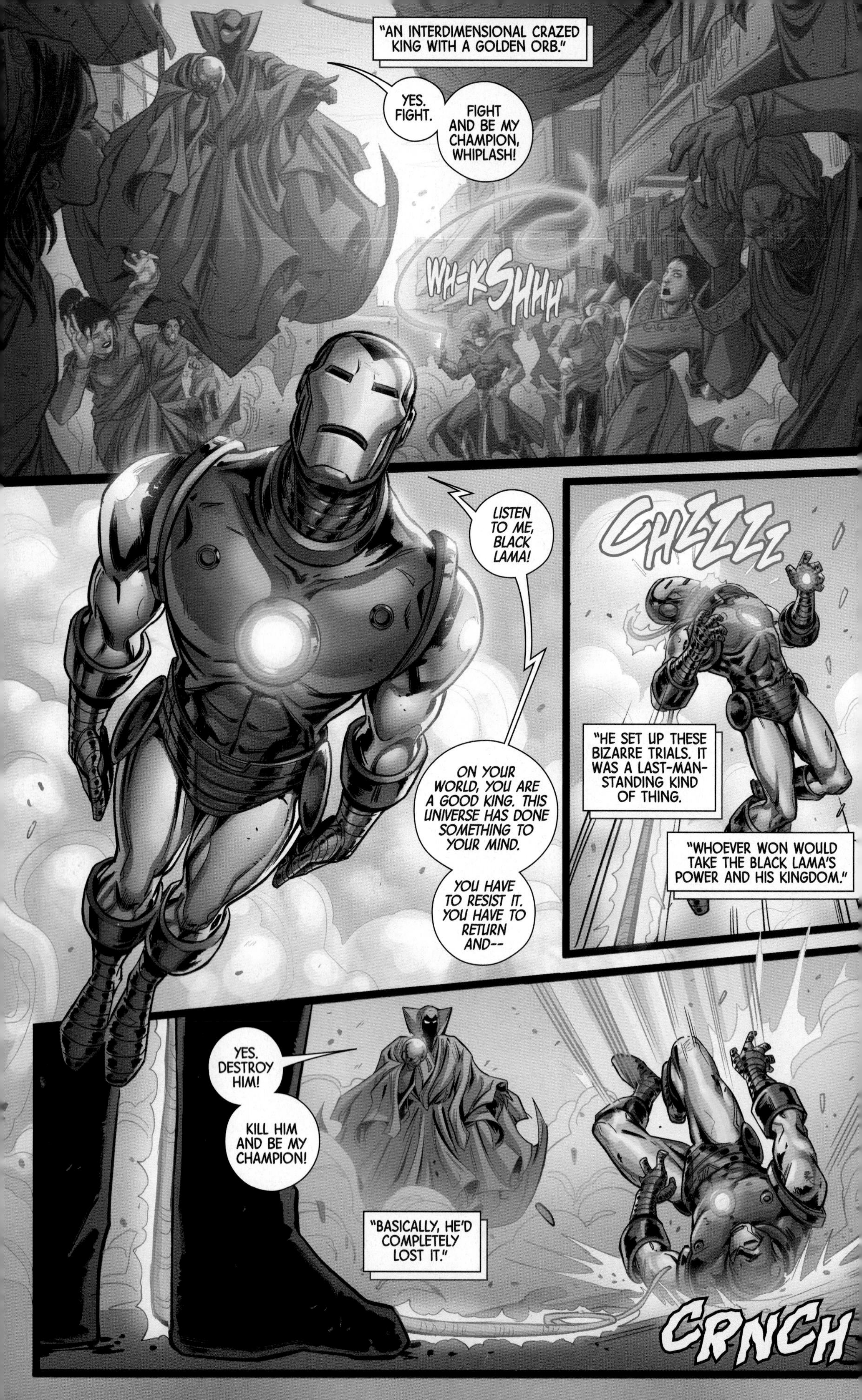
"AN INTERDIMENSIONAL CRAZED KING WITH A GOLDEN ORB."
YES. FIGHT.
FIGHT AND BE MY CHAMPION, WHIPLASH!
WH-KSHHH
LISTEN TO ME, BLACK LAMA!
ON YOUR WORLD, YOU ARE A GOOD KING. THIS UNIVERSE HAS DONE SOMETHING TO YOUR MIND.
YOU HAVE TO RESIST IT. YOU HAVE TO RETURN AND--
CHZZZZ
"HE SET UP THESE BIZARRE TRIALS. IT WAS A LAST-MAN-STANDING KIND OF THING.
"WHOEVER WON WOULD TAKE THE BLACK LAMA'S POWER AND HIS KINGDOM."
YES. DESTROY HIM!
KILL HIM AND BE MY CHAMPION!
"BASICALLY, HE'D COMPLETELY LOST IT."
CRNCH

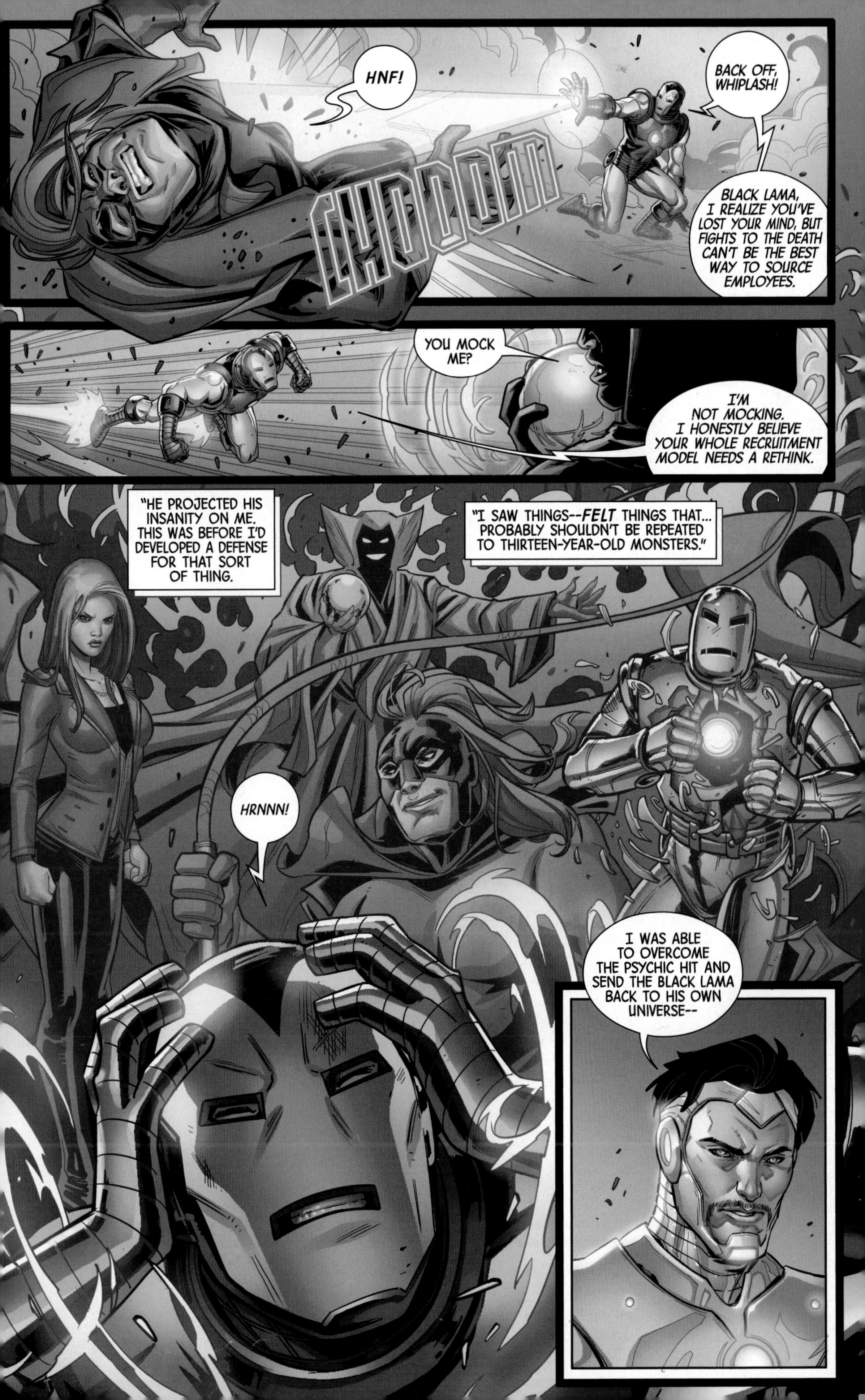
HNF!
BACK OFF, WHIPLASH!
CHOOOOM
BLACK LAMA, I REALIZE YOU'VE LOST YOUR MIND, BUT FIGHTS TO THE DEATH CAN'T BE THE BEST WAY TO SOURCE EMPLOYEES.
YOU MOCK ME?
I'M NOT MOCKING. I HONESTLY BELIEVE YOUR WHOLE RECRUITMENT MODEL NEEDS A RETHINK.
"HE PROJECTED HIS INSANITY ON ME. THIS WAS BEFORE I'D DEVELOPED A DEFENSE FOR THAT SORT OF THING.
"I SAW THINGS--FELT THINGS THAT... PROBABLY SHOULDN'T BE REPEATED TO THIRTEEN-YEAR-OLD MONSTERS."
HRNNN!
I WAS ABLE TO OVERCOME THE PSYCHIC HIT AND SEND THE BLACK LAMA BACK TO HIS OWN UNIVERSE--

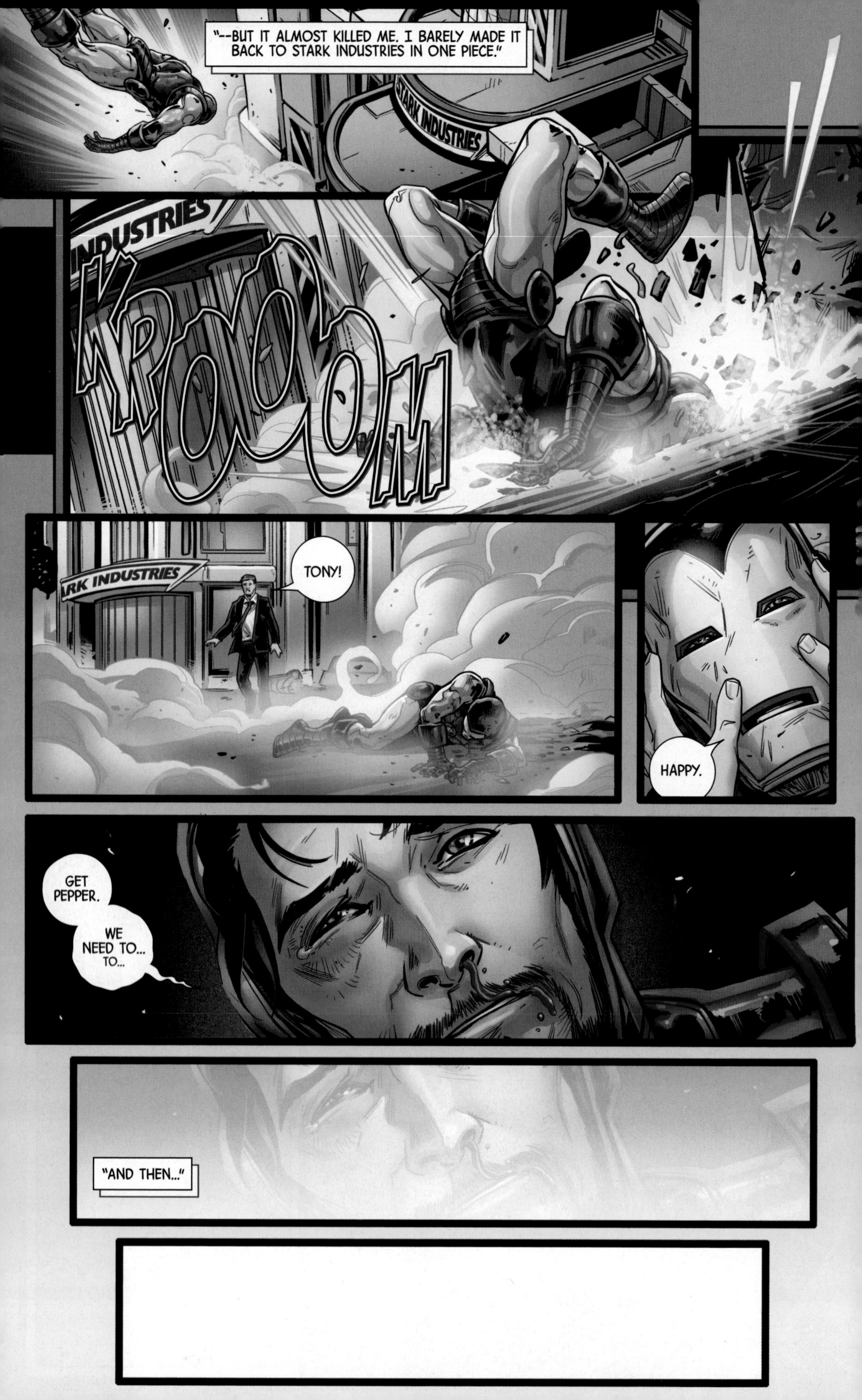
"--BUT IT ALMOST KILLED ME. I BARELY MADE IT BACK TO STARK INDUSTRIES IN ONE PIECE."
STARK INDUSTRIES
INDUSTRIES
KROOOOM
RK INDUSTRIES
TONY!
HAPPY.
GET PEPPER.
WE NEED TO... TO...
"AND THEN..."

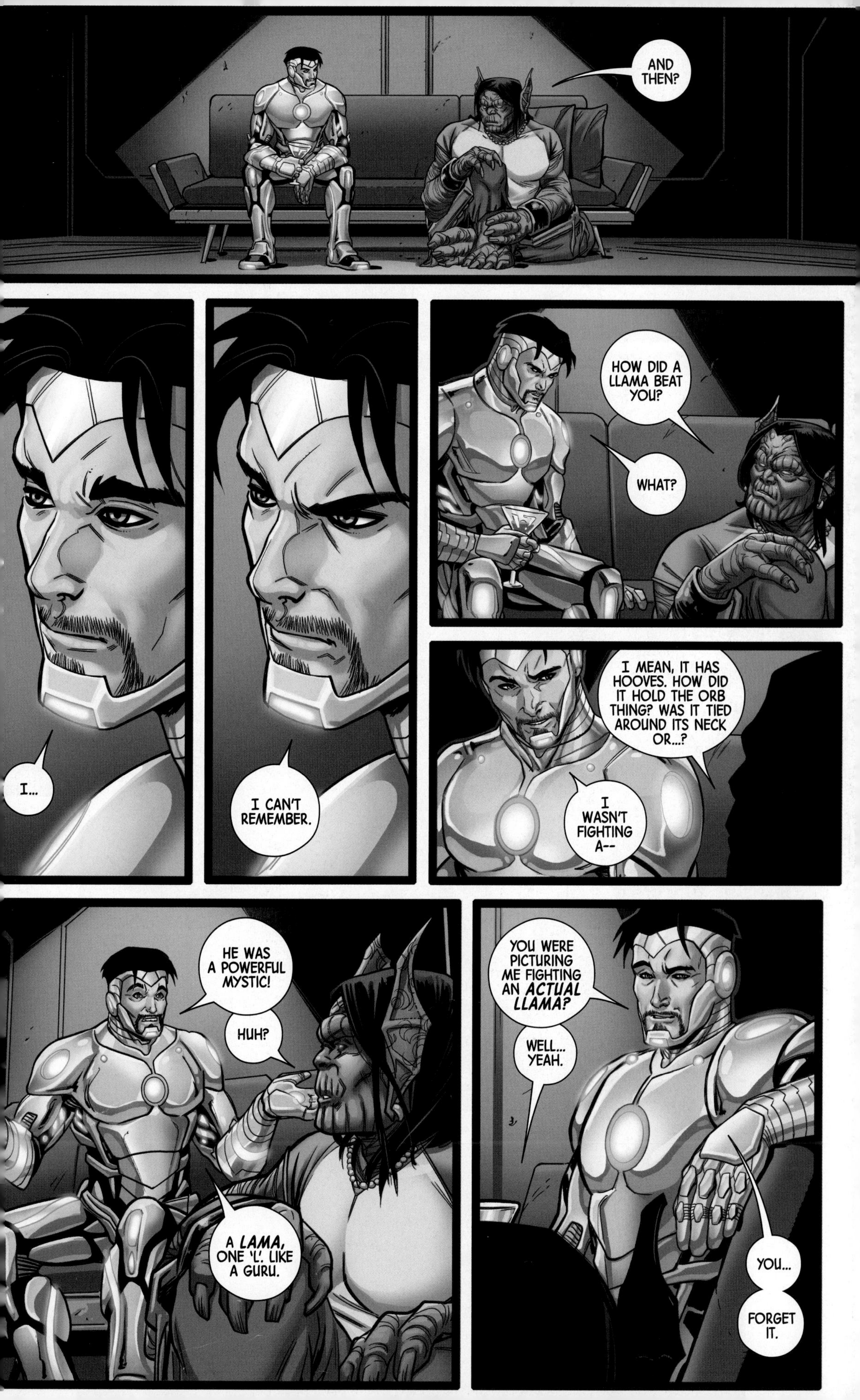
AND THEN?
I...
I CAN'T REMEMBER.
HOW DID A LLAMA BEAT YOU?
WHAT?
I MEAN, IT HAS HOOVES. HOW DID IT HOLD THE ORB THING? WAS IT TIED AROUND ITS NECK OR...?
I WASN'T FIGHTING A--
HE WAS A POWERFUL MYSTIC!
HUH?
A LAMA, ONE 'L'. LIKE A GURU.
YOU WERE PICTURING ME FIGHTING AN ACTUAL LLAMA?
WELL... YEAH.
YOU...
FORGET IT.

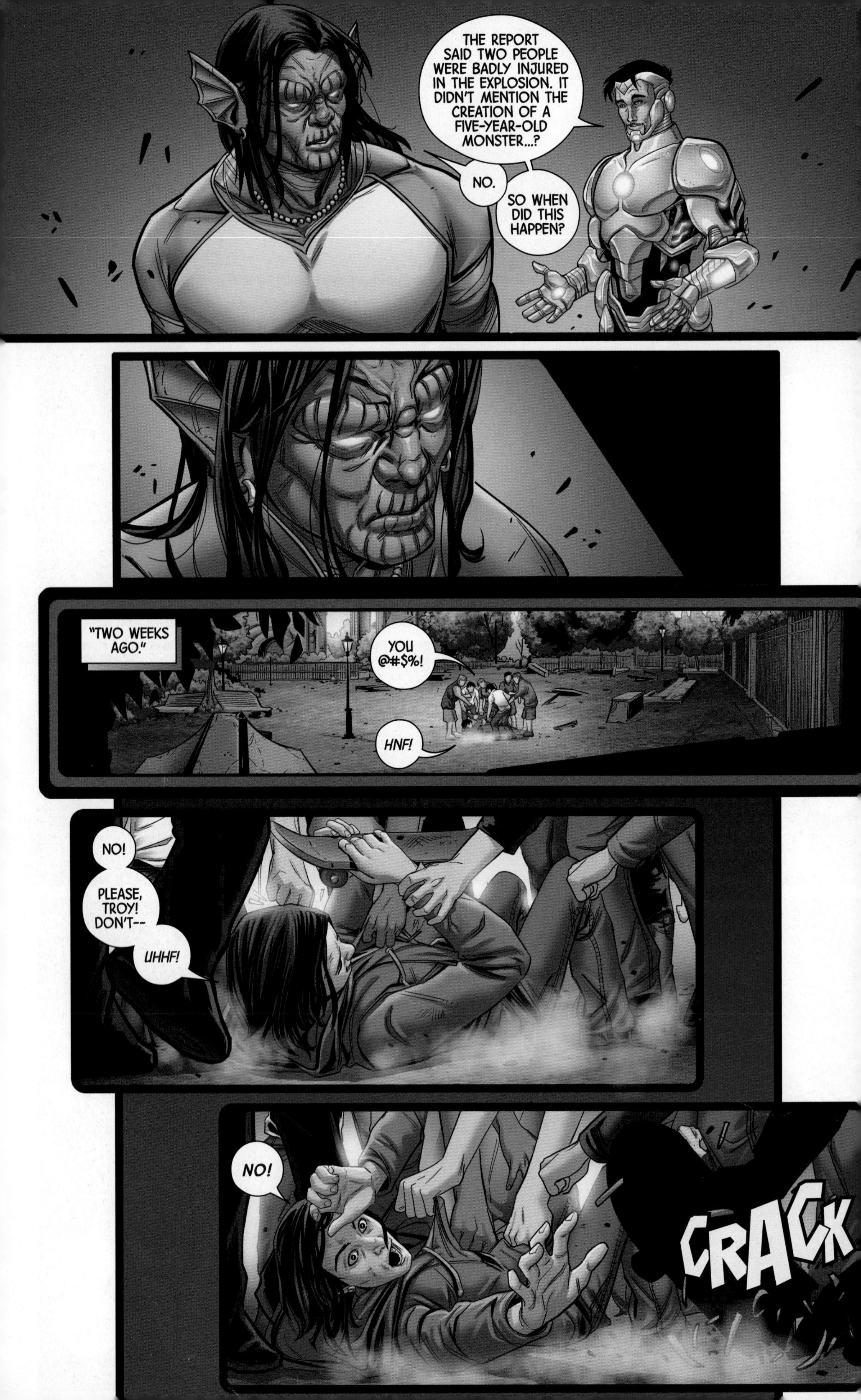
THE REPORT SAID TWO PEOPLE WERE BADLY INJURED IN THE EXPLOSION. IT DIDN'T MENTION THE CREATION OF A FIVE-YEAR-OLD MONSTER...?
NO.
SO WHEN DID THIS HAPPEN?
"TWO WEEKS AGO."
YOU @#$%!
HNF!
NO!
PLEASE, TROY! DON'T--
UHHF!
NO!
CRACK

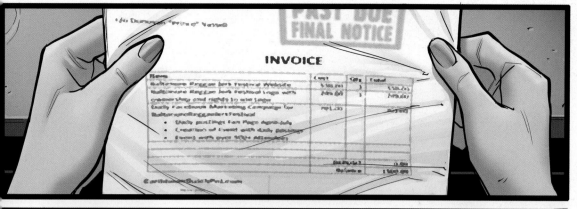

PAST DUE
FINAL NOTICE

INVOICE

JAMIE?

JAMIE!

I FELL OVER.

YOU FELL OVER?

MAYBE IF YOU JUST *TRIED* TO BE A BIT MORE LIKE THEM?

MAYBE IF YOU JUST--

CAN WE GET A NEW SKATEBOARD?

I...WE DON'T HAVE ANYTHING EXTRA AT THE MOMENT.

MAYBE FOR CHRISTMAS?

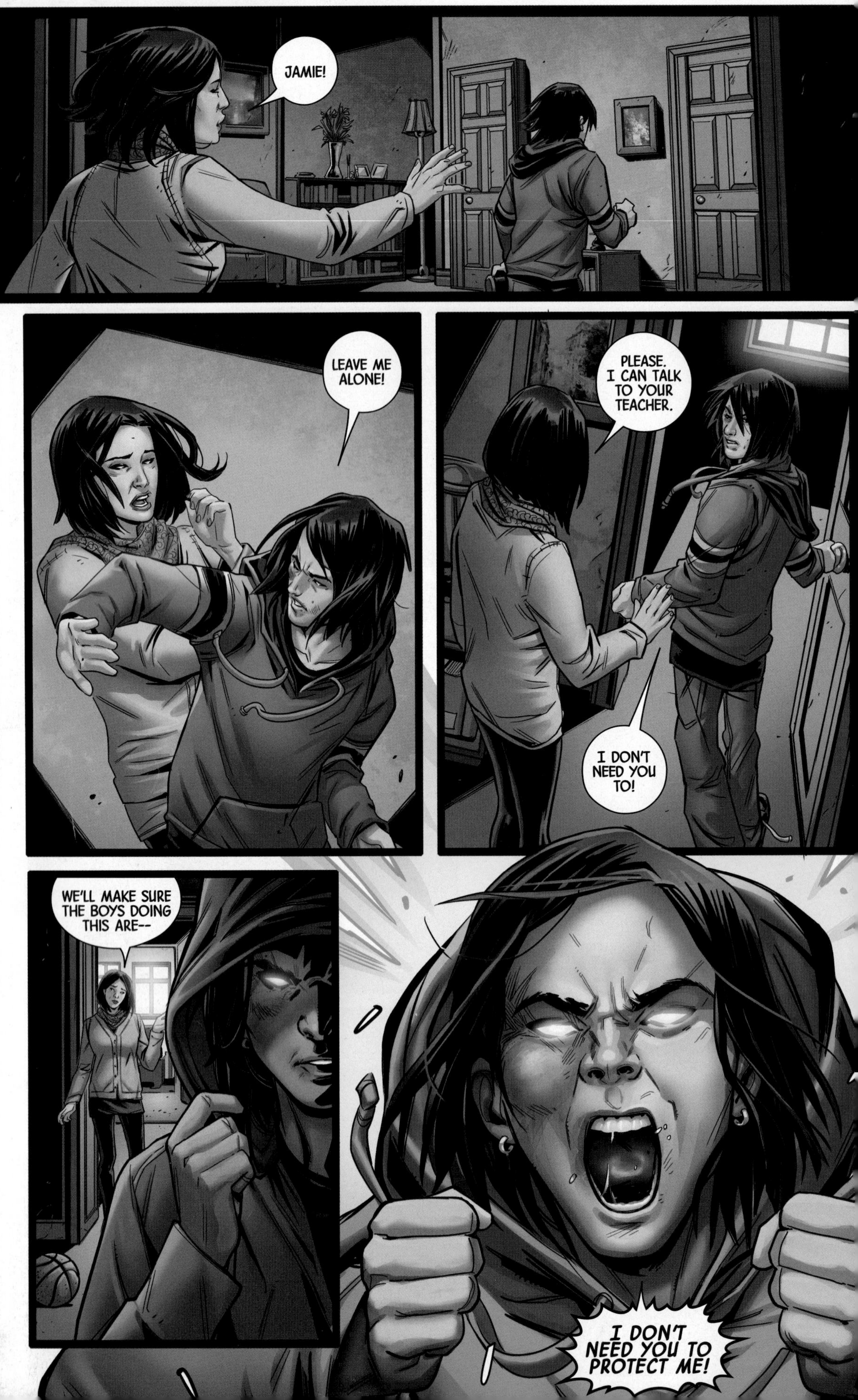
JAMIE!
LEAVE ME ALONE!
PLEASE. I CAN TALK TO YOUR TEACHER.
I DON'T NEED YOU TO!
WE'LL MAKE SURE THE BOYS DOING THIS ARE--
I DON'T NEED YOU TO PROTECT ME!

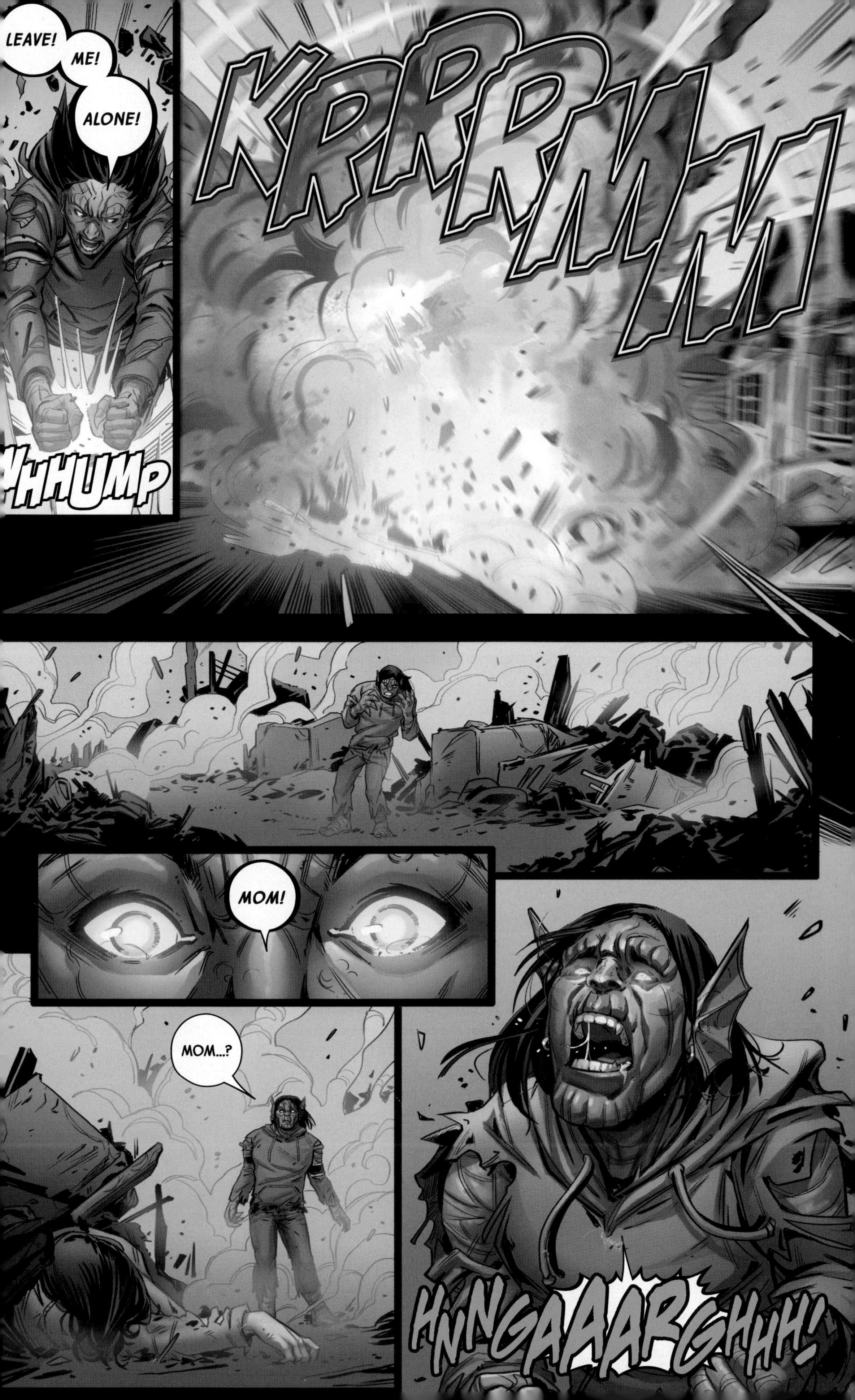
LEAVE!
ME!
ALONE!
WHHUMP
KRRRMMM
MOM!
MOM...?
HNNGAAARGHHH!

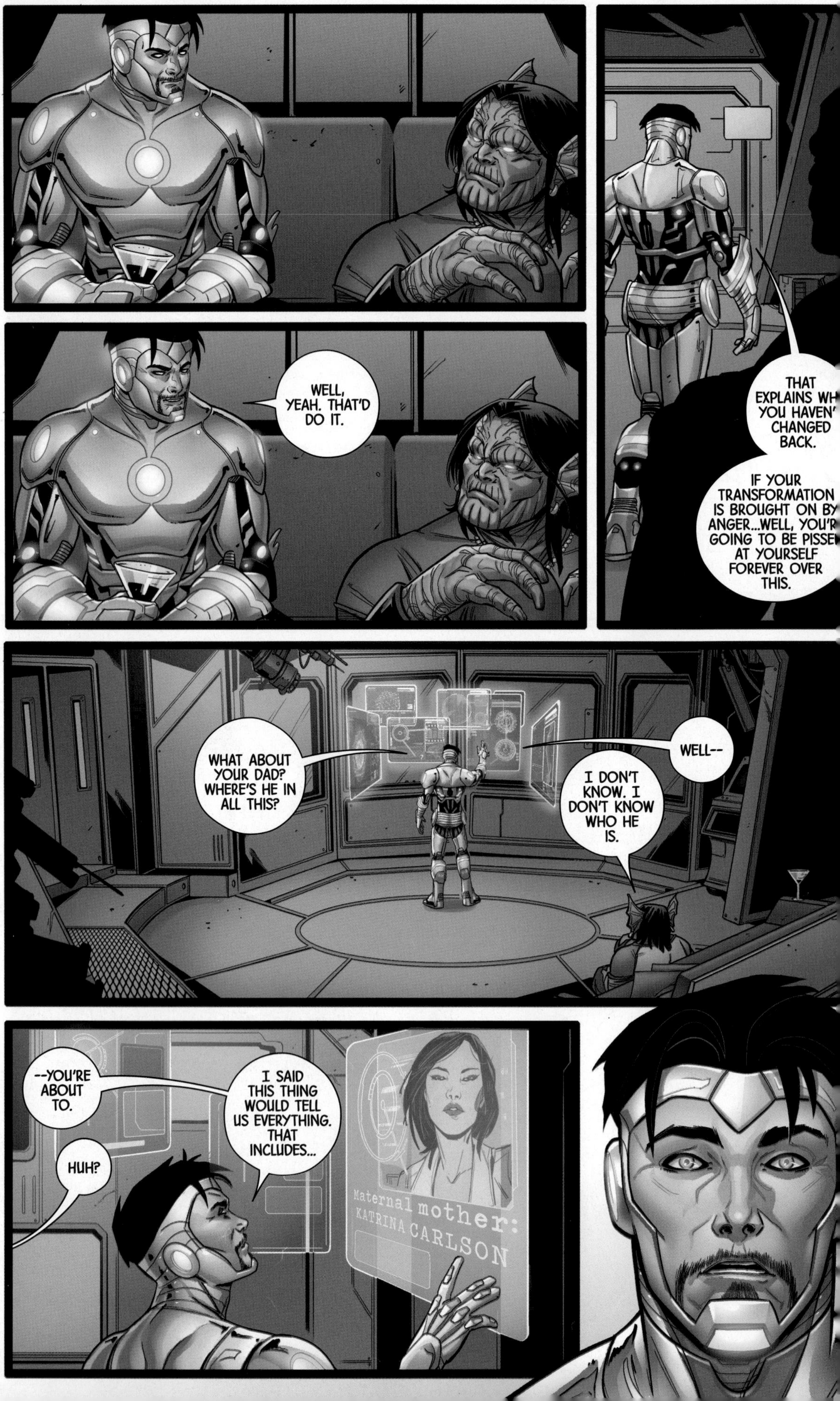
WELL, YEAH. THAT'D DO IT.
THAT EXPLAINS WH YOU HAVEN' CHANGED BACK.
IF YOUR TRANSFORMATION IS BROUGHT ON BY ANGER...WELL, YOU'R GOING TO BE PISSE AT YOURSELF FOREVER OVER THIS.
WHAT ABOUT YOUR DAD? WHERE'S HE IN ALL THIS?
I DON'T KNOW. I DON'T KNOW WHO HE IS.
WELL--
--YOU'RE ABOUT TO.
HUH?
I SAID THIS THING WOULD TELL US EVERYTHING. THAT INCLUDES...
Maternal mother: KATRINA CARLSON

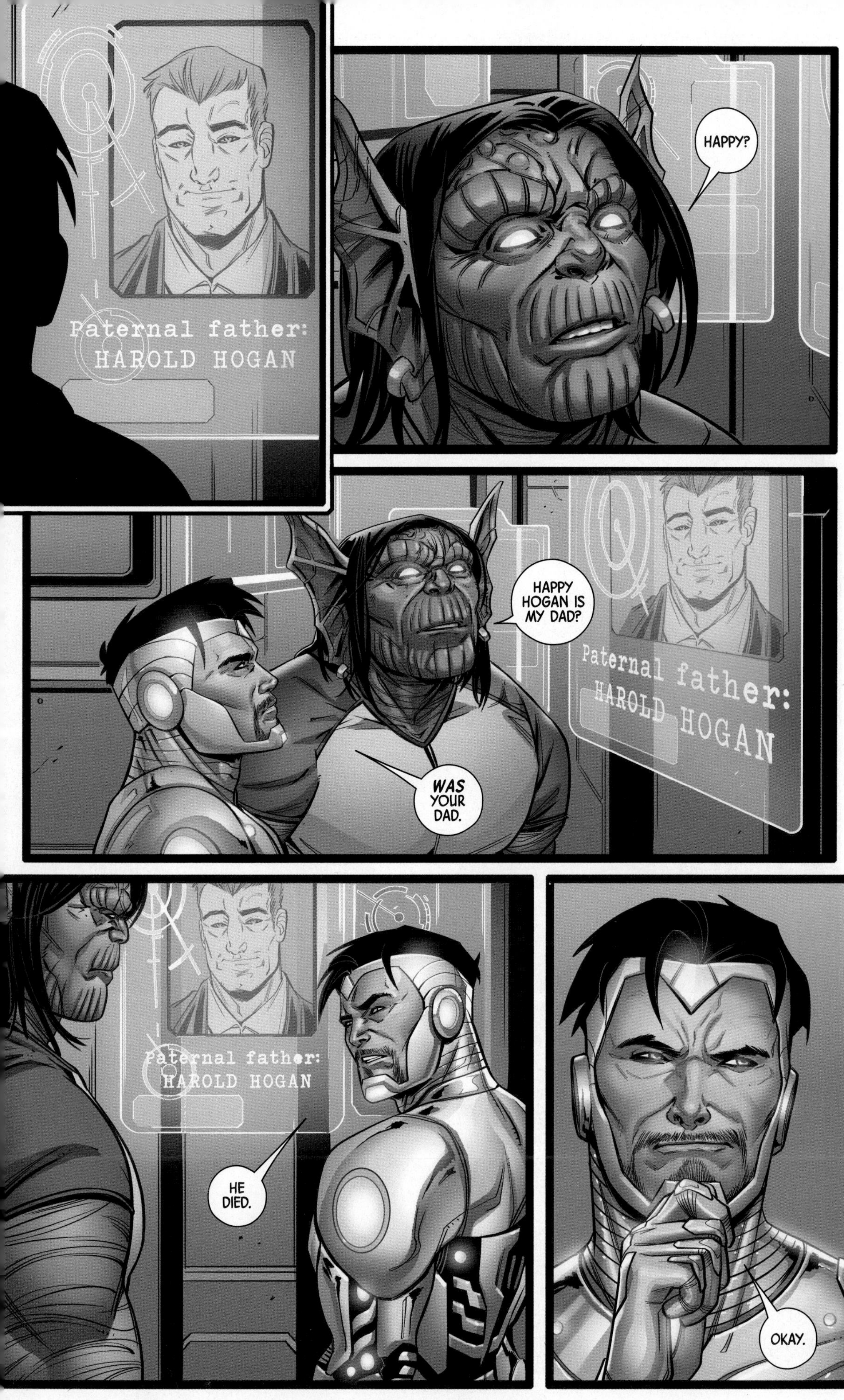
Paternal father:
HAROLD HOGAN
HAPPY?
HAPPY HOGAN IS MY DAD?
Paternal father:
HAROLD HOGAN
WAS YOUR DAD.
Paternal father:
HAROLD HOGAN
HE DIED.
OKAY.

YOU'RE THE SON OF ONE OF THE FEW PEOPLE I ACTUALLY CARED ABOUT.

I *AM* GOING TO HELP YOU NOW.

YOU ALREADY SAID YOU WERE GOING TO HELP ME...?

YES. BUT IN ACTUALITY, I WAS GOING TO PULL YOU APART AND WORK OUT WHAT YOUR CELLS ARE DOING IN ORDER TO HARNESS YOUR CONDITION FOR FUN AND PROFIT.

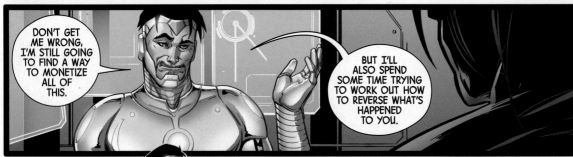

DON'T GET ME WRONG, I'M STILL GOING TO FIND A WAY TO MONETIZE ALL OF THIS.

BUT I'LL ALSO SPEND SOME TIME TRYING TO WORK OUT HOW TO REVERSE WHAT'S HAPPENED TO YOU.

WE'LL START TOMORROW.

DO YOU NEED TO GO OUT AND PROTECT THE CITY?

NO. I'VE SET UP A HUGE NETWORK OF FLOATING CAMERAS THAT MONITOR THE ENTIRE POPULACE AND CAN SEE THROUGH WALLS.

NO ONE IN SAN FRANCISCO IS DOING ANYTHING THEY SHOULDN'T BE. THEY KNOW THEY'RE BEING WATCHED. MOST OF THEM ARE JUST THINKING UP REALLY CREATIVE WAYS NOT TO BE NAKED.

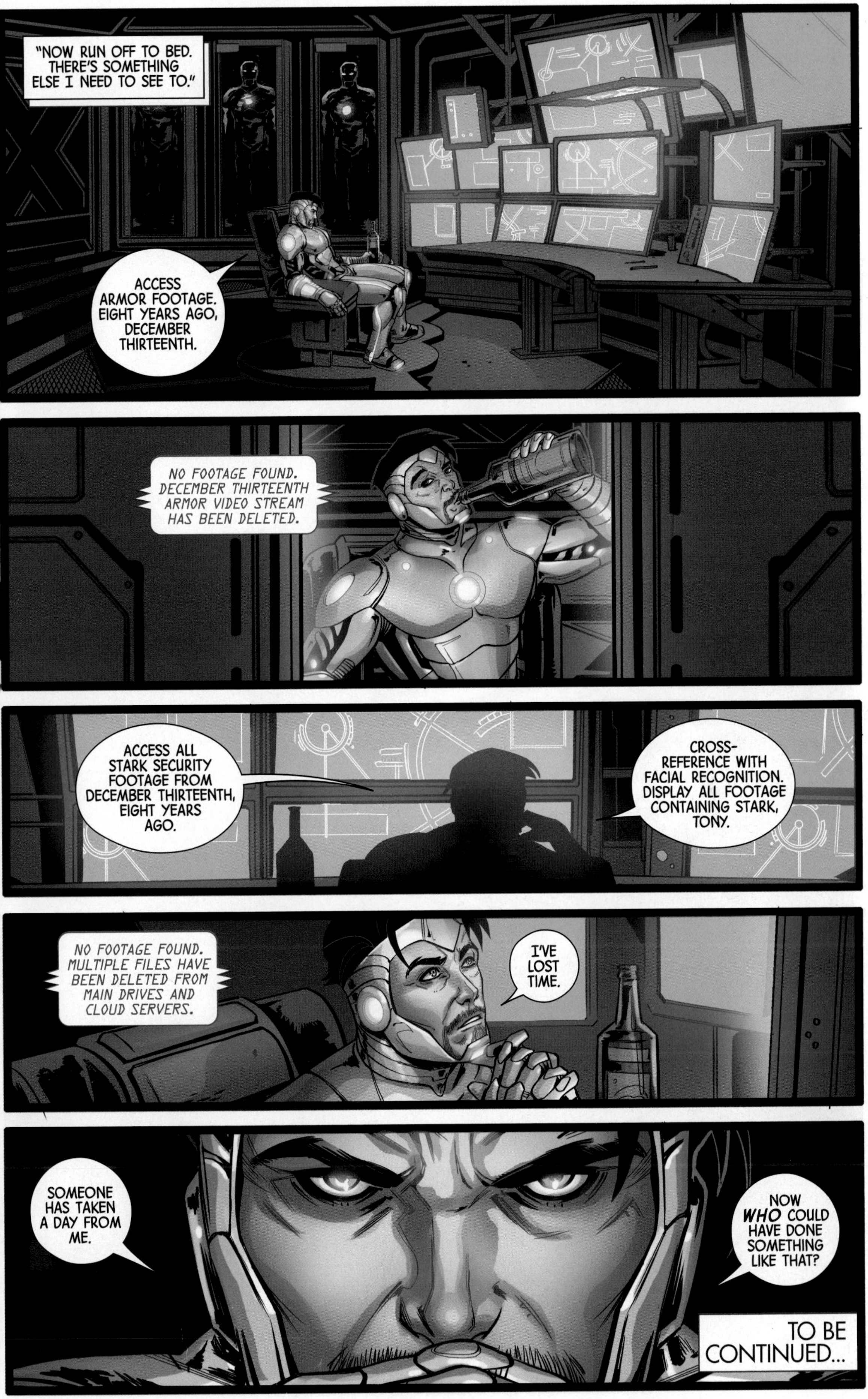
"NOW RUN OFF TO BED. THERE'S SOMETHING ELSE I NEED TO SEE TO."
ACCESS ARMOR FOOTAGE. EIGHT YEARS AGO, DECEMBER THIRTEENTH.
NO FOOTAGE FOUND. DECEMBER THIRTEENTH ARMOR VIDEO STREAM HAS BEEN DELETED.
ACCESS ALL STARK SECURITY FOOTAGE FROM DECEMBER THIRTEENTH, EIGHT YEARS AGO.
CROSS-REFERENCE WITH FACIAL RECOGNITION. DISPLAY ALL FOOTAGE CONTAINING STARK, TONY.
NO FOOTAGE FOUND. MULTIPLE FILES HAVE BEEN DELETED FROM MAIN DRIVES AND CLOUD SERVERS.
I'VE LOST TIME.
SOMEONE HAS TAKEN A DAY FROM ME.
NOW WHO COULD HAVE DONE SOMETHING LIKE THAT?
TO BE CONTINUED...

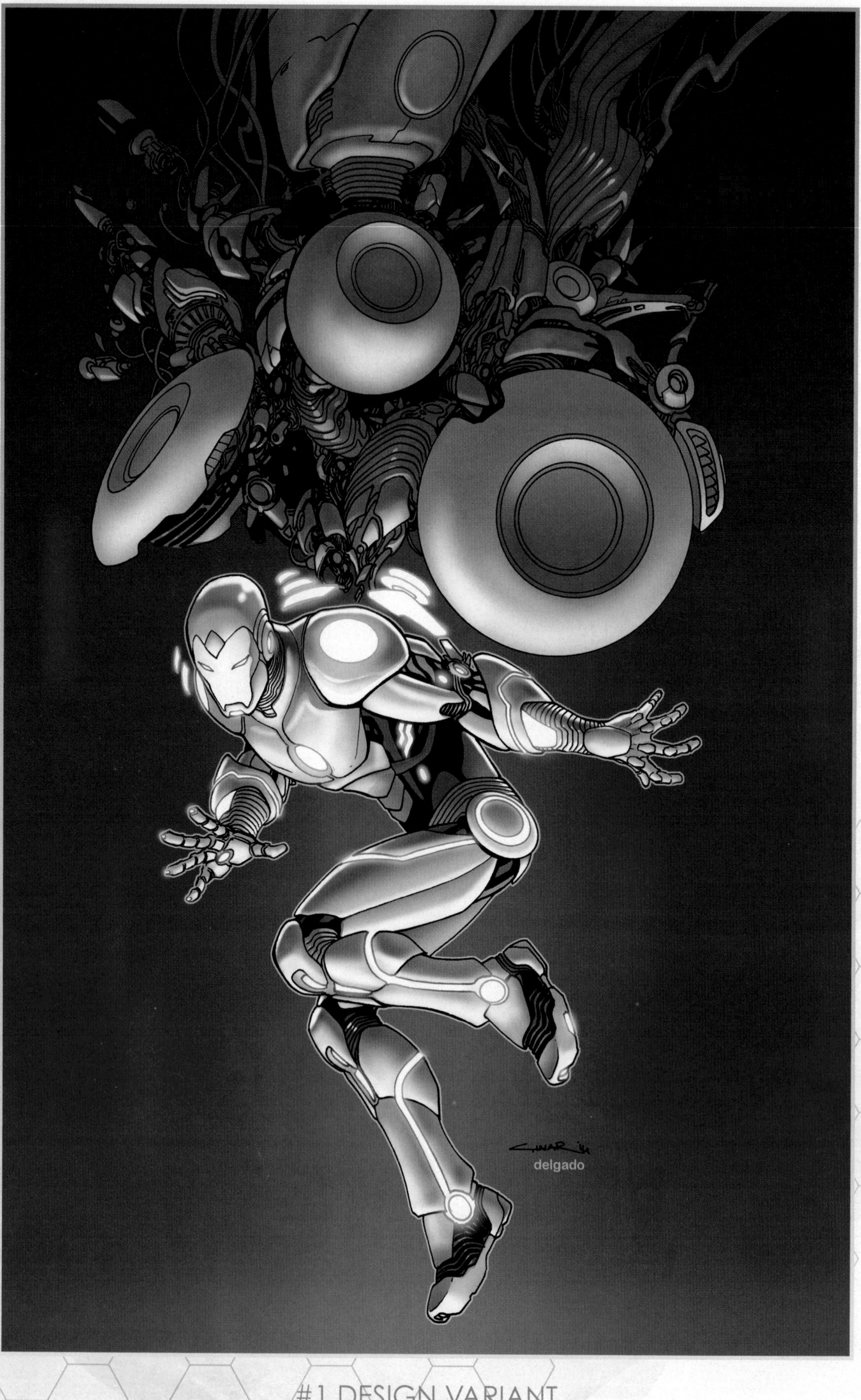
delgado

#1 DESIGN VARIANT
BY YILDIRAY ÇINAR & EDGAR DELGADO

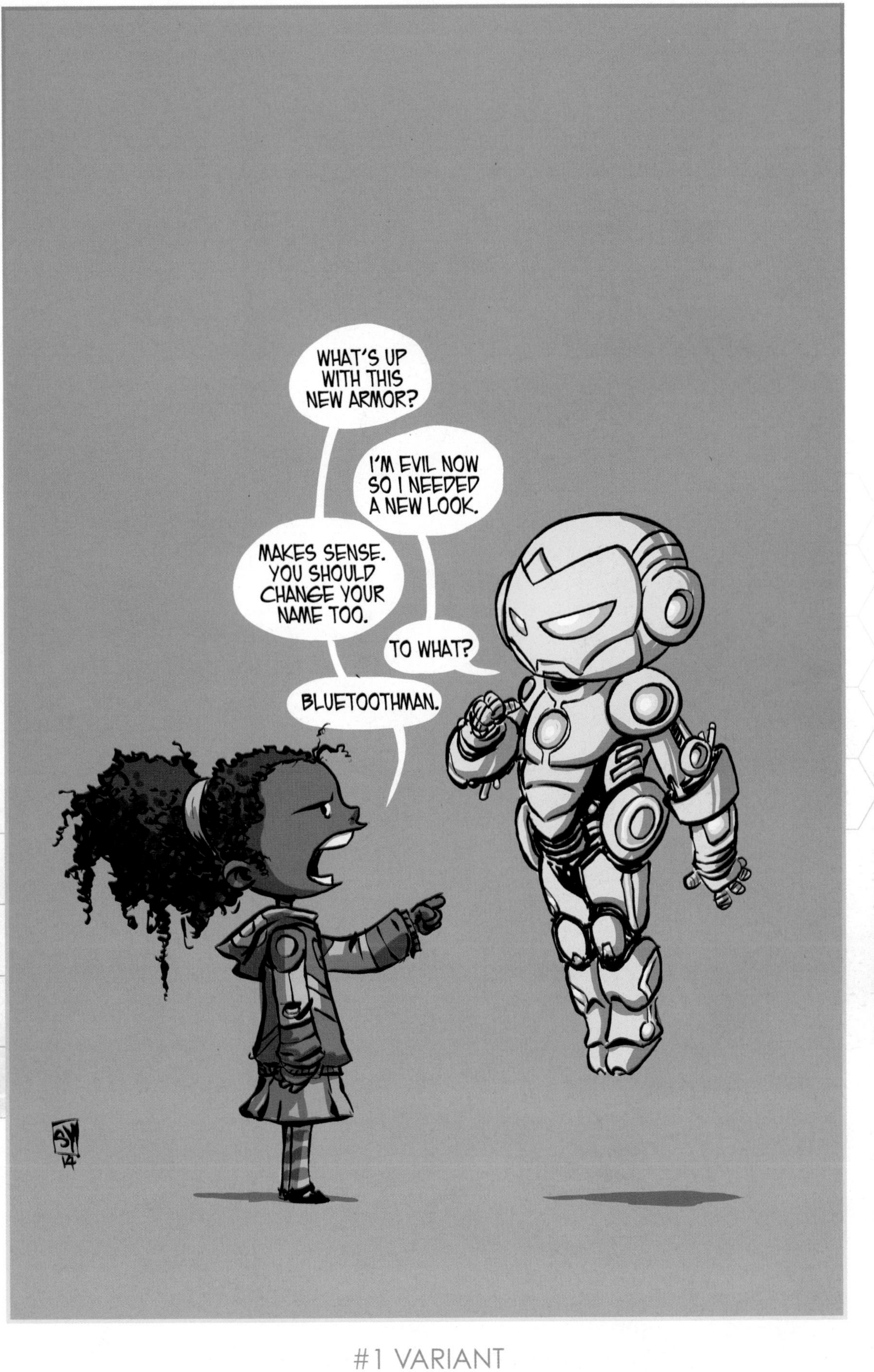
WHAT'S UP WITH THIS NEW ARMOR?
I'M EVIL NOW SO I NEEDED A NEW LOOK.
MAKES SENSE. YOU SHOULD CHANGE YOUR NAME TOO.
TO WHAT?
BLUETOOTHMAN.

#1 VARIANT
BY SKOTTIE YOUNG

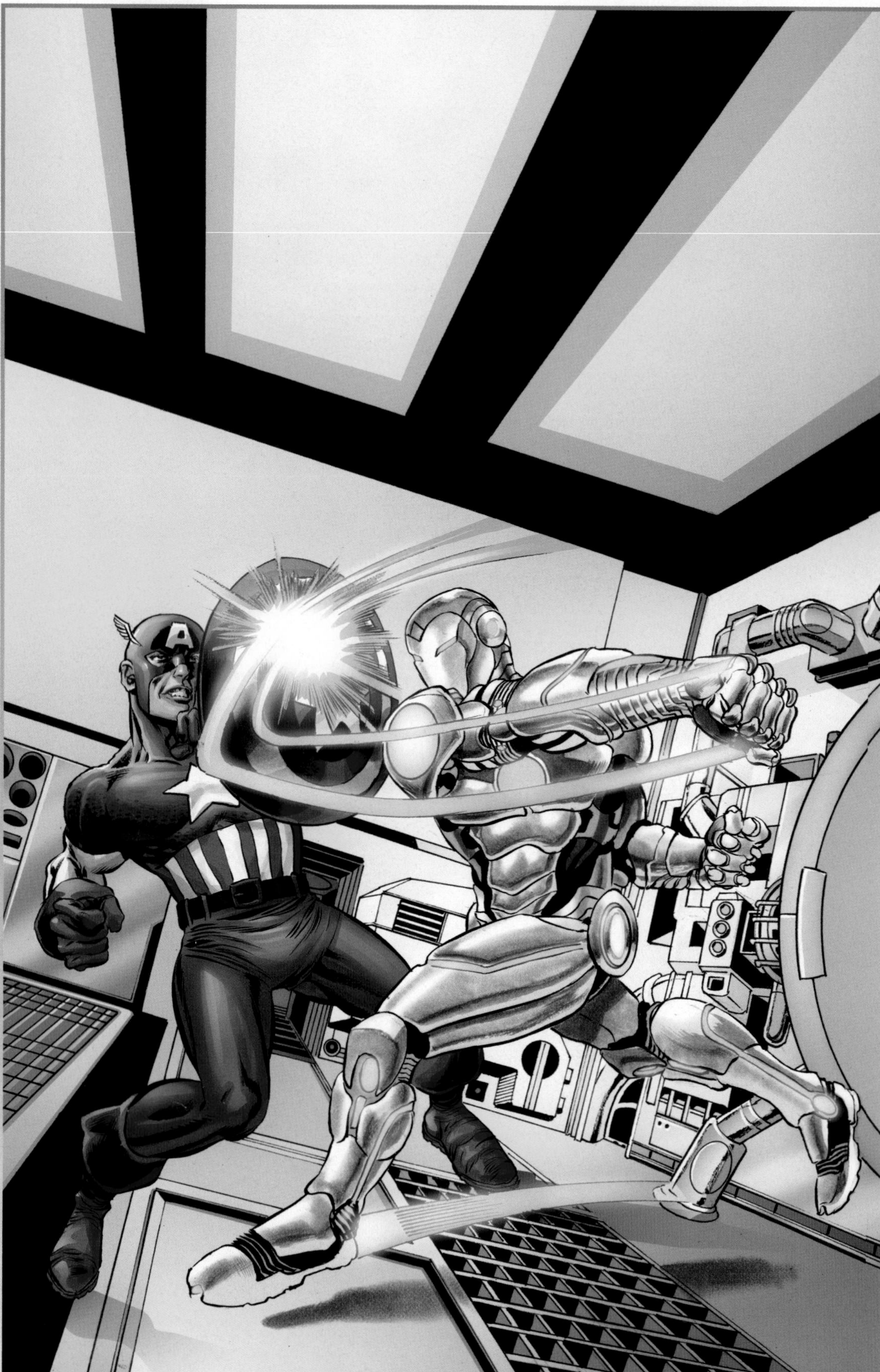

#1 VARIANT
BY MIKE PERKINS & ANDY TROY

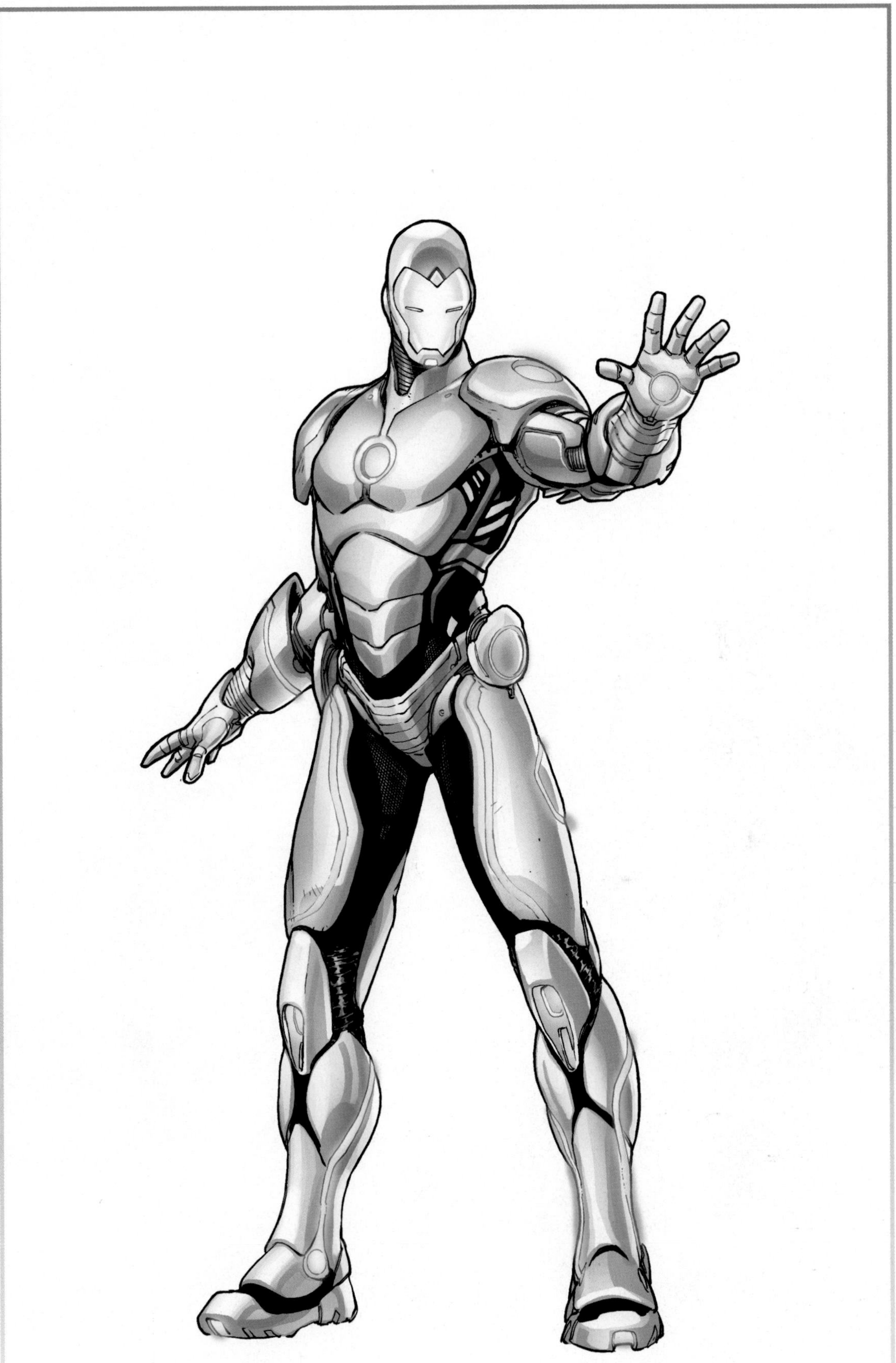

#1 VARIANT
BY SARA PICHELLI & LAURA MARTIN

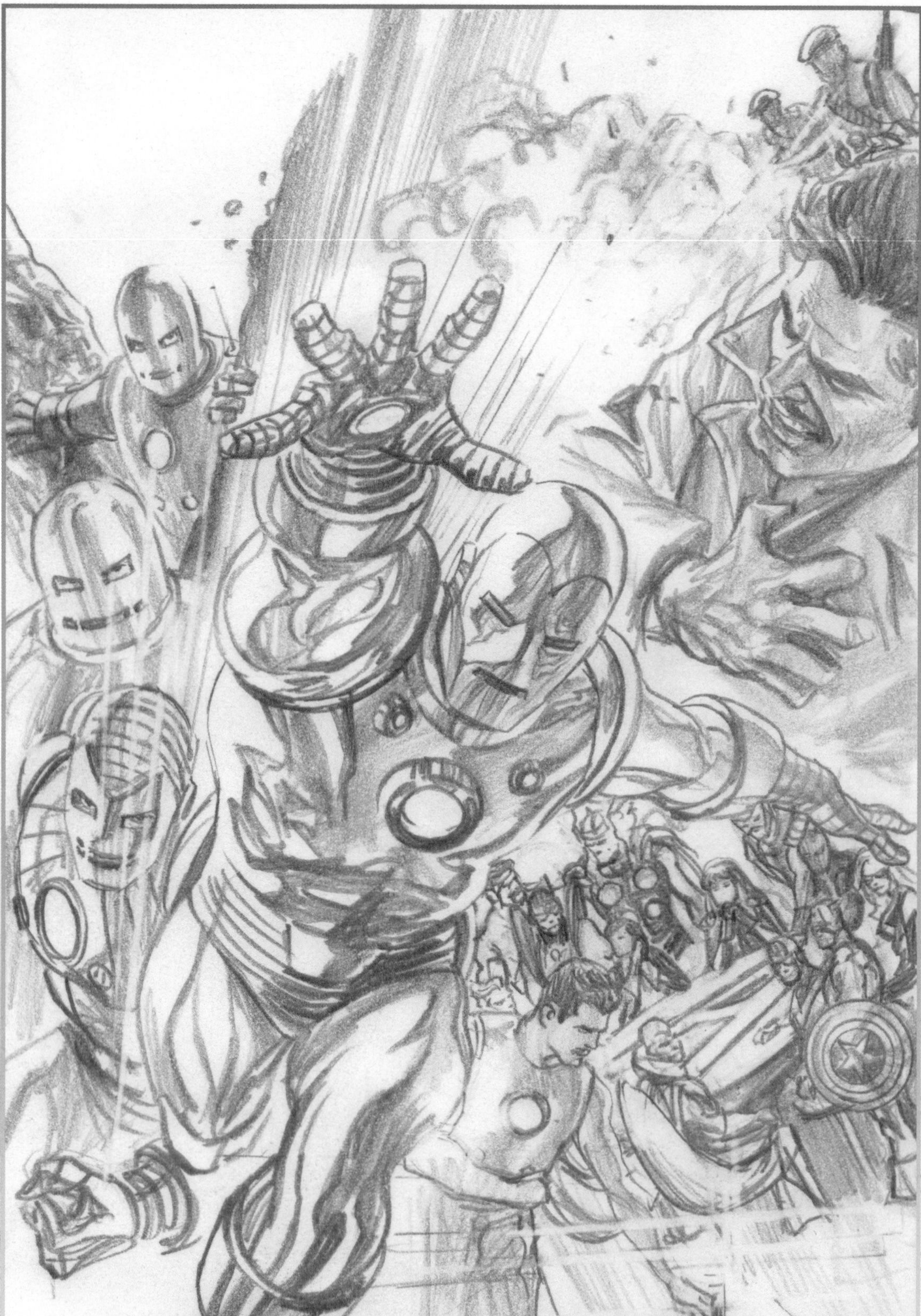

#1 75TH ANNIVERSARY SKETCH VARIANT
BY ALEX ROSS

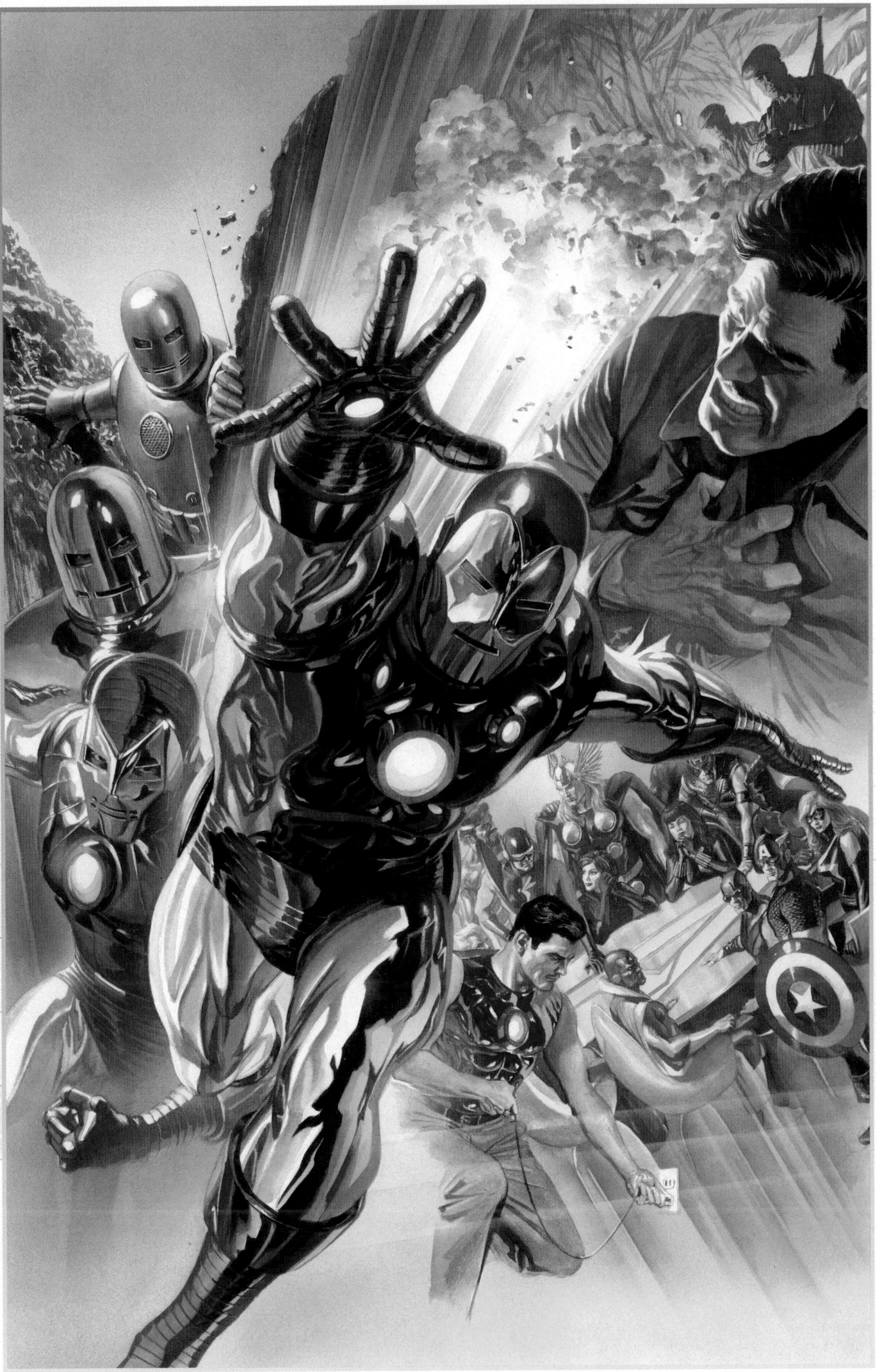

#1 75TH ANNIVERSARY VARIANT
BY ALEX ROSS

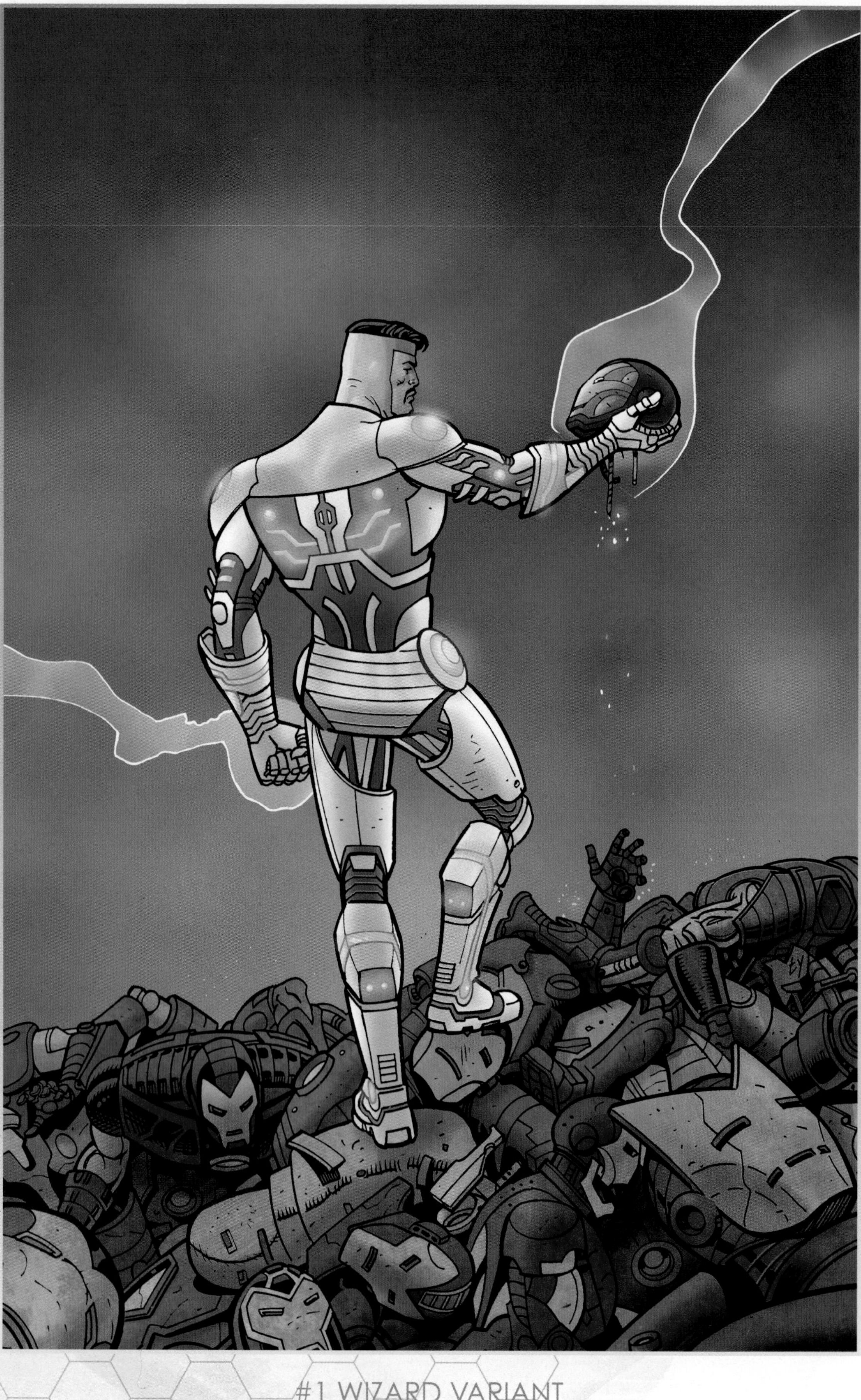

#1 WIZARD VARIANT
BY TY TEMPLETON

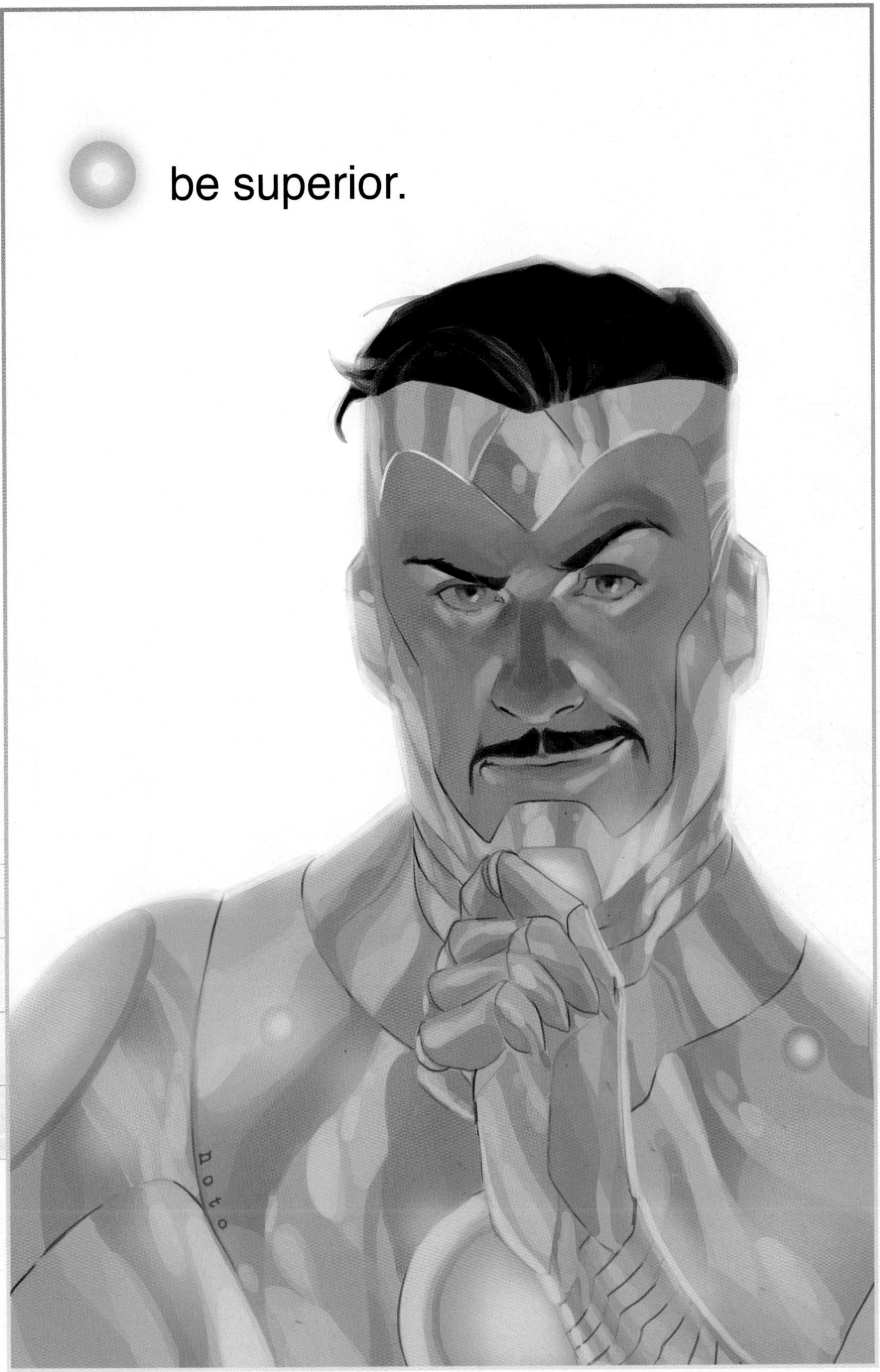
be superior.
noto

#2 VARIANT
BY PHIL NOTO

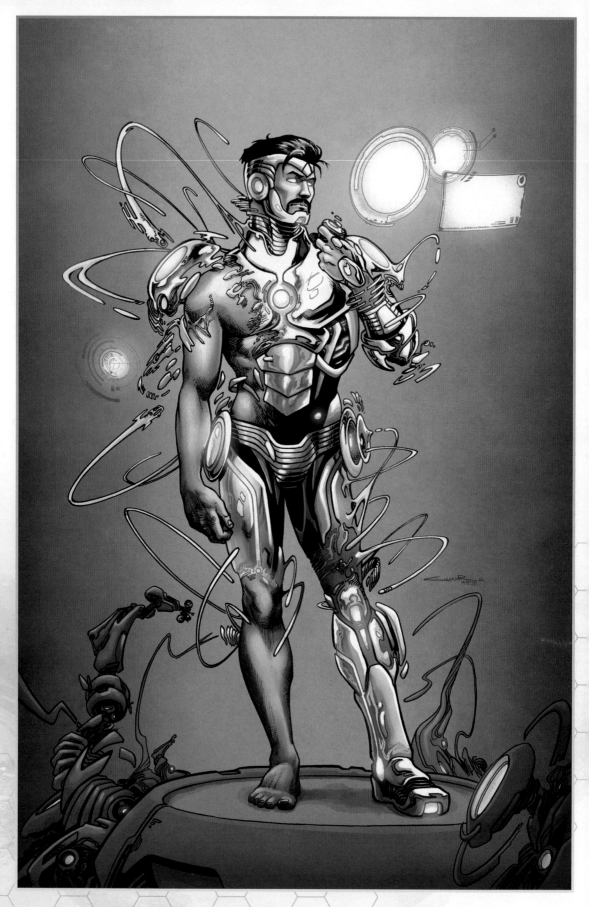

#3 VARIANT
BY YILDIRAY ÇINAR & JORDAN THOMAS BOYD

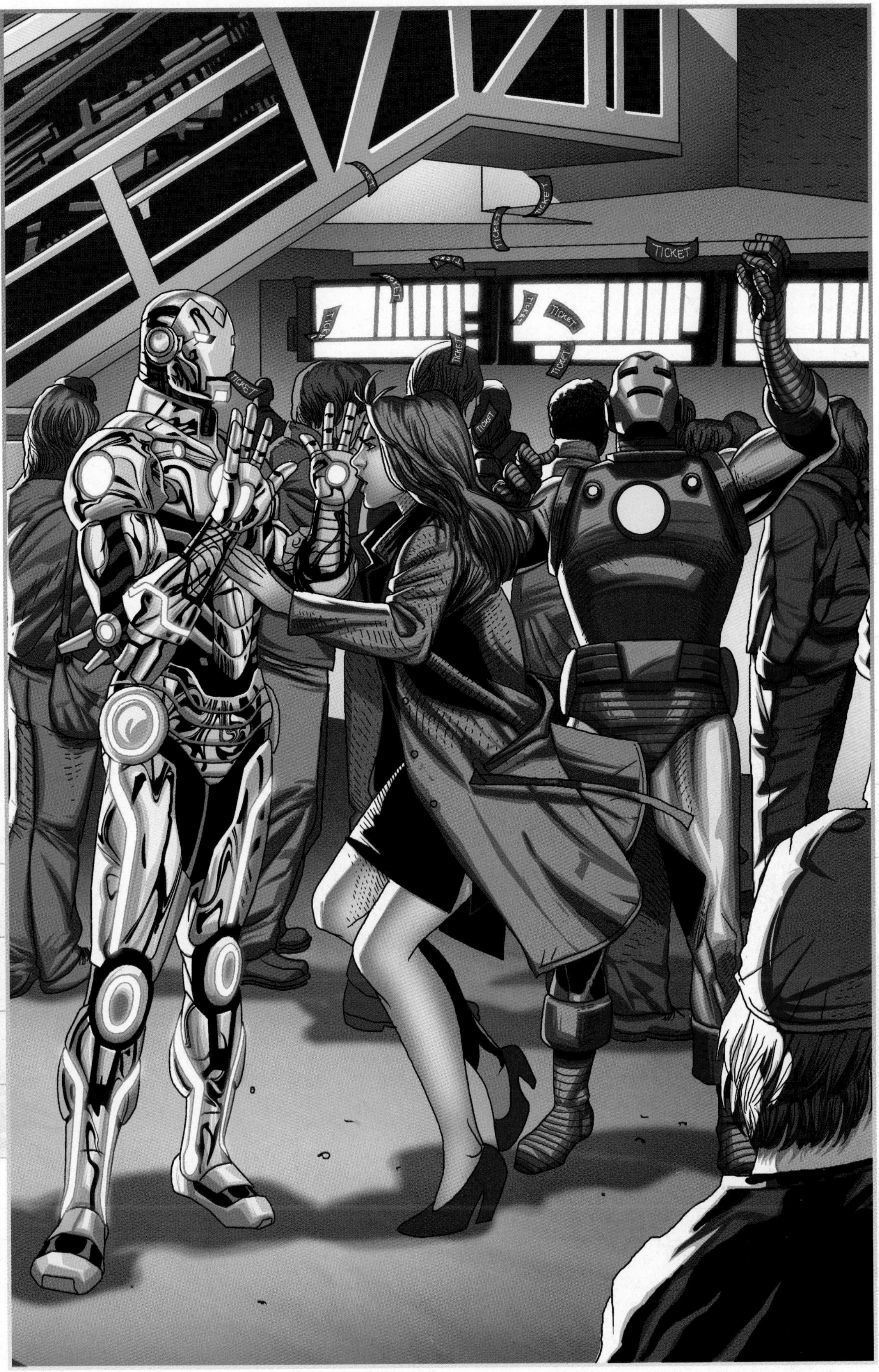
TICKET
TICKET
TICKET
TICKET
TICKET
TICKET
TICKET

#4 WELCOME HOME VARIANT
BY SALVADOR LARROCA & ISRAEL SILVA

BEHIND THE IRON CURTAIN

Hey readers! Resident shell head editor Mark Paniccia here. Thought you might like a peek behind the creative process of Marvel's latest (and most unexpected) version of Tony Stark.

While Rick Remender was planning a crazy little thing that became AVENGERS AND X-MEN: AXIS, one of the ideas everyone here at MARVEL gravitated to was seeing bad guys become good guys and good guys become bad guys. With the right characters, attitudinal adjustments and creative teams, we knew some wild stories could spin out of the event...and seeing a more devious Tony Stark unleashed on the MARVEL UNIVERSE kind of gave us all goose bumps. What would happen if the golden Avenger wasn't so golden anymore? I couldn't see Tony Stark going completely evil, but I could see him go...chrome!

Let me explain. When I talked to writer Tom Taylor about the book, we thought an extreme version of a pre-heart-injury Tony Stark personality was the way to go. As a hero, we know Tony as a good looking, stylish, confident yet fair and noble guy... but without that moral compass — that perspective he gained when Ho Yinsen sacrificed himself so Tony could escape his captors — he'd feel...SUPERIOR. He would be self-indulgent, vain and over-the-top. I'd seen a picture of a chromed luxury sports car and thought that was a pretty good example of over-the-top. We wanted to lean into the narcissism, selfishness and glam of this altered Tony Stark with a super- sleek, LED, futuristic armor, and the mirror-like quality of chrome fed into that perfectly.

Artist Yildiray Çınar's first designs for SUPERIOR IRON MAN

We told artist Yildiray Çınar and he promptly started enthusiastically sketching away at designs. We wanted to have blue LED stretch throughout and Tom had the idea that they could turn red when Tony was about to attack, giving him "a bit of menace."

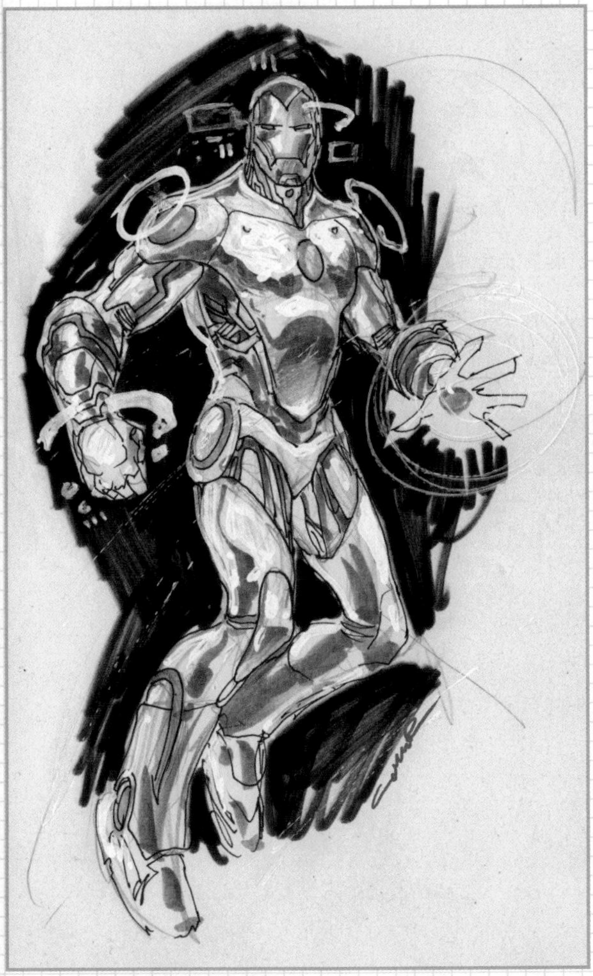

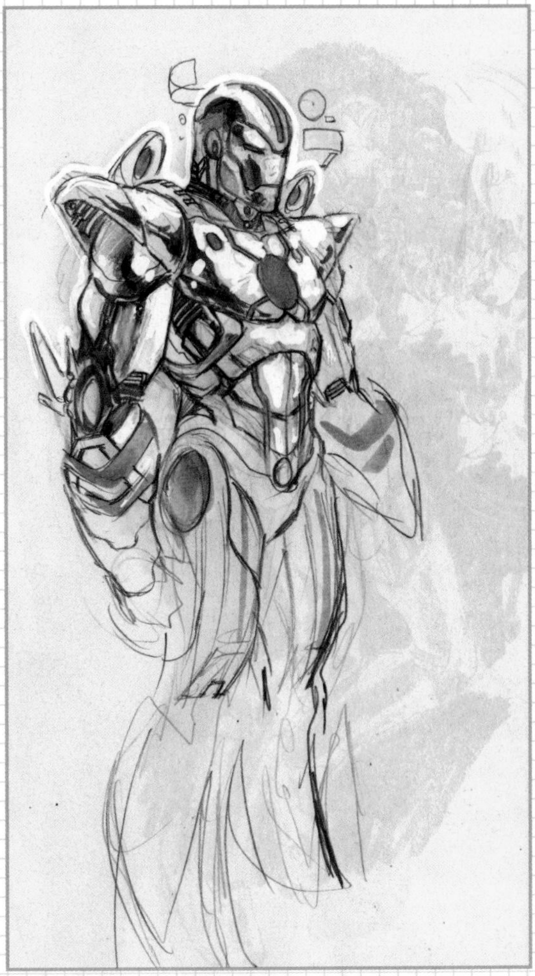

More early ideas from Yiliray

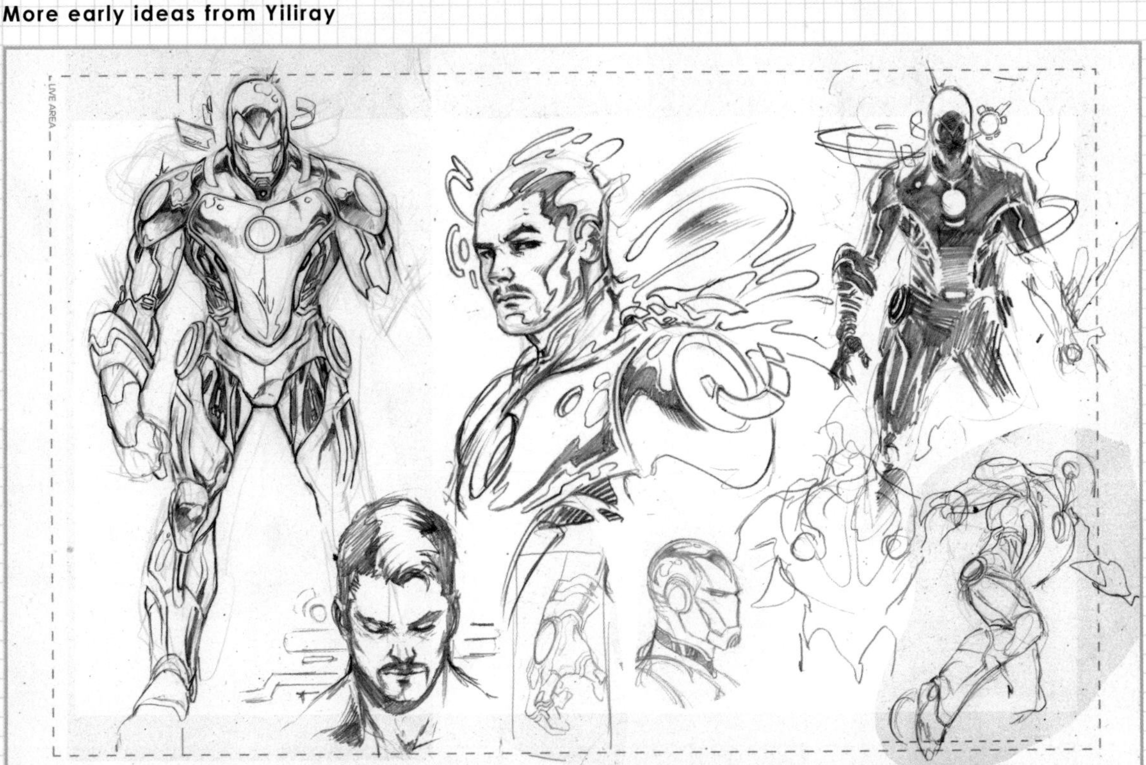
LIVE AREA

You wouldn't like Tony when he's angry (and glowing red)!

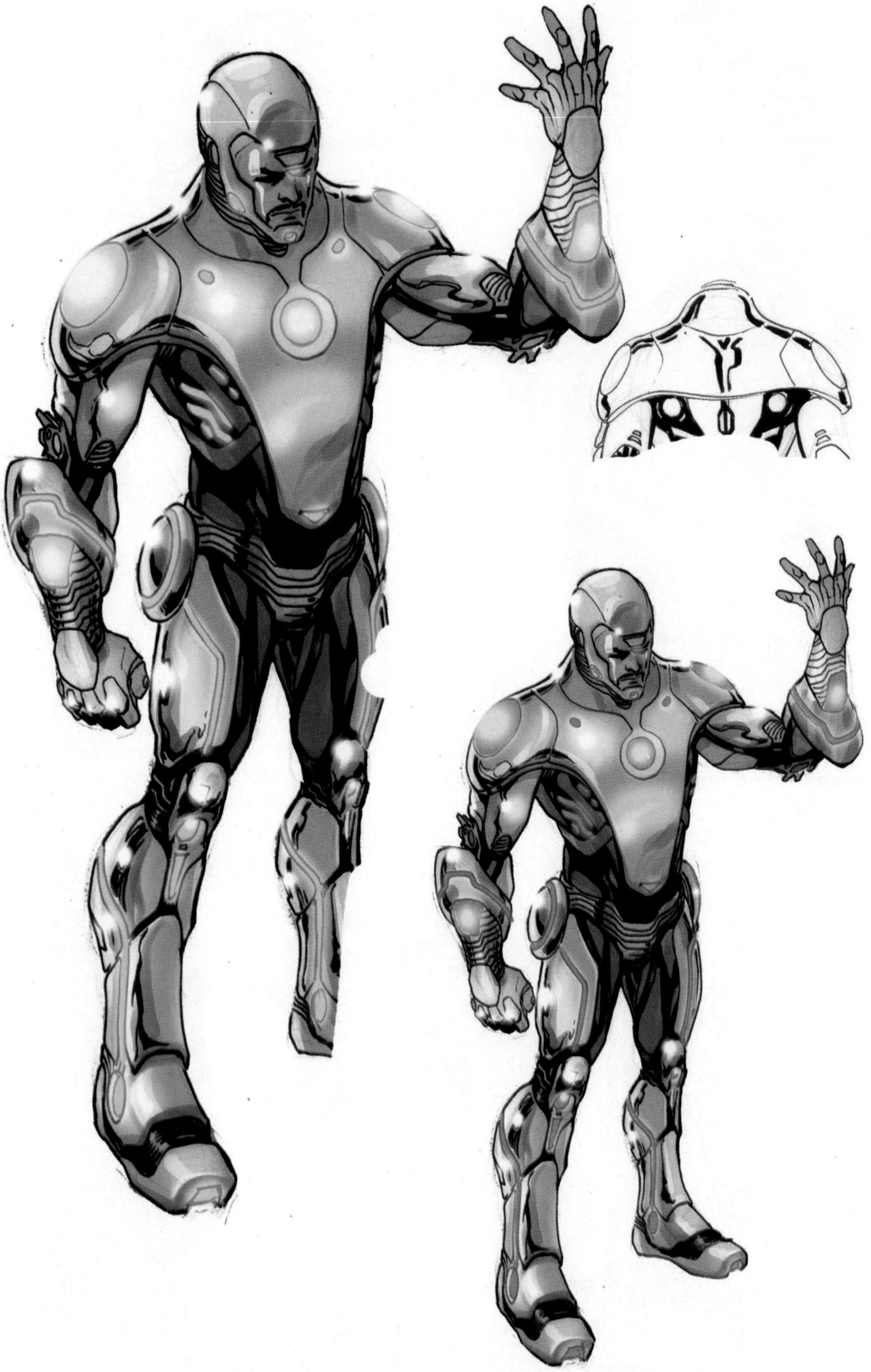

We asked Yildiray to add holographic elements and have the readouts and graphs surround Tony's head. suggested Tony not even have a faceplate. Vain Tony would want everyone to see his beautiful face. When Yildiray did helmet designs, we decided to keep the option of having the faceplate, and Tom came up with the idea of using stealth graphene for protective measures. All of Yildiary's sketches were cool but we especially liked having the eyebrows hidden, making Tony look more distant and regal.

The final helmet design incorporated many elements seen in these four versions.

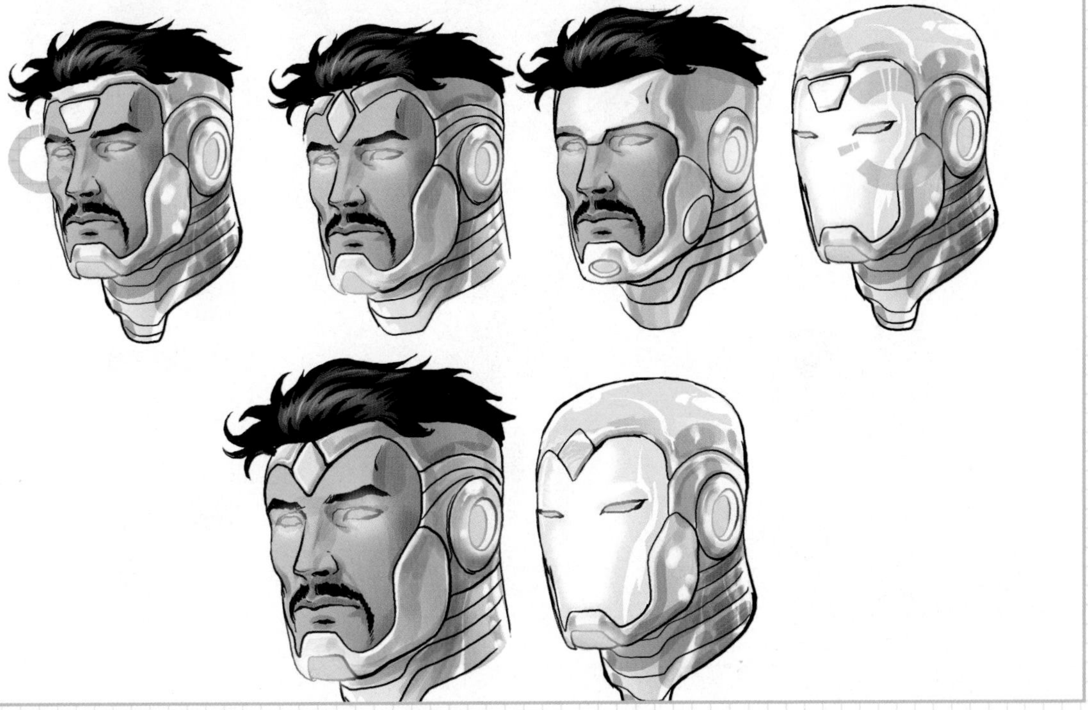

We ended up with a lot of great designs from Yildiray. The "Superior" armor still has a classic super hero vibe to it while messaging the stuff under the surface. Hope you dig it as much as we do.

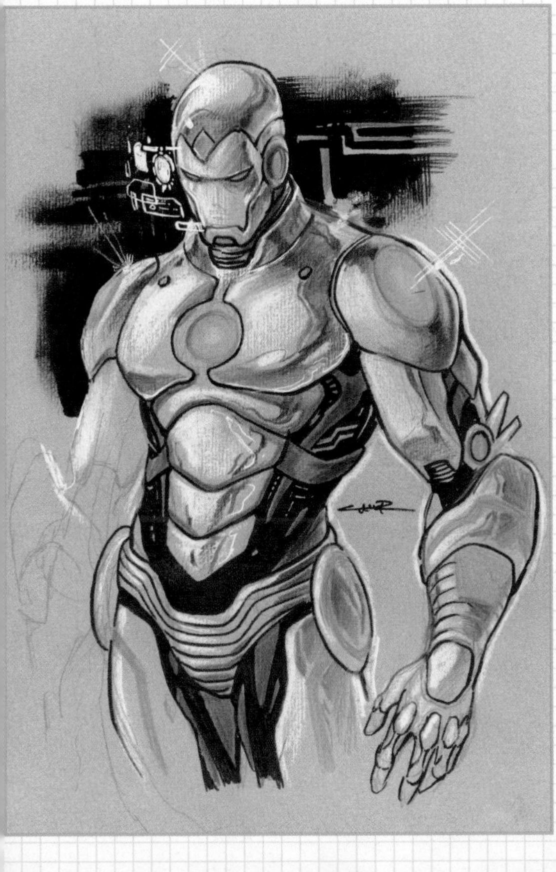

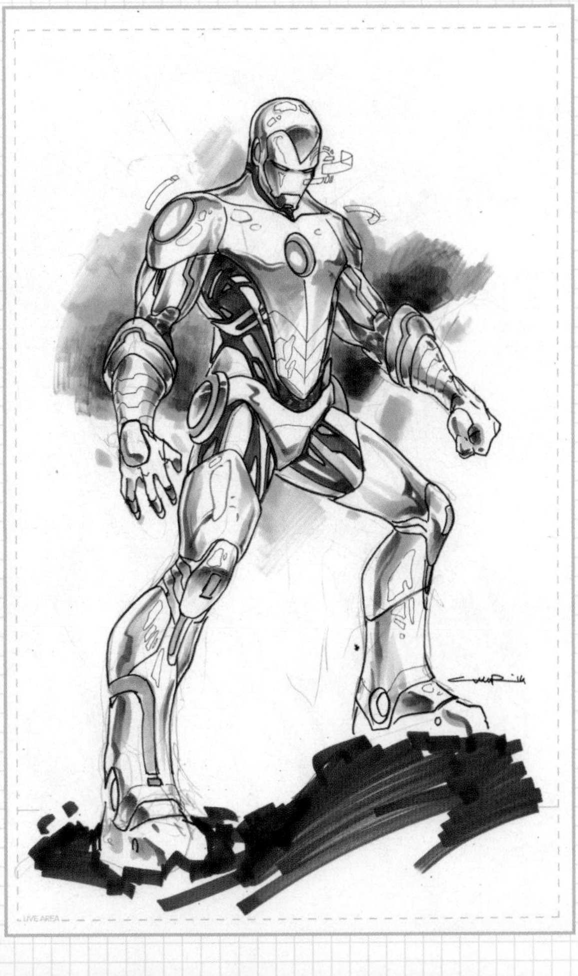

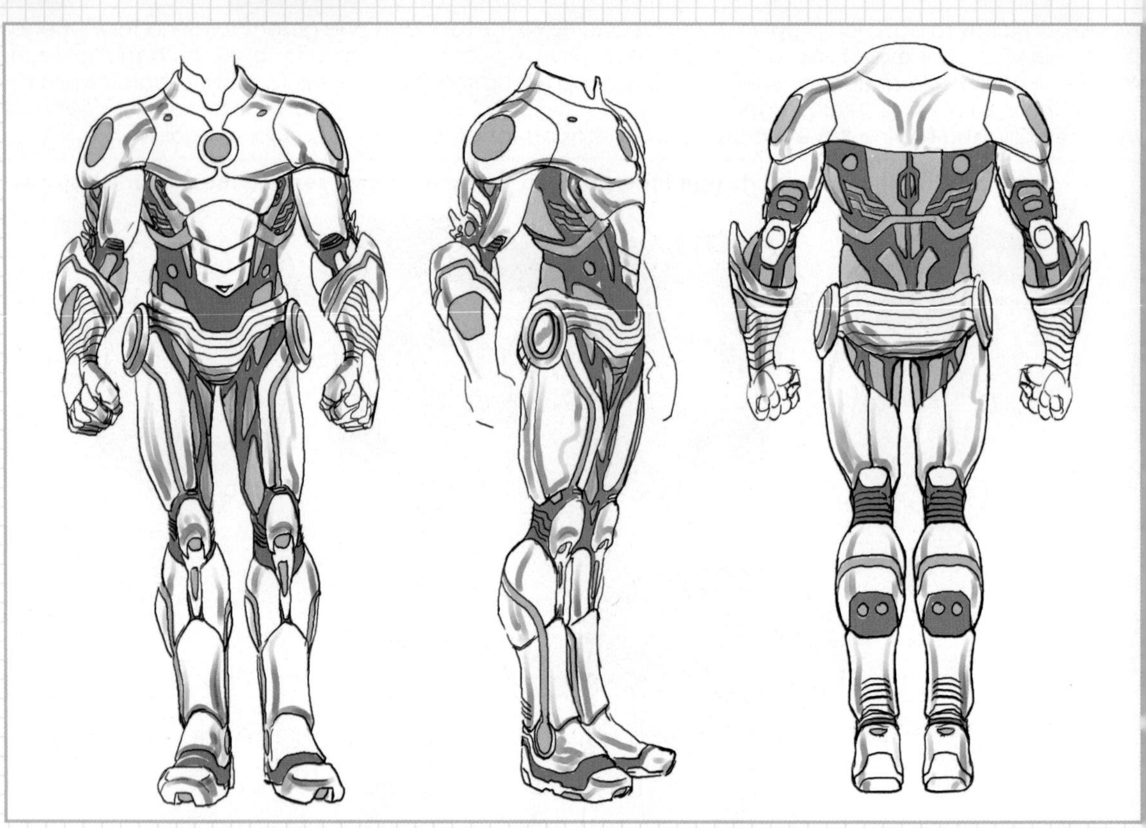

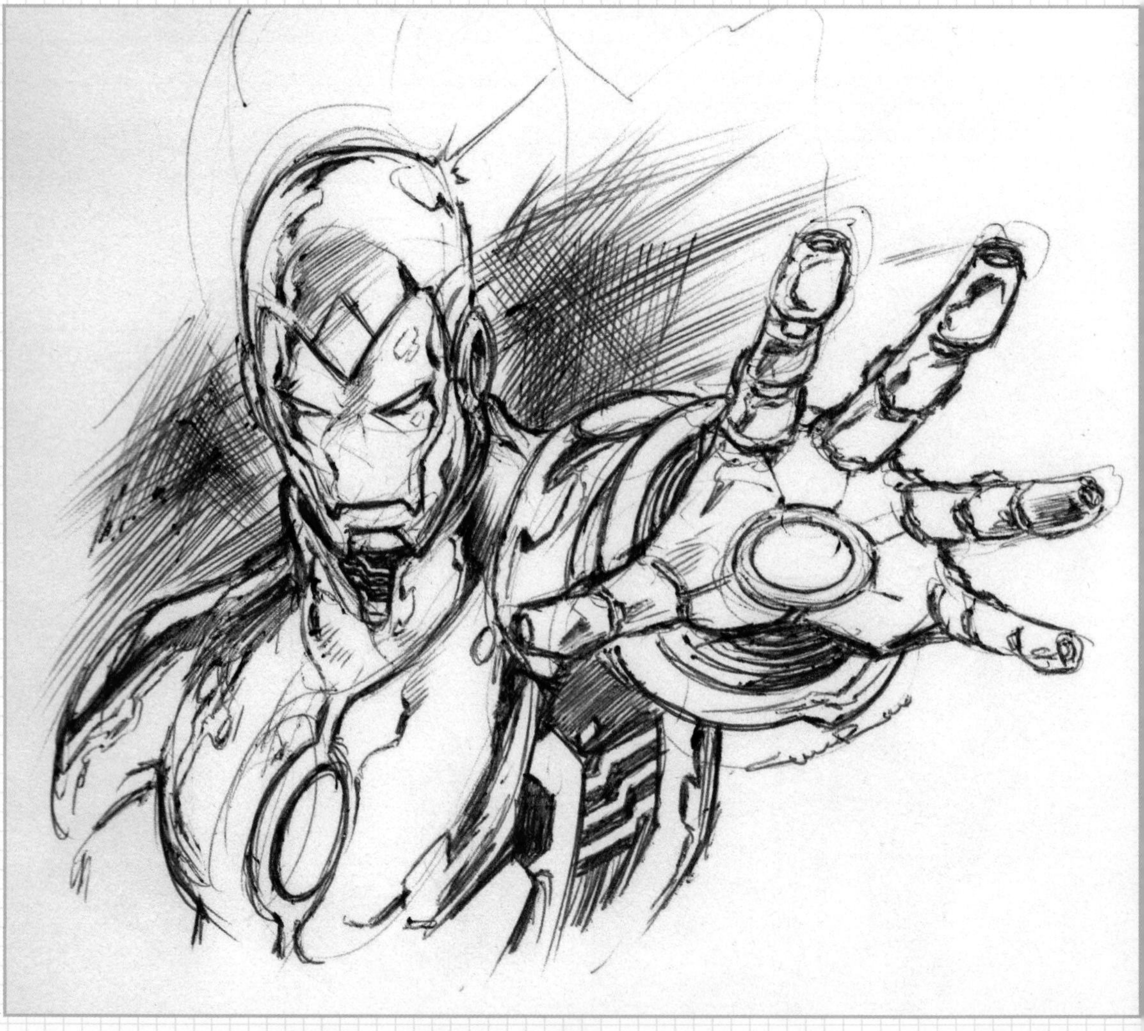

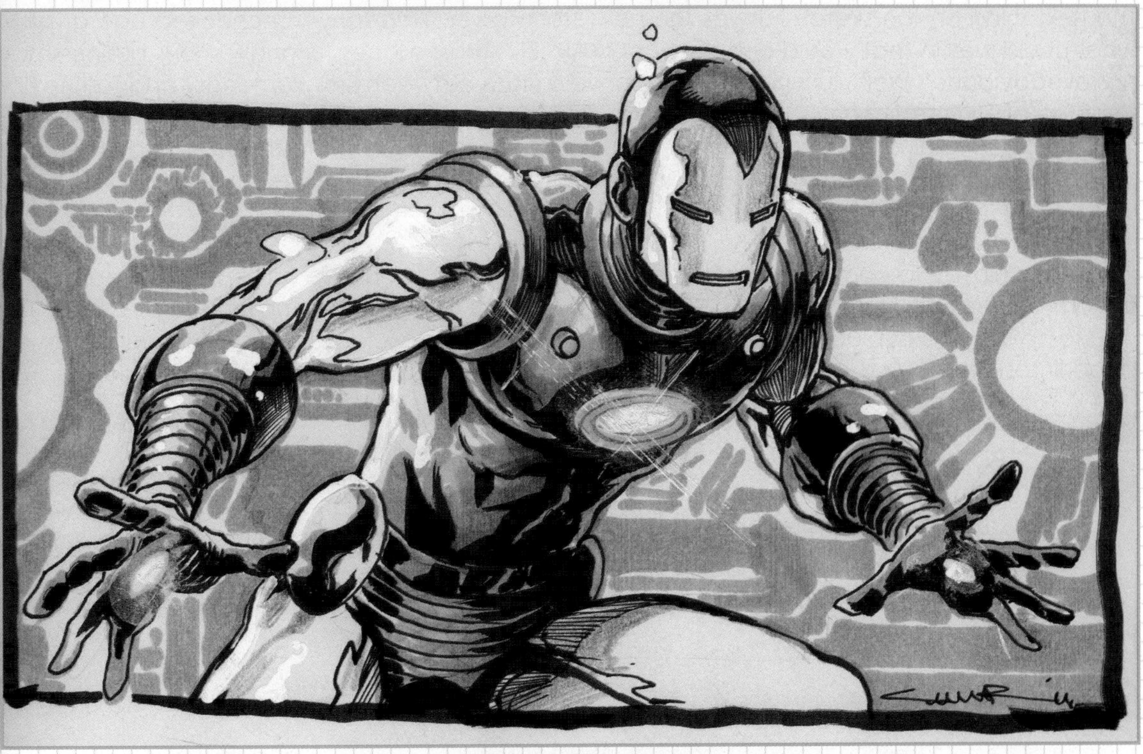

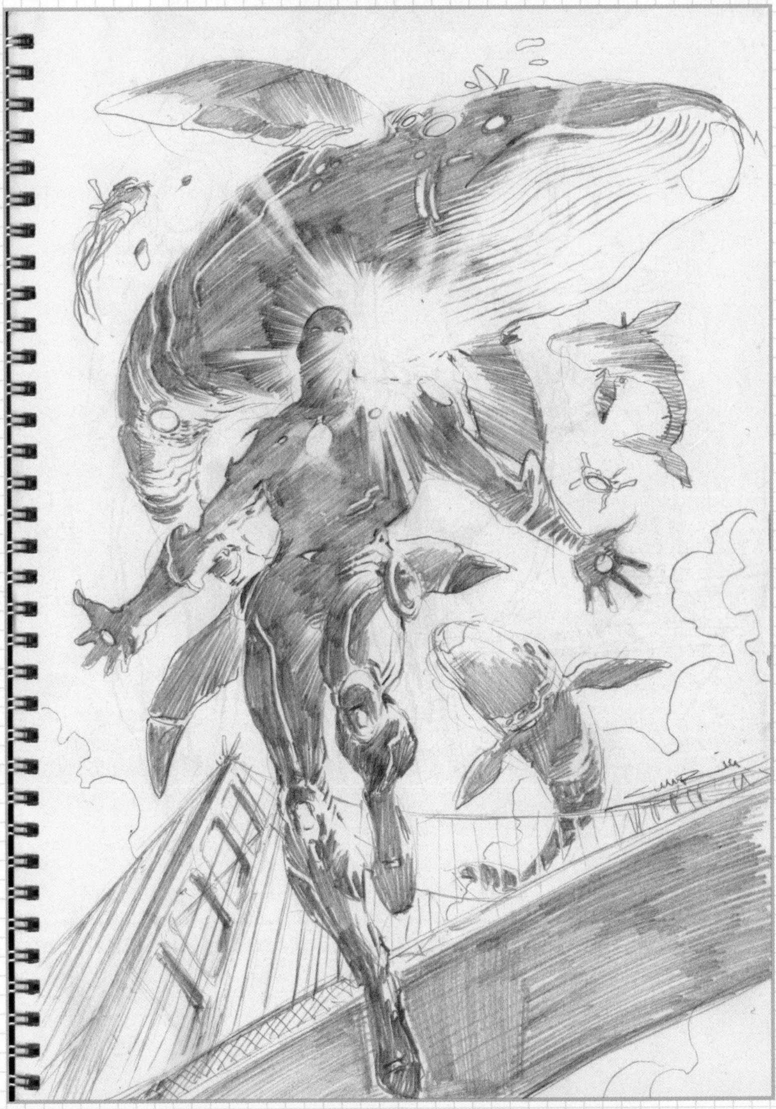

The next thing on the sketch list was the new Stark Tower. With Tony's unchecked ego at play what could we do that would one-up what MARVEL's most successful and famous businessman has already done? Well, during early AXIS conversations between Rick Remender and Tom Taylor the idea of Tony setting up shop on Alcatraz came up and dang was it a brilliant idea! Besides working on several levels, it allowed us to "upgrade" Stark Tower from the standard impressive skyscraper to a much more imposing piece of real estate. Thus what we now call STARK ISLAND was born!

We asked Yildiray to come up with something that would not only be an aesthetic extension of the armor (sleek and futuristic) but a design that exuded Tony's amped up lust for spectacle. This had to be the kind of place you'd see from a million miles away, looked beautiful and screamed good times! Personally I love it. If I could have blue LED everywhere in my house I would.

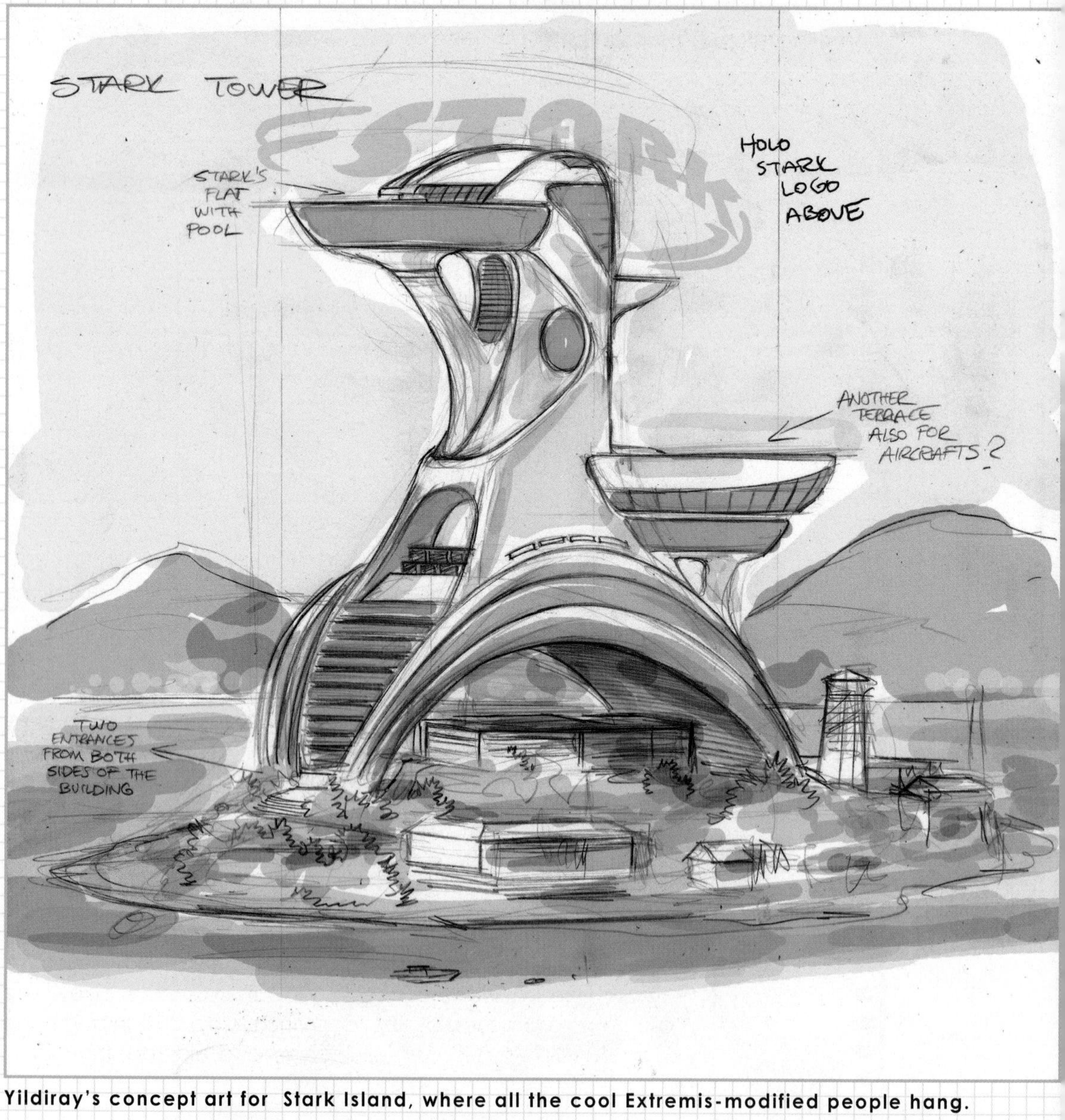

STARK TOWER
STARK
STARK'S FLAT WITH POOL
HOLO STARK LOGO ABOVE
ANOTHER TERRACE ALSO FOR AIRCRAFTS?
TWO ENTRANCES FROM BOTH SIDES OF THE BUILDING

Yildiray's concept art for Stark Island, where all the cool Extremis-modified people hang.

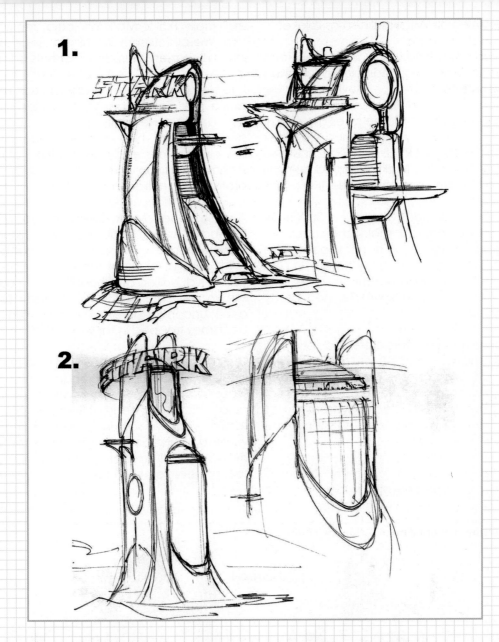

1.

2.

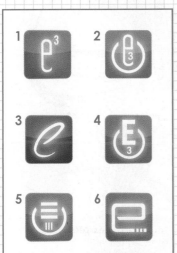

1 e^3 2

3   4 E_3

5   6

Extremis 3.0 app designs. All so good I wished there was an app to help us choose.

Another important visual element was the app design for Extremis 3.0. In-house designer Summer Lacy provided us with six different options. And we loved 'em all. Tom was especially drawn to #5, commenting that it was "all kinds of genius." It was a hard decision but after going back and forth a few times we finally settled on #2, beautifully simple yet layered in meaning. Summer was good enough to design the recap page where the app icon is a key image really helping to give the book a unique vibe.

Before I go I'd like to give a shout out to Summer Lacy who did an awesome job on the logo and recap design and Irene Y. Lee and Nelson Ribiero for their great design contributions.

Mark Paniccia
Senior Editor
MARVEL COMICS

So…TEEN ABOMINATION started as a joke.

In fact, at one stage, he wasn't even Teen Abomination. He was, ridiculously, named TEEN MAN-THING.

Some jokes stay jokes. Some jokes grow legs, grow long hair, grow green, and get their own origin in the MARVEL UNIVERSE. This joke did this because he quickly stopped being a joke and became something else.

One of the challenges with writing SUPERIOR IRON MAN is that our main character is… well, kind of a *jerk*. You're not supposed to like him. Sure, you can enjoy his antics and his humor and his ego but this isn't the Tony we all know and love anymore. He's pretty unlikeable.

But stories need characters readers can root for. This was one of the reasons MATT MURDOCK was chosen to stand against Tony in our first arc. Matt is a guy we all root for, and seeing this twisted Tony from Matt's perspective really helped us shape our SUPERIOR IRON MAN.

While Teen Abomination was originally created pretty much just for Tony to poke fun at and dismiss, our whole team, and especially Editor Mark Paniccia, really liked him. We all felt sorry for him as soon as we saw his humanity through Yildiray's art.

I remember Mark actually asked me to make sure Teen Abomination didn't really hurt anyone. He really liked the character and wanted him to be redeemable. Mark became really protective of Teen Abomination. So much so, he was even protecting him from me.

And so, when Mark asked me to write a flashback issue for Laura Braga in issue #5, I knew what I wanted to do. I wanted to tell the tragic origin of Teen Abomination. A young kid, bullied at school for being outside the mainstream, who was already feeling a bit uncomfortable in his own skin, who becomes trapped in far worse skin.

The challenge was then to tie him to our story and our characters in a fundamental way - to tie him to Tony. And I wanted even the cold, calculating heart of Superior Tony Stark to see what we saw in Teen Abomination. I wanted to give Superior Tony Stark someone he would feel protective of. We hope you'll feel protective of him too.

Tom Taylor

First version of Teen Abomination by Yildiray Çınar.

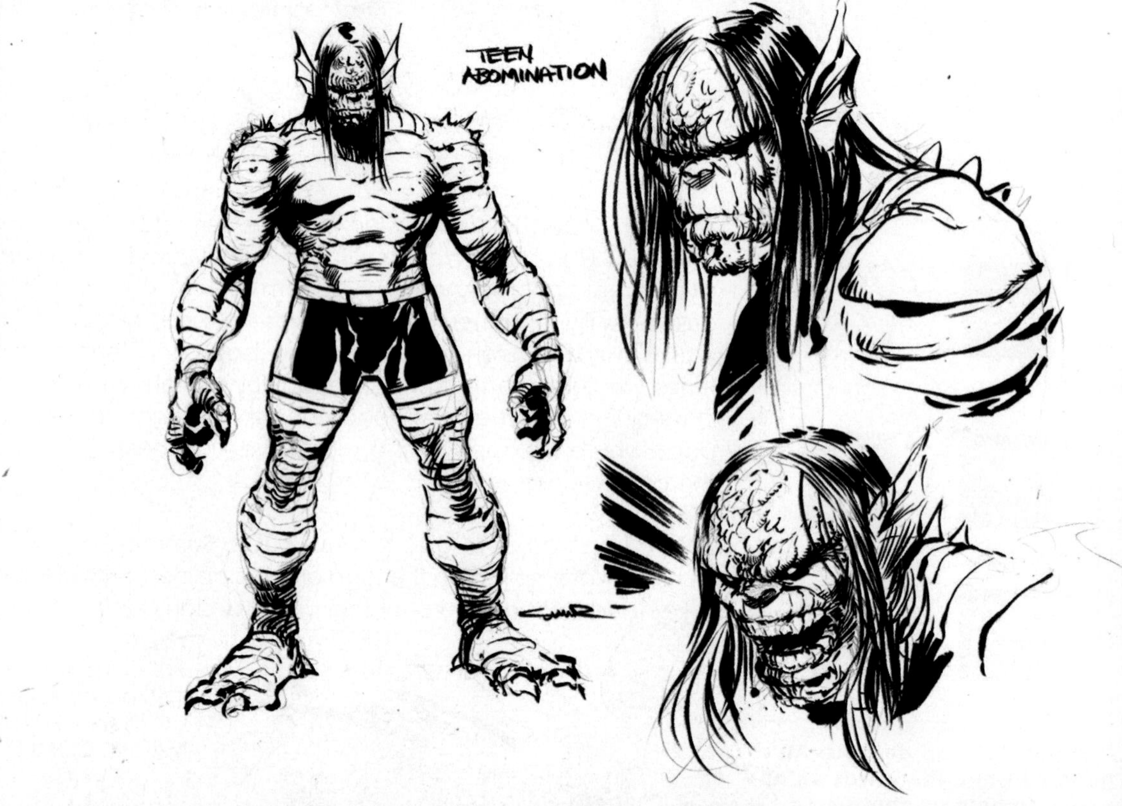
TEEN ABOMINATION

Take two leaning more towards a Hulk vibe.

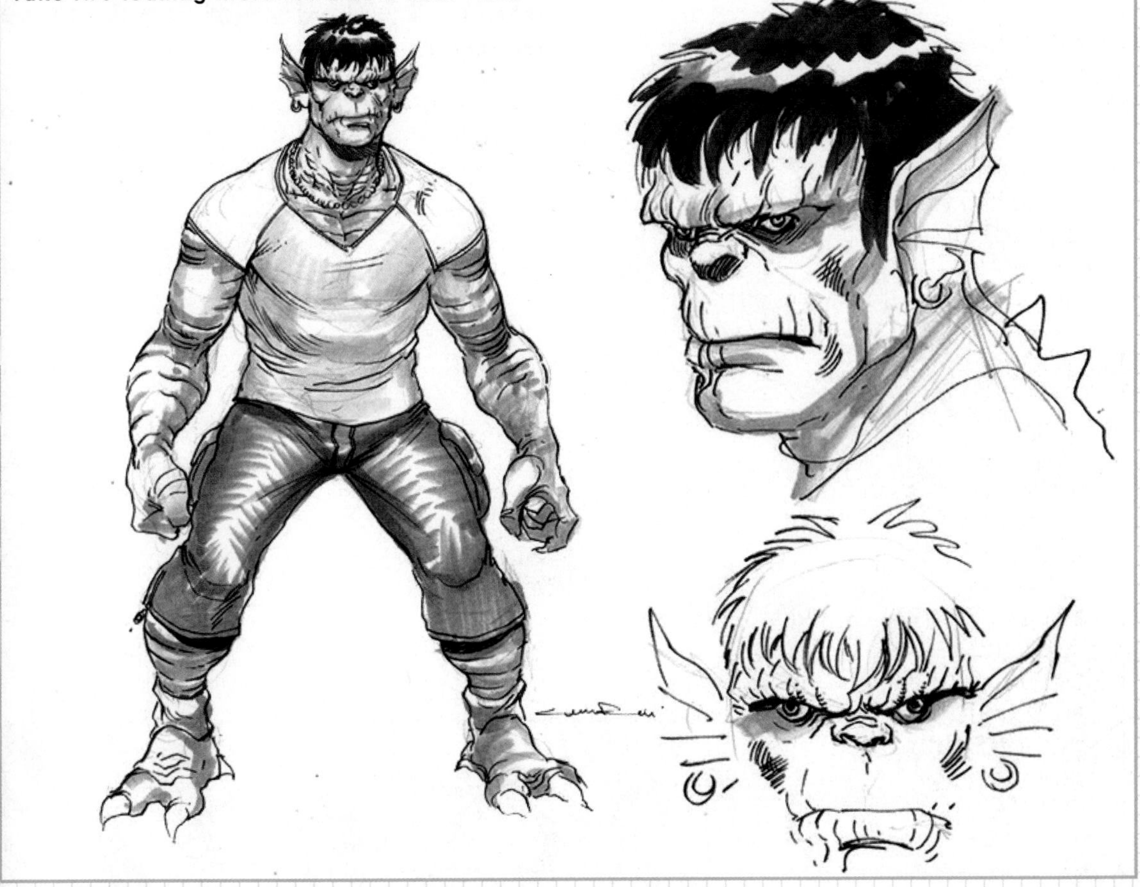

Teen Abomination from issue #4, page 14

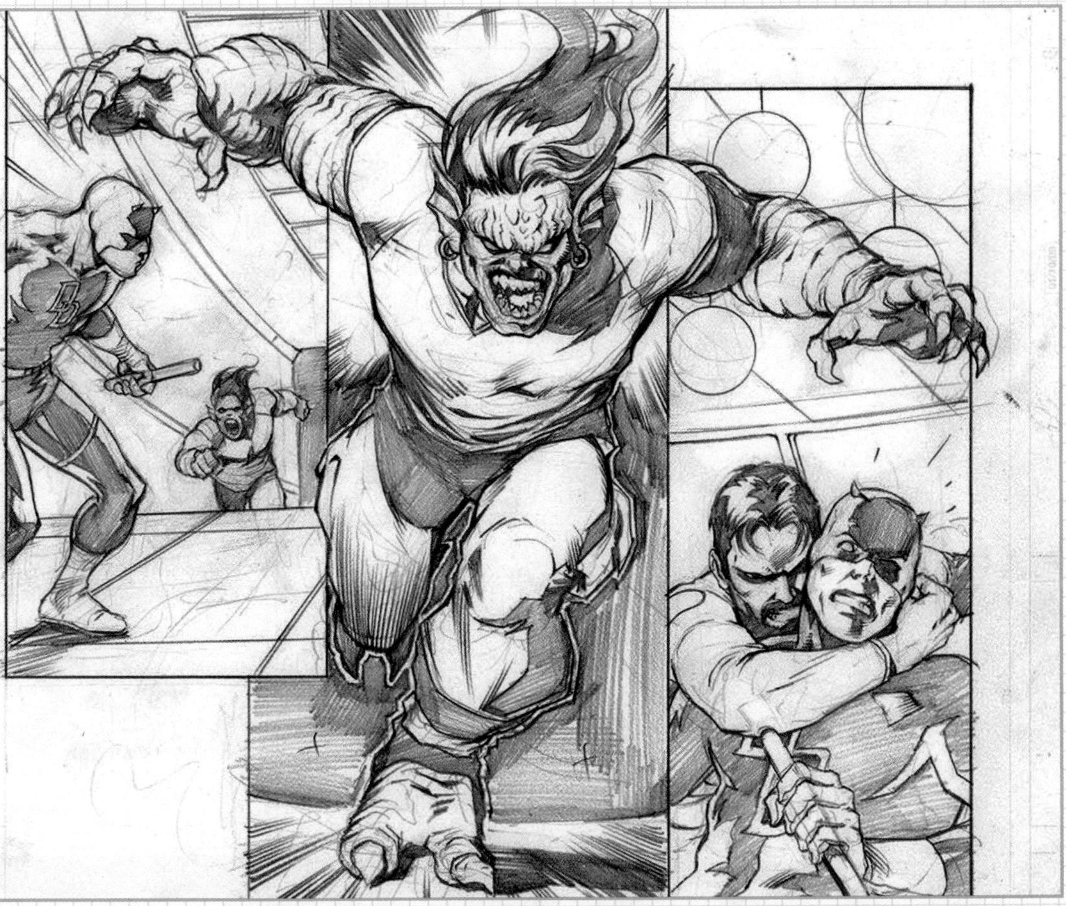

ART PROCESS

#3, page 15

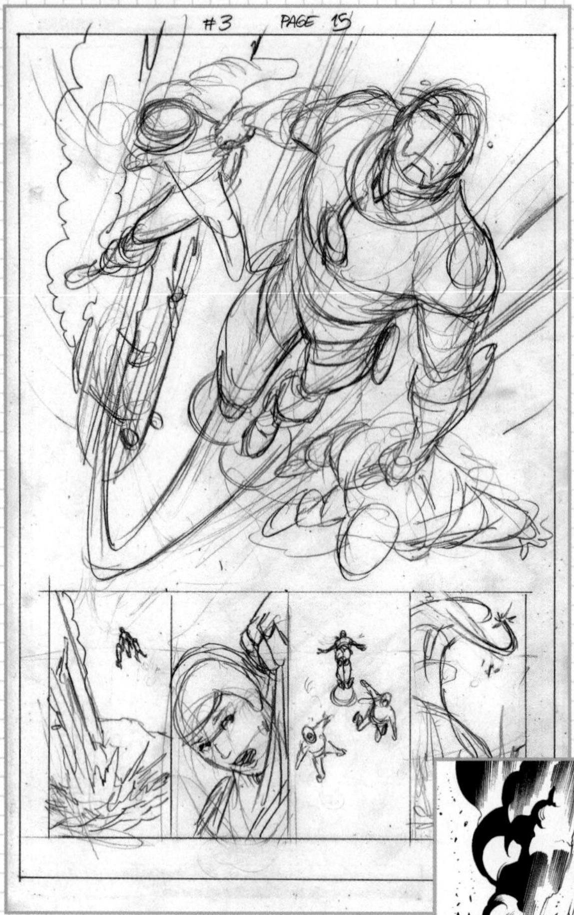
#3 PAGE 15

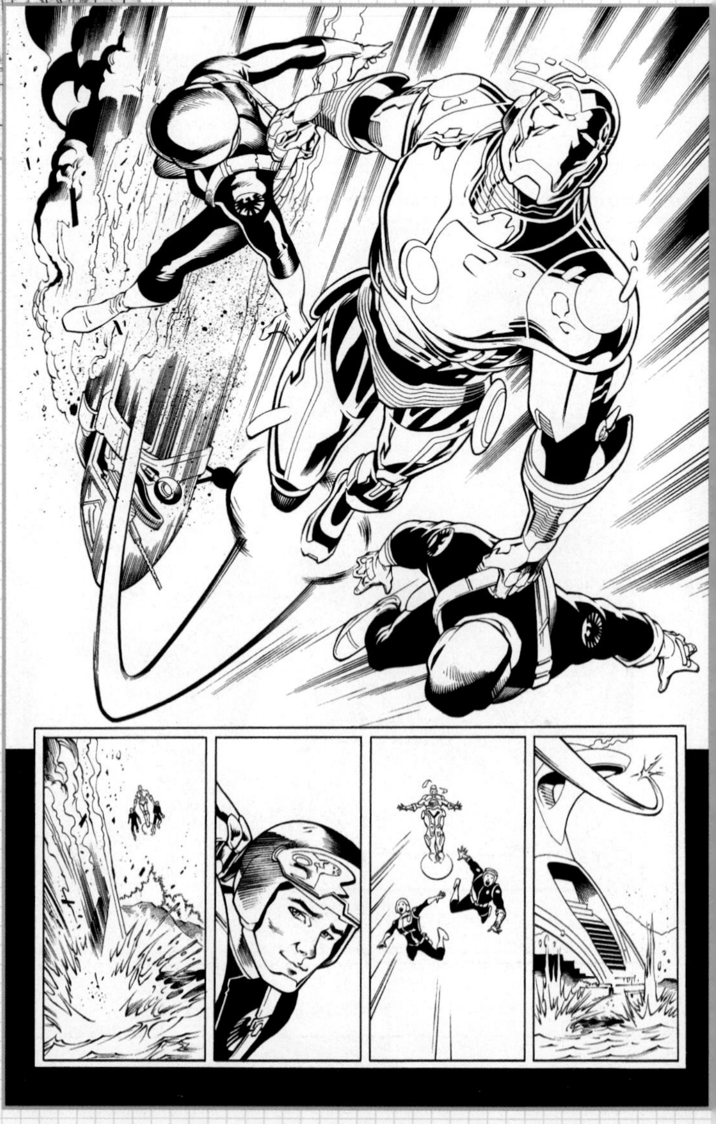

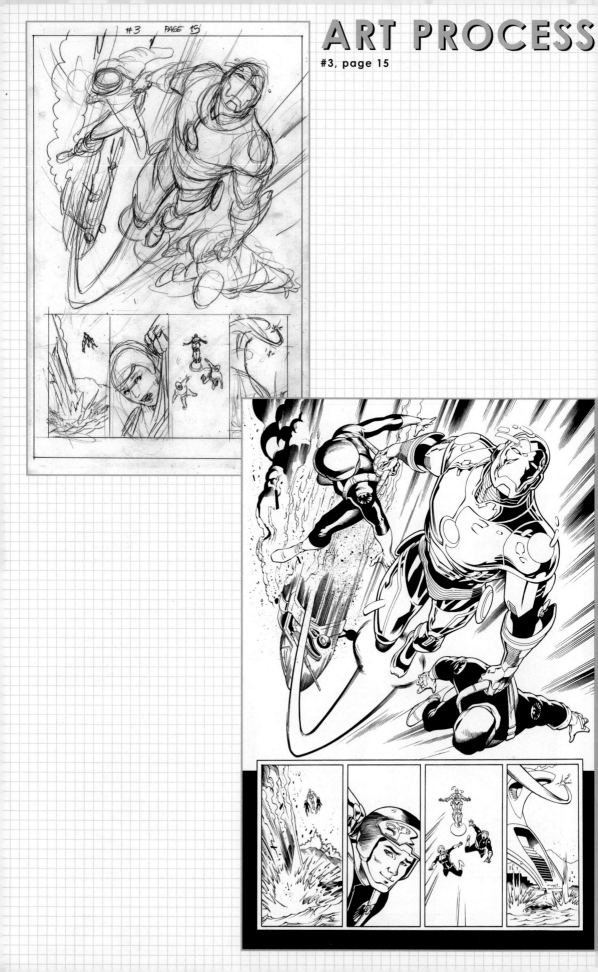

SUPERIOR IRON MAN #3 PAGE 15

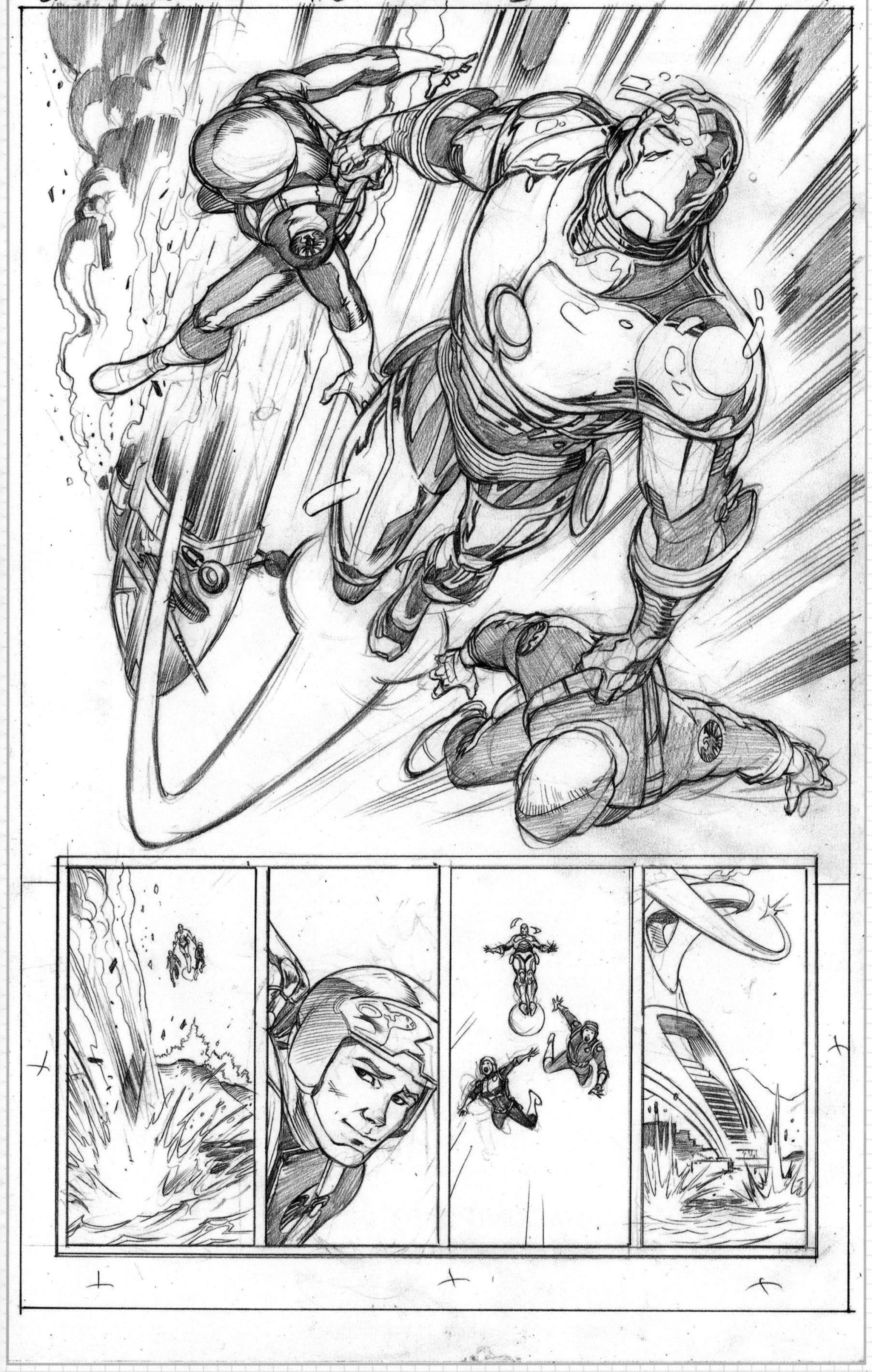

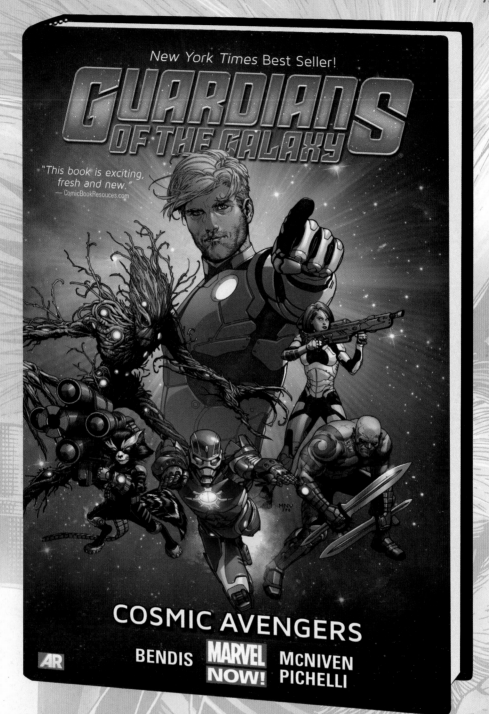